*I think that Mr. Kozak-Holland's book is **perfect for any manager** as well as IT management. Having had my own business I felt when I read this book that the advice applies not only to IT but can be offered as helpful hints and warnings to just about any business, big or small. I am currently contracted in IT and often see the same re-occurring problems at all levels. Mr. Kozak-Holland's book should make us all look at our past downfalls and ensure we all learn from them. This book works well on many levels's being **entertaining, insightful and a fun read** for anyone interested in history.*

- Al McGuinness

*Being a history buff, I was intrigued with a book that could link a historic non-IT project with modern so-called new wave online IT projects. I was not disappointed, it clearly demonstrated the more things change, the more they stay the same. The flow was pragmatic, thorough and easy to follow. The **language was geek free** and informs the reader on what they should expect from their deliverables and why they are needed. More importantly why certain decisions are made and their overall impact on any project. In the end, the book clearly demonstrates, through the Titanic reference, that it is rarely a single decision that creates the failure but a series of smaller seemingly unrelated decisions that cause us to fail. Failing to plan does cause your plan to fail. I would **recommend this book to any NON-IT person**, and any IT professional who is about undertake a project that does involve Information Technology.*

- Tim Lalonde, Director of Information Technology, Manitoulin Transport

*I feel that Mr. Kozak-Holland's book is ideal for technical IT managers, and also for non-technical managers having to be involved with computing solutions. A great analogy using the Titanic as an example of over-confidence in building, and running a ship. **If you don't plan to avoid "IT Icebergs," then you will likely hit one....and then what happens? A great read!***

- James Chillingworth

*The use of historical reminders to present to readers some very practical lessons is both entertaining and insightful. The author has me **looking forward to his next book** in this "Lessons from History" series. **A great value** most of us in the IT industry can get from this book is the large number of practical reminders that (without the proper foundation) it is too easy to lose focus on the details that count and the result is often a failed project. Used properly, **this book can help project managers and participants "steer clear" of potential disaster.***

- Tony Tolleson

To Barbara

[signature]

Avoiding Project Disaster

Titanic Lessons for IT Executives

by Mark Kozak-Holland

Second Edition

Multi-Media
Publications Inc.
Lakefield, Ontario

Avoiding Project Disaster: Titanic Lessons for IT Executives

By Mark Kozak-Holland

Published by:
Multi-Media Publications Inc.
R.R. #4B, Lakefield, Ontario,
Canada, K0L 2H0

http://www.mmpubs.com/

Editor:	Kevin Aguanno
Copy Editor:	Josette Coppola
Typesetting:	Tak Keung Sin
Cover Design:	Cheung Hoi

Copyright © 2002, 2006 by Mark Kozak-Holland.

ISBN (Paperback):   1-895186-73-0
ISBN (Adobe PDF eBook): 1-895186-74-9

Published in Canada.

This first edition of this book was published in 2002 under ISBN 1-931182-34-5 by IBM Press and MC Press. The original title was *On-line, On-time, On-budget: Titanic Lessons for the e-business Executive*.

Library and Archives Canada Cataloguing in Publication

Kozak-Holland, Mark
       Avoiding project disaster: Titanic lessons for IT executives / by Mark Kozak-Holland. -- 2nd ed.

(Lessons from history)
Previous ed. published under title: On-line, on-time, on-budget: Titanic lessons for e-business executives.
Includes bibliographical references and index.
Also available in electronic formats.
ISBN 1-895186-73-0

       1. Business enterprises--Computer networks--Management. 2. Electronic commerce--Management. 3. Information technology--Management. I. Title. II. Title: Titanic lessons for IT executives. III. Series: Kozak-Holland, Mark. Lessons from history (Print).

HD69.P75K69 2006	658'.05	C2006-902327-1

Dedication

To my wife Sharon and children Nicholas, Jamie, and Evie.

Contents

Preface

In today's world, delivering Information Technology (*IT*) projects on-time and on-budget is not enough. You also need to be on-line—connected to the Internet. With that Internet connection comes the high expectations of your customers and partners, and the rigors of a "24/7" operation. This raises the bar for IT projects in an industry with a notoriously high[1] project-failure rate.

This book is for the business executive and manager responsible for IT spending. You are responsible for approving new IT projects in your organization. Just as important, you are responsible for the delivery of business services to your customers.

Consider this scenario: You have just reviewed another urgent proposal for a large IT project that falls outside of the annual fiscal budget. You are under a lot of pressure to approve this type of project because it is deemed strategic. You are concerned, as you're not sure that last year's expenditures on IT projects really lived up to their promises. Your customer-service department still complains about lost calls, and the accounting department still processes paper invoices, despite thousands of dollars of technology. However, the business-service metrics presented to you are at best confusing, as they indicate minor improvements in service levels. Instinctively, you know that technology alone can't be the answer. Instead, it is a combination of procedures, technology, and organizational realignment that builds lasting value. In this book, you'll learn why your instincts are correct and what you can do, systematically, to get the most out of your IT expenditures.

This book outlines the stages involved in IT projects. Specifically, it provides a step-by-step guide to the deliverables that the IT department or service provider should produce at each

---

1. Only 26 percent of all IT projects finish on-time, on-budget, and with all the features and functions originally specified. (Source: "Chaos, a recipe for success," Standish Group, 1998.)

stage of the creation process. Knowing the rationale for and the timing of deliverables enables the non-IT manager to be a full participant in the creation process.

To simplify some of the more complex concepts and to elaborate key points, this book uses *Titanic's* story. Each chapter contains a *Titanic*-based narrative woven into the book's structure.

This book will help you solve these six problems:

- *How can I improve the probability of success and mitigate the risk in my IT projects?* Every day, organizations are presented with new IT projects based on emerging technologies that attempt to solve all kinds of business problems. As a business manager, you are challenged to discern the value[2] and risk of these projects. You need to balance this against current investments in IT projects for maintaining, improving, and evolving business services, and their services levels.

  In this book, you learn how to determine whether past IT investments have been worthwhile, and what future IT investments are required to meet service-level goals. Based on this, you can select the appropriate IT projects and understand their associated risks, and then determine whether your IT department or service providers can deliver them. You will discover how to measure the uncertainty and risk of going on-line, determine the exposure, and then take appropriate actions to mitigate the risk.

- *How can I deliver my goods and services in an environment of uncertainty?* Uncertainty in terms of the risk of doing business on-line (through intranets, extranets, Internets, portals, or other electronic channels) differs from the risk associated with more traditional channels. As your organization moves its operations on-line through IT projects, you expose the inner workings of your business operations to potentially millions of customers, partners, and suppliers around the world.

  Many organizations fail to recognize how difficult it actually is to maintain business services continually on-line and to meet the "up-time" expectations of the Internet. Nor do they recognize the ever-increasing business dependence on services and information, and the interorganizational dependencies that consequently develop, in 24/7 availability. If you fail to provide stable, highly responsive business services that can withstand the onslaught of weekly changes, demanding customers will readily switch or "click" to a competitor. In fact, continuous business-service

---

2. 84 percent of companies either do not do business cases for their IT projects at all, or just do them on a select few key projects: (Source: 2001 META Group Inc., Stamford, CT-USA)

availability is becoming a major competitive advantage. This book describes how you can mitigate the uncertainty and risk of remaining on-line continuously.

- *How can I anticipate and mitigate on-line outages to save money, customer goodwill, and maybe my job?* Organizations providing on-line services are continuously surprised by outages. Even with all the major advances in reliable technology and systems, organizations struggle to get stability and availability in their service-delivery environments. By going on the Internet, your organization becomes even more vulnerable and seriously affected by outages. These are horrendously expensive and highly visible because of the global exposure of the Internet.

  This book describes the difficulties of creating and maintaining continuous 24/7 business services. It outlines how you can evaluate your organization's ability to de-liver business services, work out infrastructure weak points, and determine the pit-falls and costs in running a service continuously. It also outlines how you can create a business case, based on potential outage costs, for going on-line. As a business manager, it is important for you to understand the investment requirements for busi-ness availability before making any financial commitments.

- *How can I ensure my investments in individual IT projects, related to on-line operations, are well-directed?*[3] In improving and evolving business services, investments in IT projects are usually apportioned towards technology first, but meeting customer-service levels is only partially dependent on technology availability. At least as important is establishing processes and aligning the organization to adhere to them.

  This book questions why service levels are improved with expensive technology so-lutions when much simpler, nontechnological approaches are available. It describes how you can understand what is required to design, create, and support business ser-vices and environments that are mission-critical. This includes navigating the vast set of technology options for availability and determining the trade-offs necessary to maximize IT investments. It also examines finding the right balance of effort for the deliverables, in terms of technology, process, and organization, in every stage of the IT project.

- *How can I run with the IT-jargon "wolves" without being devoured?* The IT industry is notorious for its use of jargon and the overcomplication of technology. Jargon is often presented in a manner that preserves the mystique of computer technology and

---

3. 83 percent of companies are unable to align their budgets with business needs more than once or twice a year. (Source 2001 META Group Inc., Stamford, CT-USA)

buries it under confusing acronyms. Very often, IT departments instigate, lead, and run IT projects that become too focused on IT itself, rather than on business.

On-line operations, however, are the lifeblood of companies, so as a business manager, you can no longer stand back from IT projects. This book provides you the ability to get involved in IT projects and work with the IT organization by asking the right questions at the right stage in the IT project. As a consequence, you can influence incremental investments that are well-directed. You can also review and understand various alternatives available at each stage of the project. Likewise, IT managers looking to improve business services need to involve you and provide the right information for decisions to be made regarding IT investments. IT projects can only be truly successful if they receive the continued full support of your business.

- *How do I know what and how to measure?* Many organizations continuously collect metrics related to the availability of business services. However, very often the wrong types of metrics are collected, as these relate to the availability of the technology in terms of the hardware, like servers and networks. This provides for a disparate, bottom-up view that is extremely misleading. It deceives organizations into thinking they are meeting customer expectations when, in fact, they are not. Metrics need to originate from a customer standpoint and have a top-down, holistic view.

This book describes which metrics you need to collect, how to analyze these metrics, and how to interpret availability reports. You can then rapidly determine which current business services are critical, and their actual service-level measurements and performance. As a result, the past performance of your IT organization or service provider can be carefully scrutinized.

Why Titanic*?*

Every chapter of this book uses *Titanic* as an analogy. *Titanic's* construction took four years, but in the course of just four days, it was destined to go to its grave because of a number of bad decisions. Modern interpretations of *Titanic's* story point to the inadequacies of technology, like the brittle steel and the shortage of lifeboats. However, this is very misleading. Rules and procedures were not adequately tested, incorrectly implemented, and blatantly and continuously violated by the very people who were ultimately responsible for the ship, its safety, and the passengers and crew. This provides a very important lesson for today's complex service-delivery environments.

Today, society's faith in computer technology is extraordinarily high. This is reflected by the way businesses, industries, factories, and offices are being automated at every level. More and more of the business world is rushing to get on-line. Statistics pour out every week on Internet growth, e-business, the increased levels of automation, and the electronic provision of every conceivable service imaginable. As consumers, we have become very reliant on performing everyday activities through electronic business services. In fact, our relationship with electronic business services has become one of complete dependency.

However, on-line is getting more and more vulnerable and overworked. Time after time, glitches crash a mission-critical business service at enormous cost[4] to the organization. Very often, only when a significant outage is widely reported and falls under the scrutiny of the public do we begin to appreciate how dependent we have become on this electronic world of the service-delivery environment, and the impact the outage has on an organization. In your own personal experience, how often have you encountered the message "Service Temporarily Unavailable" at a bank machine, could not access a Web site, lost an electronic transaction, or been trapped in a voice-mail system?

In going on-line, you need to be prepared and know that your IT people are prepared, as well. Investing in reliable technology is not enough. In the past few decades, the quality and reliability of computer technology has increased by an astounding rate, while the quality of business services does not seem to be getting any more reliable. The problem goes beyond computer technology, into other factors such as the environment, infrastructure, operations organization, and processes. Improving business services and availability requires an intelligent, aggressive, and proactive approach. It requires a balancing act between business needs and the revenue stream. Some committed organizations have been able to master availability, but these organizations are far and few between. This book provides an insight on how they achieved this balance.

Rationale for Using Titanic

This book leverages case studies to demonstrate that the same mistakes that were incurred in the construction and operation of *Titanic* are constantly repeated in today's organizations. The story of *Titanic* is reviewed in light of an IT project, as a lesson for today's organizations.

Most Infamous Disaster of All Time

Titanic was the largest ship afloat. It was billed as unsinkable, with all the latest safety features, like a double hull, bulkheads, electric water-tight doors, and powerful engines. Everyone onboard, from the captain and crew to the 53 millionaires believed in the mystique of the *Titanic*, much like most IT and non-IT managers believe in the infallibility of technology. By examining the flow of the *Titanic* story, you can avoid disaster in your own technology epic.

---

4. A large financial institution could lose $90,000 per hour or $40 million per year in outages. AT&T's network broke down for nine hours at an estimated loss of $70 million.

The *Titanic* disaster had a huge impact on society and its attitudes. The disaster stunned the world and brought the populations together for a short time, very much like the first landing on the moon did 60 years later—although for completely different reasons. *Titanic* was a microcosm of Western society, in class, nationality, race, and culture. Many historians write about the event as the end of the nineteenth century because it briefly unnerved Western society's faith in progress. However, the timing was also a prelude and an omen to the First World War, where technology not only failed to prevent the war, but greatly increased the slaughter through the machine gun, mustard gas, and total warfare waged on land, sea, and air. In fact, the First World War was probably the greatest disaster of the twentieth century.

Classic Mistakes

The same classic mistakes are repeated today, in designing, constructing, delivering, and managing leading-edge technology in service-delivery environments. This is very significant to this book. Technology was pushed to its limit in *Titanic*, and the disaster forced changes, specifically a rethinking in procedures and how these were followed.

---

5. At Caisse Populaire Desjardins (CCPEDQ) the Business Availability Project established an unprecedented 24 month availability record for CCPEDQ in an extremely dynamic environment, resulting in the public recognition of the project and awards for outstanding achievements. OCTAS is a competition honored by the Fédération de l'informatique du Québec, a major occasion in the province: http://www.fiq.qc.ca/evenements.htm#laureats.

Introduction

In this book, you learn how to move from a business that is not on-line or only partly on-line to a business that has its operations fully on-line[1]. In the progression, you discover the technology, processes, and management issues that affect the move. The key to profitability is the availability of on-line resources, and the key to availability is planning. This book helps you plan your on-line operational presence, understand that presence, and most important, continually evaluate that presence.

Don't be fooled into thinking that being on-line is all about technology. IT integration projects using emerging technology carry a certain inherent risk when the project starts with a new technology. Many organizations fall into a trap when they fail to examine other considerations, such as changes in business requirements, business processes, organization, new business drivers, existing business practices, and habits that will affect the on-line operation. The result is projects that are technically perfect, but that do not come close to meeting business goals.

The framework for the chapters is based on a project or business life-cycle model. This lifecycle is used to highlight all the stages required in the creation of a new on-line operation, and how mistakes are commonly made in the evolution of such a project. Each chapter in this book has two intertwined threads that make a complex subject easier to understand:

---

1. The term *on-line*, in this book, refers to electronic services provided by commercial transaction systems through channels like the Internet.

- The first thread is the story of *Titanic* within the context of each of the project life-cycle stages. The lifecycle and models clarify what happened from an operational point of view.

- The second thread examines how to build on-line operations within the context of the project lifecycle.

Target Audience

This book has been written to help organizations deliver operations on-line. Decision makers want to have answers to the following questions:

- What can go wrong in creating or maintaining an on-line operation?

- What is the cost and impact of it going wrong?

- How can I prevent it from going wrong?

- What is my return on investment for creating a strong on-line operation?

What Is "Mission Critical"?

A mission-critical environment implies a part or whole of a service-delivery environment that is absolutely critical to support the life of a business, or the livelihood of an organization. Whatever your organization does as its primary activity is its mission-critical task. If you are putting that mission-critical task into on-line operations, you want close to 100 percent availability of that operation.

You do not want to be an organization that fails to invest adequately to protect on-line operations. As you go through this book, you will learn that the biggest task isn't buying the technology, it is managing the implementation of that technology into the complexity of a service-delivery environment. Because consumers, business partners, and employees expect 24-hour-a-day access to on-line operations, failure to provide that continual and uninterrupted access can have a serious business impact.

If you think you can afford a few minutes of downtime a month, think again. Consider the banking industry. For every minute a critical on-line business operation is down, it costs the organization over $1,000. For an organization achieving 90 percent, this calculates to a loss of $50,000,000 per year. Even a figure of 99 percent, considered to be high by the industry, calculates to a loss of $5,000,000 per year.

Potential Bankruptcy

Market studies show the level of availability for on-line operations is a key differentiator for many organizations. If your on-line business services are unavailable, your customers could be switching to your nearest competitor. The cost can be quite staggering when downtime minutes are multiplied by the number of lost customers, or lost user productivity. Here are some examples of organizations that have suffered this:

- In January 2006, a four-hour system outage affecting ticketing, baggage check-in and boarding pass printing caused delays of United Air Lines flights.

- In April 2006, Microsoft's MSN search engine, the third most popular in the U.S., suffered an hours-long outage as queries returned an error message instead of Web page results.

- In January 2006 Salesforce.com faced several 4 hour outages caused by a problem with the interface that connected to the back office sales reporting.

- In July 2005, HSBC admitted hardware failure caused a major systems crash that hit thousands of customers for ATM, credit/debit, online services and internet, and it was the worst in its history.

- In December 2004 Walmart.com online store suffered outages, two days after online retail giant Amazon.com faced significant performance problems that stretched back over 11 days.

- In November 2004, a mistake while performing an upgrade to Windows XP at the UK Department for Work and Pensions stopped 80,000 staff from processing new pensions and benefits claims for several days.

- In October 2004, a routine monthly code update for PayPal.com only allowed users intermittent access to the online payment site. There are 50 million user accounts.

- In October 2004, a computer failure at Waikato Hospital (NZ) left thousands of health workers out of pocket and forced the manual processing of patient records.

- In October 2004, Avis Europe took a €45m hit due to problems with a new ERP system. Development was halted with delays & higher costs due to implementation and design problems.

- In September 2004, hundreds of flights were grounded for 3 hours at Western US airports. A computer failure knocked out radio contact between pilots and air-traffic controllers. In five instances airplanes passed very close to each other.

- In August 2004, a computer crash prevented thousands of UK pensioners collecting benefits payments on the busiest day of year after the £500m Benefits Transfer system went down.

- In June 2004, RBC fell behind processing salary deposits thousands of Canadian workers as millions of transactions were affected by a computer glitch that caused payroll delays.

These examples are just the tip of the iceberg. Most outages are unreported, as organizations will avoid the harmful effects of publicity and the likely loss in customer confidence.

Difficulty in Providing Continuous On-line Operations

Why is it so difficult to deliver continuous on-line operations? Why do service-delivery environment fail, and services become unavailable? Here are a few reasons:

- The dependency on service delivery environments is rapidly increasing because of the rate at which on-line operations are being adopted and used. This will continue to increase even more rapidly well into the twenty-first century.

- A widely held view within organizations and industry has promoted an unquestioning belief in the benefits of technology and the unlimited introduction of technology to increase the number of business services and functions available. As a result, the scale of service-delivery environments has become more complex, and hence more difficult to manage.

- As more business functions are introduced through new applications, the functional complexity increases. Software or applications are typically pervasive within an environment. Applications are overlayered rather than replaced, while hardware is upgraded and changed every two to five years. As a result of this complexity, it is becoming more difficult for staff to understand the whole service-delivery environment.

- Through continual miniaturization, more and more of the components are hidden in a "black box." For example, video-recorder technology is so complex, with the integration of electronics and mechanical cassette components, that outside of the manufacturer, very few specialists even try to repair a VCR. Our ability to access technology is becoming increasingly difficult because of the understanding of technology and its interations is decreasing.

- In the pursuit of operational efficiencies and lower cost of service, organizations continue to automate and eliminate staff. Automation can further complicate the service-delivery environment by hiding the inner workings. Many service-delivery environments are run with a skeleton staff who have a limited understanding or knowledge of the environment or its workings.

- Knowledge of emerging technologies and new solutions being implemented into a new environment can be rapidly lost when the integration teams involved with the project are disbanded. A concerted effort is required to transfer the knowledge to operational staff.

If It's So Hard to Provide On-line Operations, Why Is Everybody Doing It?

The answer to why everyone is rushing to go on-line is complex, as there are a number of trends or external pressures in business that drive the need for the continuous availability of on-line operations. Consumers today expect 24/7 access to banking, telephone, travel, emergency, healthcare, and other services. They bank, shop, and do business with the companies that are available when needed. When a particular company's business services are not available, customers will go to a competitor to make their reservations, purchase their goods or services, or complete financial transactions. Customer loyalty is not a given; it has to be earned. Organizations are under tremendous external pressures to provide continuous electronic business services.

Global economic trends and the globalization of business have pushed interactions to a 24/7 basis. It is always 9:00 A.M. somewhere in the world, as customers start the day. It is critical for corporations to be available through the Internet to a wider global market. There are huge competitive pressures for businesses to be continually on-line and not get left behind.

Time is becoming a very precious commodity in people's personal lives. Extended customer services and new service-delivery channels set expectations for even higher levels of service availability with customers. For example, a single interaction or engagement that cannot be performed at a certain point in the day might mean a missed deadline. Time is becoming so valuable that it soon could be the most important criteria in purchasing a service or a product.

Competition has greatly increased, as new players have jumped into traditional markets with fresh ideas and approaches. These range from alternate organizational structures to the way emerging technology is leveraged. For example, consider the impact of Walmart on retail, ING on retail banking, and Amazon on bookstores. As a result, competition has forced traditional organizations to adopt emerging technologies, re-engineer, downsize, restructure, and emerge as flatter organizations. These organizations have fewer staff, but rely more on continuous on-line information to more people across the organization, to enable better decision-making.

Intense competition and common service-delivery environments have meant more services are chasing fewer customers. Consumer choice for electronic business services is continuously growing. As a result, products and services are being standardized at a faster rate. "Commoditization" is a process whereby a service is continually up-valued, to stay ahead of a competitor's commodity.

Regulation has opened up new markets, as monopolies have been broken up and competition introduced. This is related to competitive pressures, as more competitors jump across traditional industry boundaries. For example, gas stations that traditionally sold gas have evolved into 24-hour mini-market convenience stores, with fast-food restaurants attached.

Businesses will see fewer of their customers face-to-face. The customer will interact more with the organization's nonhuman channels, like phones, automated tellers, the Internet, kiosks, and wireless devices. If the service-delivery environment stops, the service stops, and the business stops.

e-Business has become a predominant mechanism for how businesses interact, interchange transactions, and exchange information in an automated fashion. e-Business has created a linked electronic environment from the consumer, to the retailer, to the distributor, to the manufacturer/supplier. Information is not just pertinent to one organization, but to many. Suppliers need to know the details of an organization's deadlines, purchase orders, and stock levels to better schedule shipments and replenishments. The whole supply chain works without human interaction and requires continuous business operations for information. All the businesses (partners and suppliers) depend on all the links. Being a weak link in the supply chain means trouble as customers switch to the competition, or co-dependent partners hit you with penalties.[2]

Boundaries between industries are disappearing quickly where organizations need to have many associations electronically cross-industry, cross-business, and cross-competition. With this approach comes the problems of scheduling many partners and running an effective project. In fact, dissimilar organizations and cultures are being forced to work together effectively and competitively. Decisions have to be made today with the information available on-line. All this has brought about a need for continuously available information in a 24/7 environment.

---

2. The handful of companies who have linked their systems directly to their suppliers say the effort has been worth it. For example, Nordstrom.com can offer customers 20 million pairs of shoes because the inventory of its suppliers is easily accessible. Herman Miller, a leading manufacturer of office furniture, completes customer orders on schedule more than 95 percent of the time, thanks to improvements in internal processes and electronic links with suppliers. (Source: *San Jose Mercury News.*)

Service-industry organizations worldwide have been rapidly implementing emerging e-business technologies and building service-delivery environments. These organizations are doing so in an effort to meet customer demand and cut operational costs. As a result, these environments are becoming more and more integrated within and between organizations, possibly heading toward a common environment through the Internet. These environments are becoming the de facto standard for the provision of all on-line business services.

What Are the Different Industries Doing about On-line Operations?

This section establishes a clear definition of what a mission-critical business service is within various industries and sectors. It also outlines how emerging technologies and the Internet have changed business services to e-business services. Reading it—and seeing your company in the descriptions—will help you get a feel for the possibilities that technology can bring you.

- *Financial institutions*—The banking industry has long provided a broad range of electronic business services, from personal retail banking to commercial business. Retail services are provided through channel devices like ATMs and POS devices (instant cash, debit and credit), phones (tele-banking), and PCs with modems (home-banking). These services allow users to complete basic and complex transactions without the assistance of bank staff.[3] Banks provide commercial customers with business services that include electronic purchase orders, invoices, and automated payments. The advent of e-business and the Internet has seen the evolution of e-banking, including services like e-statements, e-bill presentment, and e-money. Portals have integrated products and services more closely, providing a more personalized and consolidated financial picture, linking customers with brokers, wholesale lenders, and other parties. Financial institutions can now place customers within segments and track all customer interactions across multiple channels. A growing number of global Internet banks threaten to take on traditional financial institutions. The requirement for continuous availability has become essential.

- *On-line brokers*—For many years, full-service brokerages have provided automated trading and clearing services to their brokers and clients. Automated systems execute and confirm trades, and handle clearing and settlement. These transactions have been low in volume but high in value. With the advent of e-business and the Internet, brokerages have put e-business infrastructures in place to support millions

---

3. The profitability of handling an electronic transaction is 10:1 over a traditional branch-teller transaction. Therefore, most financial institutions look to channel 95 percent of all transactions towards electronic delivery, and move staff to a relationship-banking role.

of customers in low-cost e-trading, and even perform surveillance functions. The value of the transactions has dropped, but the volume has grown exponentially—along with the requirement for continuous availability of service.

- *Telecommunications providers*—Telcos provide long-distance service, as well as other business services such as call management (caller ID, call waiting, call forwarding, etc.) and paging. The telephone system today is a multilevel computer network, using software switches in the fault-tolerant network nodes, to route calls quickly and reliably to their destinations. The advent of e-business and the Internet has seen the evolution of widespread email access, high-speed Internet services, personalized calling cards based on individual usage patterns, digital phones, digital cable for entertainment, video on demand, interactive TV, and numerous other services. All of these require continuous availability of service.

- *Cellular service providers*—These companies provide a breadth of mobility services, like home location register, pre-call registration, automatic roaming, call delivery, portability of custom features, and accurate billing on out-of-area operations. With the advent of e-business and the Internet, cell providers are now entering the world of wireless Internet, where high availability leads to better and faster responses to customer requests. Service is a competitive differentiator and secures customer loyalty. Wireless devices might well become a de facto means of cheap and quick Internet access and making electronic payments.

- *Retailers*—Traditional brick-and-mortar retailers have used electronic business services to provide faster and more convenient checkouts through credit- and debit-card transaction services and bar-code scanners. The advent of e-business and the Internet has tied stores electronically and directly to the supply warehouse, distributor, or manufacturer in one supply chain, integrating warehouse operations, inventory management, transportation operations, and return and repair services. The whole process maintains a rapid and reliable flow of products to the customer. e-Business has also introduced the micro-merchandizing of stores, target marketing of the consumer, and revolutionized procurement and distribution.

- *E-tailers*—Dotcoms, e-channels, B2Bs, e-Marketplaces, global transaction-processing hubs, and e-auctions are driven completely by the advent of e-business and the Internet to provide interactive on-line commerce through the Internet. Although many products and services can be bought and sold on the Web, certain retail products have proved particularly successful, such as books, CDs, software, electronics, consumer goods, and computers. Continuous availability is life and death to these providers, as they are completely dependent on the service-delivery environment. Without it they cannot conduct business. e-Marketplaces, e-auctioneers, and financial exchanges bring suppliers and vendors together, and are typically sponsored and driven by a market leader. e-Channels take on traditional distributors.

- *Manufacturers*—The last few decades have seen the continual automation of the production floor and the introduction of concepts like just-in-time. The advent of e-business and the Internet, with the integration of solutions like Manufacturing Resource Planning (*MRP*) and Supply Chain Management (*SCM*) has allowed the automation of distribution and logistics, from accepting raw materials to outputting the finished product. It has also allowed manufacturers to implement build-to-order strategies and custom-configure every order. This has happened across all types of manufacturing, from food, to automobile production, to computers. Customized products are ordered electronically on-demand, and every interaction and transaction from the consumer to the retailer, to the distributor, to the manufacturer/supplier is electronic, across the whole supply chain. e-Manufacturing designs products, procures components, and drives machinery. Further, manufacturers can buy raw materials and goods through B2B marketplaces, turning to bid management and Web-based purchasing. e-Marketplaces also offer manufacturers a liquid market for their goods, and the ability to sell finished goods directly to consumers, bypassing distributors. Manufacturers of automobiles and complex machinery are adapting monitoring technologies to monitor the status of critical components within their product for remote maintenance.

- *Oil and gas*—Petroleum retailers provide card-payment services directly at the fuel pump. The advent of e-business and the Internet has helped petroleum retailers collect data for use in stock control and marketing databases that allow retailers to build purchasing profiles of their customers. Personalized promotional offers and price discounting are offered automatically at the fuel pump.

- *Healthcare providers*—Hospitals and clinics provide electronic health services through electronic medical records. Within a hospital, each patient has a comprehensive medical history that follows the patient around. It is accessible from different parts of the hospital by different specialists. Each nursing care floor records data on patient status, medications administered, and other relevant information. This provides an official record of the nursing care given to patients. The advent of e-business and the Internet has connected physicians to the hospital's business office, so that changes can be made to each patient's account for services rendered and medicines provided. Patients discharged have their records of stay automatically transferred to their local physician's Clinical Management System (CMS), including X-rays and medical information. Electronic claims submitted electronically are processed in 24 hours. Insurers deposit payments into providers' and physicians' accounts.

- *Drugstores*—With the advent of e-business and the Internet, drugstores are now becoming integrated into the healthcare value chain and provide 24-hour prescription services, which cannot afford any downtime.

- *Utility providers*—Utilities use business services to provide essential public utilities 24/7. The advent of e-business and the Internet has helped utility companies shift from meter-based to customer-centric service delivery and improved customer service. This includes services like e-bill payment/presentment/statement, e-payment remittances, and other e-service requests through on-line applications like account information for both consumers and businesses (B2C and B2B).

- *Government agencies*—The advent of e-business and the Internet has had a significant impact on cash-strapped government agencies, which have been moving a vast array of public services to the Internet and kiosks in convenient public places. For example, these services include the delivery of e-licenses, public assistance e-benefits, the filing of e-taxes, e-learning to schools, e-justice, and even e-voting/e-democracy. Governments worldwide are using this technology to reduce the cost of service delivery and make their services citizen-centric around "life events."

- *Law enforcement agencies*—These organizations provide life-critical 911 services through Command and Control Systems. The advent of e-business and the Internet has introduced sophisticated profiling solutions for identifying suspects; matching old cases; and providing immediate information and services like rapid license-plate or photo-identity searches on suspects or stolen vehicles, intelligence on cases, geo-positional maps, and building plans for entry planning. These services are available to officers through Mobile Data Terminals.

- *Couriers*—Many national couriers offer a service that guarantees next-day delivery. This requires sophisticated systems for transportation, warehousing, tracking, and billing, available continuously around-the-clock. Service levels and penalties support the guarantees. The advent of e-business and the Internet allows for real-time shipment status and enables customers to directly track packages through the system.

- *Airlines*—Air travel has long relied on flight-management systems. The advent of e-business and the Internet has allowed airlines to handle flight planning, route optimization, gate and crew assignments, catering, baggage handling, and refueling. The whole operation is electronic, and without it, planes cannot fly.

- *Transportation*—The advent of e-business and the Internet has allowed transit companies like airlines and rail to offer on-line, integrated booking that responds to inquiries with the best routes and fares. As well as guaranteed seating, every plane or train is booked as close to maximum capacity as possible. The scheduling of information is done on-line, so that timetables can be changed based on changing travel patterns or engineering work. Similarly, trucking companies provide current on-line information to customers about the location of goods in transit or to facilitate on-time delivery of goods to just-in-time manufacturers.

- *Travel and reservations*—The advent of e-business and the Internet has introduced e-reservations across industries like travel, leisure, hospitality, and entertainment, enabling everything from hotel and car rentals, to tickets for sports events and concerts. This allows individual on-line buyers and e-agents (personal agents) to determine the best deals and purchase e-tickets. Discount pricing can be adjusted electronically to maximize capacity.

- *Broadcasting*—Many cable television companies offer 24-hour broadcasting services. The advent of e-business and the Internet enables TV broadcasting systems to provide a mixed communications environment with easy data exchange. It streamlines the production process and helps to promote and deliver programming content in a more discrete and re-packaged form. It also allows automatic broadcasting operations, streamlined news reporting, and improved record management. Intranets help leverage enterprise resources and knowledge for collaborative purposes.

- *Weather*—Meteorological offices offer forecasts and weather information services to aviation, commercial, and media customers. The advent of e-business and the Internet has made e-weather services very popular. Meteorological centers process a high volume of messages on a 24/7 basis.

- *Telemarketers*—The advent of e-business and the Internet has allowed telemarketers to match products more accurately to an audience by predicting the profiles of inbound callers and likely repeat callers.

- *On-line gaming*—State and provincial governments provide a variety of electronic gaming services like lotteries through convenient public-access points, and these have proved to be an enormous source of revenue. The advent of e-business and the Internet has further spread e-gaming and sports betting. Virtual-reality technology with advanced graphics will further enhance the experience.

- *Professional service providers*—The service industry has been greatly affected by the advent of e-business and the Internet, as knowledge and its management takes center stage in the value proposition taken to clients. A single portal guides service providers to all company knowledge harvested from all worldwide projects. In addition, e-collaboration and Web-based tools allow colleagues to work interactively across all hemispheres around the 24-hour clock, in service-development lifecycles and multinational projects.

Chapter Organization Using a Project Lifecycle

This book explores how to create on-line operations and explains some of the complex issues you will encounter. The framework for the chapters is based on a project or business lifecycle model, shown in the following figure. The chapters are laid out in this format so that you can appreciate the evolution of a business-services project from conception to implementation. It also allows for a rapid audit of your organization's ability to support your on-line operation. Each chapter is written so that a business manager has a better appreciation of the kind of questions that need to be asked at each stage in the project lifecycle.

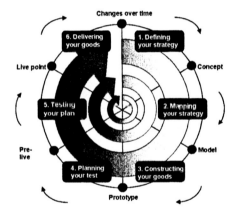

Figure I.1: The project lifecycle used through the chapters.

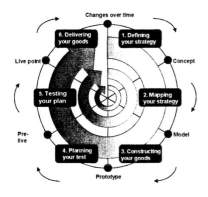

Defining Your Strategy

I found that defining my strategy for any project makes it easier to go into meetings and ask for money. Half the time, when you know what you want and can describe it clearly, people fund you on that alone.

Klaas Westra, President,
Centre for the Study of Insurance Operations (CSIO)

Chapter Objectives

When you are done with this chapter, you will be able to define the business requirements for your on-line operation. With these, you will be able to move on to chapter 2, in which you start to map the strategy for reaching your goals.

In this chapter you learn how to articulate the business problem or opportunity, specify the solution, and justify its value. This will allow you to make a go/no-go decision about whether to proceed with your on-line operation.

What Steps Do I Need to Follow?

You go through the following four steps to identify your own business requirements:

1. Articulate the business problem or opportunity.

2. Define a business solution to the problem.

3. Specify what the on-line operation is required to do.

4. Justify the value (or cost) of the on-line operation.

To get you warmed up to the subject, let's walk through these four steps with *Titanic* as a backdrop.

What Are Business Requirements?

Business requirements are the driving factors behind the creation of your on-line operations. Requirements are driven by an organization's desire to meet and exceed customer's expectations and to match or stay ahead of the competition.

Why Do We Need Requirements?

External change acts as a catalyst for the organization to respond and initiate ideas for projects. For example, the competition introduces a new on-line operation, or a new emerging technology opens up a new opportunity to solve a pervasive business problem. The first steps are to recognize these changes, determine their impact on the organization, outline responses, and then carefully document all these as business requirements.

Business requirements are continuously referred to through the project lifecycle in a number of different ways to help successfully design and implement on-line operations. The architect uses the business requirements as a basis for building the on-line operation. They are also used as a baseline in the user-acceptance activity, to measure the deliverable against what was planned for, and to define service targets. Finally, they form an important checkpoint at the project conclusion, when the business sponsors sign off.

Articulate the Business Problem or Opportunity

The first step in articulating the business problem or opportunity is to explore and clarify the changes affecting your organization. You also need to determine the gap between your current and desired capabilities. Let's see how the owners of the White Star line saw their business opportunity.

At the turn of the twentieth century, White Star's fleet of aging liners was affecting its ability to compete. The White Star liners were hopelessly outclassed by Cunard's faster liners, and another competitor, North German Lloyd, was already in the planning stage for new ships using the latest in technology. So, White Star's business problem was to meet or exceed its competitors on these two fronts.

Likewise, in today's world, an aging and inflexible IT infrastructure can cause you to become outclassed by your competition. You cannot afford to allow your technology to age by more than two years.

For White Star, a major business opportunity lay in transatlantic traffic, carrying everyone from nouveau riche industrialists to the immigrants working in their factories. Your opportunities are not with transatlantic traffic, but with providing on-line operations. In today's world, many companies recognize the major business opportunities that proliferate with the Internet and on-line operations, such as the ability to reach new markets and potential customers, or to just better serve existing customers.

The changes related to White Star's business problem or opportunity included an aging technology infrastructure, an attractive marketplace opportunity, and competitive pressures. The desired capability had to compete effectively with Cunard and fend off the challenge from North German Lloyd.

Define a Business Solution to the Problem

The second step, defining a solution, involves examining all the choices and selecting the best one, and then setting out the short- and long-term objectives for addressing the business problem. As the first solution, White Star had the choice of copying Cunard's "speed of service" strategy. Transatlantic crossing time had decreased over the previous 200 years, and having fast, "blue ribbon" ships was very prestigious. However, fast ships are limited by a sleek and narrow hull, and therefore cannot carry as many passengers and cargo.

Likewise, in today's world, you can copy successful business strategies. By emulating these with newer technologies, you can hope to gain the advantage of better service and an increase in revenue, or more functionality with lower operational costs.

A second choice for White Star was to leverage new technologies that allowed builders to vastly increase the size of the ship, by up to 50 percent in gross tonnage. A much larger ship provided a capability to greatly increase the level of luxury and comfort by providing more space in all three classes of quarters, as well as more overall cargo capacity.

In today's world, you can leverage new emerging technologies and open up new options for new business strategies. For example, new channels open up access to a new customer base. However, what channels are best suited for your organization? What type of channel strategy do you deploy? And with the pervasiveness of technology in the infrastructure, what technology do you use?

A third choice for White Star was to offer improved second- and third-class passage, equivalent to first- and second-class on other ships, which would attract the growing second-class and booming immigrant third-class traffic. To achieve this, the ship had to be made to look and feel like a magnificent floating palace.

In implementing a solution in today's world, you are faced with many choices of channels and technologies. For example, how do you deploy your channel strategy to better serve your many classes of customers? You must pick the on-line operation that best meets the business requirements of your organization.

So, what solution did White Star pick? To exploit their business opportunity, they decided to build three gigantic luxury liners over a four-year period. The selected solution was a combination of choices two and three. In today's world, you might choose a new business strategy based around new, emerging technologies. In selecting a solution, you change your business model. This solution becomes your *on-line operation.*

Specify What the On-line Operation Needs to Do

In step 3, describing what your on-line operation is supposed to do, start by articulating the desired output and new capability. Again, let's look at White Star.

Cunard could sail a ship between Southampton and New York in six days, at a speed of 25 knots. With larger ships, White Star would do it in seven days, at a speed of 21 knots. The crossing time was approximately 15 percent longer, but this was not significant over a seven-day trip, where comfort was a critical service factor. A modern comparison is in building an inexpensive, fast sports car versus a very expensive, luxurious sedan. The White Star business solution would provide three ocean-going liners sweeping the Atlantic on a weekly basis. In hindsight, the differentiation on service seemed a good strategy for White Star to pursue.

Likewise, the on-line operation that you pick for your company must be available and deliver your product or service. After all, this is the core of your business requirements. Otherwise, there would be no business reason to implement the solution. Of course, like many terms in business and in on-line operations, "availability" has many definitions. There are so many variations and "gotchas" in this term that a special section later in this chapter is devoted to helping you figure it out.

Justify the Value of the On-line Operation

The objective of this last step is to make a "go/no-go" decision on whether your on-line operation is viable. Hence, you need to start by conducting a quick cost-benefit analysis to highlight viability. Then, you can go through a more detailed business case, to forecast a return on investment (ROI). Sounds simple, right? Well, with technology solution projects, this is never really simple. That's why the following section is entirely devoted to it.

What Are the Cost Benefits of Your On-line Operation?

"ROI" is a general term that encompasses several different financial measures.[1] However, your objective here is a cost-benefit analysis, where you calculate the profit of implementing the on-line operation by subtracting its investment costs from its benefits, and determining whether this is a positive number.

Let's look at the basic elements of ROI more closely. Profits are increased by increasing revenues and/or reducing costs (or expenses). Revenue generally relates to sales. Increasing sales revenue can be done by selling products or services to new customers, or selling more products or services to existing customers.

Costs, or more accurately, on-going operational costs, are both *fixed* and *variable*. Fixed costs relate to amortized spending, such as monthly payments for hosting costs, leased hardware, or licensed software. Variable costs tend to relate to projects, marketing, people, and organization. Reducing operational costs can be done through leveraging resources more effectively, increasing productivity through automation, improved processes, or consolidating for better scale of economy.

In summary, you can look at the formula this way:

Profit = revenue – (costs)

Profit = revenue – (operational costs + solution investment)

Profit = revenue – ((fixed costs + variable costs) + solution investment)

Therefore, you can justify an on-line operation so long as the following is true:

Revenue > fixed costs + variable costs + solution investment

Revenue-generating On-line Operation

Let's examine the ROI formula by applying it to a revenue-generating on-line operation. This could be a Web stock-trading application, a business commerce site, or a credit/debit transaction-based solution. Assume that, before on-line operations, you had the graph on the left of Figure 1.1. After on-line operations begin, your revenue stream looks like the graph on the right. Going on-line, therefore, gives you revenue of $150, operational costs of $60 (fixed and variable), an investment of $30, and a profit of $60.

---

1.   The elements of the ROI equation are Net Operating Income over Investments costs. However, it encompasses financial terms like Return On Assets, Net Present Value, and Internal Rate of Return.

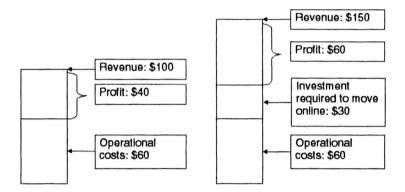

Figure 1.1: Real costs of a revenue-generating on-line operation.

Cost-reducing On-line operation

Let's now examine a cost-reducing on-line operation, which lowers processing costs or produces productivity gains through the automation of paper handling, back-end functions, or workflow processes. Examples of this kind of solution are a corporate HR intranet portal, a financial back-end system, or an Enterprise Resource Planning (ERP) package.

Typically, cost-reducing on-line operations are more difficult to measure. How do you quantify productivity gains or improvements in efficiency? Figure 1.2 shows one possibility. The graph on the left is before on-line operations, and the one on the right is after on-line operations begin. In this case, going on-line requires an investment of $20, but reduces operational costs by $50, for a profit of $30.

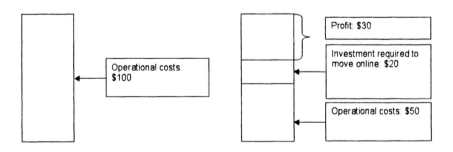

Figure 1.2: Real costs of a cost-reducing on-line operation.

What Are the Total Unavailability Costs?

So, if revenue is greater than the sum of fixed, variable, and investment costs, the project is a go, right? Wrong. One more cost must be included in the formula: *total unavailability costs.* Since profit is entirely dependent on your on-line operation being available, is the value of availability equal to the profit, as the logic suggests? Well, if the on-line operation is unavailable, you can't deliver the operation to gain profit. Do you spend all your profit on availability? In short, no. But how much do you need to spend?

In answering these questions, a lot depends on whether your on-line operation is mission-critical to your business. This affects the real unavailability costs. At this point, we need to explore the concept of *availability* more.

What Is Availability?

Every on-line operation has, at its core, availability. One consistent way of defining availability is in terms that customers and end-users care about: availability of on-line operations.[2] Any time users cannot access your on-line operation, regardless of the reason (whether a hardware problem, a software bug, a communications error, or planned maintenance), it is not available to deliver its intended benefit. Customers cannot purchase, interact, and/or do their jobs until the on-line operation is available.

In putting operations on-line, especially on the Internet, you are faced with the challenge of providing a 24/7 operation to your customers. You need to accurately measure your availability first to maintain this operation, and then to improve it. The traditional approach is to use percentages, but these are aggregated and not very accurate. The best way to measure end-user service availability is by outage minutes per year, assuming a 24-hour, seven-day, year-round clock. From a business and customer viewpoint, these *User Outage Minutes (UOMs)* provide a more meaningful measure and baseline to organizations.

How Do I Factor Availability into the Cost?

Now that you have a better understanding of availability and how to measure it, let's go back to factoring its cost into on-line ROI. When you implement an on-line operation, it won't always be 100 percent available. The question is, how much unavailability can your organization tolerate? Let's go back to the formulas:

---

2. Some vendors measure availability in terms of mean time between failure (MTBF). However, this only assesses the average availability of hardware components and has no significance in terms of application availability. Other vendors count only unplanned downtime in their calculations.

Revenue > fixed costs + variable costs + solution investment
+ total unavailability costs

Total unavailability costs = Unavailability cost[3] x UOMs[4]

For each user outage minute to which you agree, you need to calculate this formula:

Unavailability cost = (average revenue per minute – absence effect value)

However, with on-line operations, sales revenue is not evenly generated. More revenue is generated in peak periods. Knowing the revenue per minute is very significant for those peak period minutes because they are a lot more valuable. The "absence effect value" is what it would cost your company if that minute of operation disappeared:

Absence effect value = (average revenue per minute + repercussion value)

The "repercussion value" is the ripple effect of the outage minute; some minutes will be higher than others. This value is expressed in a dollar amount. You might know this value based on your experience in the industry, but you need a formula that brings out the hidden costs. Too often these costs are overlooked; check these with your organization's accounting department. (Once you have a calculation, you can compare it to estimated industry minutes in Table 1.6.)

Revenue-generating On-line Operation

You know the average value of the outage minutes based on average revenue, but not the real value of each minute. To calculate the repercussion value, you need to consider the following:

- The outage could be devastating during a critical period like a peak sale or "flash crowd," whereas a failure in the middle of the night might have minimal impact.

- The overall duration time of a single outage has an exponential impact on the cost. For example, a 24-hour outage will affect significantly more customers than a two-hour outage. Further, a customer might return in two hours, but not after 24 hours. Costs to service and customer retention increase exponentially for every minute of an outage.

---

3.   In terms of revenue per minute lost.
4.   Based on the total number of outages, the duration time of an outage, and the number of users impacted.

What about Other Costs?

The calculation is still not complete. There are more severe, but less obvious, costs that you need to consider.

In this era of the Web, telemarketing, and micromarketing, brand loyalty might not be as important as fast and efficient service. Customers affected by service downtime are likely to switch to a competitor and remember the incident. The cost to your organization is dissatisfied or lost customers.

Just as important is the value of the customer affected by the outage. For example, the value of a first-class passenger's minute of satisfaction is significantly more important than that of a steerage-class passenger's. In short, your organization can afford to lose some customers. However, it is not always easy to discern the customer's profitability or long-term value. In most organizations, 80 percent of the business is driven by 20 percent of the customers. Losing any of that 20 percent can have a devastating effect.

Many companies guarantee specified service levels of availability to their customers. If the environment fails, these service levels cannot be met, and often the result is a penalty paid to the customer. This varies widely from a single fixed penalty to a time-based amount. In some situations, you might have to consider the potential costs of legal actions. Stock markets and shareholders, always sensitive to downtime, are known to punish companies by dumping their stocks.

It is easier to measure the revenue you lost during a specific outage than to quantify the brand erosion and lowered company prestige that could be used competitively. Regaining service levels and fixing the problem might be straightforward compared to the problem of regaining customer trust, which might take years.

Continuous availability makes it possible for your organization to guarantee a certain service level, and thus create a new competitive edge. A major freight-delivery company guaranteed a refund of customer money if the package did not arrive by 10:30 A.M. A telecommunications company set a 99.9 percent call-completion performance standard for premium toll-free service, and guaranteed refunds when that standard was not met.

Table 1.1 outlines how to calculate the repercussion value for unavailability costs. These should be done on a UOM basis. The parameters in repercussion value calculations are very specific to an organization. For example, loss of shareholder confidence is a heavily weighted parameter for financial institutions.

If you examine total unavailability costs without the repercussion value, you might get the impression that you can sustain a lot of short outages (of one or two hours), as the individual impact of each outage might not seem very high. For example, with a new on-line operation, this might calculate to a low 5 percent of the profit. Most organizations will not worry about a loss relative to the 95 percent profits retained. However, the customer base might be tolerant of only four or five outages before defecting in droves (the repercussion value). So, the 95 percent profit retained could be offset by a potential 30 percent customer loss, which would result in negative profitability in the following year.

Table 1.1: Other Availability Costs for Revenue-generating On-line Operations

Repercussion Value for Unavailable Service	Definition	Calculation (Formula)
Lost transactions	Transactions are completely lost, requiring recovery.	Lost transactions × time for recovery
Cost of adjustments and settlements	The number of transactions incomplete, multiplied by the cost of adjustment.	Transactions × adjustment cost
	The number of errors, multiplied by the cost of manually correcting each error.	Errors + cost
Penalties paid for missing service-level guarantees	The time of unavailable service penalties per minute.	(Time + overtime) × penalty/hour
Loss of customers and goodwill	The number of customers lost, multiplied by the lifetime value cost.	Customers lost × lifetime value
	The number of customers lost, multiplied by the cost of attracting new customers as replacements.	Customers lost × replacement cost
Loss of profitable customers	The number of most-profitable customers lost (based on profitability segmentations), multiplied by the lifetime value cost.	Most-profitable customers lost × lifetime value
Loss of shareholder confidence	The market reaction to downtime.	Drop in share price
Damage to image, brand-name erosion	Damage to image and brand-name erosion have a long-term and serious impact.	Additional marketing costs
Lawsuits	Customers are dissatisfied with service. Service receivers might sue vendors.	Lawsuit costs + loss
Losses due to unfortunate timing	The number of lost opportunities, multiplied by the value of opportunity.	Lost opportunities × value
Repercussion value (of the outage) =		**Total**

Cost-reducing On-line Operation

The profit is entirely dependent on your on-line operation being available. To calculate the repercussion value, you need to consider the following:

- The time of the outage. For example, if it occurs during a critical period like month- or year-end, it could have a significant impact on processing. Different minutes have different values to different companies at different times.

- The overall duration time of a single outage has an exponential impact on user and support costs. This is caused by hidden interdependencies to other applications or services, which in turn affect different and unexpected user populations who use the service indirectly. This underlines why the speed of recovery is so imperative and is part of the business case.

What about Other Costs Outside of Processing?

There are still more severe but not as obvious costs that you need to consider. Depending on the industry, when on-line operations or services are down, many employees cannot perform their jobs properly. Lost productivity can be even more costly than lost revenue. Besides, catching up lost work results in wasted compensation and overtime costs. An indirect cost might be associated with your employees and their inability to complete their own activities or tasks because of the dependence on the service. Just as important is the value of the user affected by the outage. For example, the value of a department head's minute of time is significantly greater than a clerk's.

Unexpected service downtime means unanticipated bills for the repair of your environment, including support, consulting services, specialists, and user or administrator retraining. In cases where error causes a serious problem, the cost of recovering the environment can be very significant. The cost of recovery might result in additional cost if it is done during off-hours or involves other support organizations.

To conduct worldwide operations efficiently, you must make your basic business operations available 24 hours a day, seven days a week. A manufacturing facility in Germany or Korea might need to access information from headquarters' databases in New York, regardless of the time of day. Table 1.2 outlines the repercussion-value calculations that are specific to an organization. For example, lost user productivity is a heavily weighted parameter with most organizations.

Table 1.2: Other Availability Costs for Cost-reducing On-line Operations

Repercussion Value for Unavailable Service	Definition	Calculation (Formula)
Cost of user employee productivity lost	Directly (average loss of productivity)	
	The number of users affected multiplied by unavailable service time	Users × time cost/hour
	The number of users affected multiplied by the catch-up time required	Users ((time × cost/hour) + (overtime × cost/hour))
	Other employees affected indirectly multiplied by unavailable service time	Employees × time × cost/hour
Cost of adjustments and settlements	The number of incomplete transactions multiplied by the adjustment cost	Transactions × adjustment cost
	The number of errors multiplied by the cost of manual correction of error	Errors + cost
Additional support and maintenance expenses	The number of staff required to put the on-line operation back to normal	Support staff × (time + overtime) × cost/hour
Penalties paid for missing service-level guarantees	The time of unavailable service multiplied by the penalty costs per minute	(Time + overtime) × penalty/hour
Loss of confidence in service	User loss of confidence in the services, which might affect morale and satisfaction	Additional internal marketing costs
Losses due to unfortunate timing	The number of lost business opportunities and their values	Lost opportunities × value
Repercussion value (of the outage) =		**Total**

As you can see, the repercussion value is a significant factor in the formula. Figure 1.3 shows that the actual cost of unavailability is not linear. The repercussion value has a much greater real impact than actually perceived.

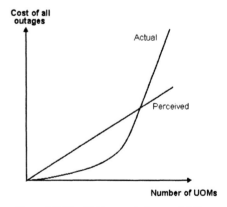

Figure 1.3: The hidden cost of unavailability.

Creating a Technologically Savvy Cost-benefit Calculation

So, how much of the profit should you spend on availability? Where do you want your organization to be positioned along the curve in Figure 1.3? The answer is very specific to your organization, but it is based on completing the following formula:

- If you know the repercussion value of each minute, you can calculate the absence-effect value.

- If you know the absence-effect value of each minute, you can calculate its unavailability cost.

- If you know each minute's unavailability cost, you can add them together for each outage, to create the total unavailability cost.

- With the total unavailability cost, you can evaluate the following relation:
  Revenue > fixed costs + variable costs + solution investment
  + total unavailability costs

If the relation is true, then you are ready to move on to Chapter 2.

Calculating Titanic's Projected Cost Benefits

White Star's business case for its three liners was based on increasing revenue through superior service. The projected revenue from one round trip assumed the following revenue opportunities:

- The price of a first-class suite was $4,350, with four passengers to a suite and 905 passengers in this class.

- The price of a second-class suite was $1,750, with four passengers to a suite and 564 passengers in this class.

- The price of a third-class ticket was $30 per passenger and 1,134 passengers in this class.

- *Titanic* carried 900 tons of baggage and freight at a total price of $5,000.

As you can see in Figure 1.4, a staggering 75 percent of the total revenue was based on first-class passages.

Projected revenue per trip		
Passage fares	**# of passengers**	**Revenue**
First	$4,350	900	$978,750
Second	$1,750	564	$246,750
Third	$30	1,134	$34,020
Cargo		
Revenue		$5,000
Gross revenue per trip		$1,259,520

Figure 1.4: Projected revenue per trip.

To find the revenue per minute, start by determining the total minutes in the trip. If the crossing time is seven days, then the number of minutes is

$$7 \times 24 \times 60 = 10,800$$

or 20,160 minutes on a round trip.

Adding all the passenger minute types together, the revenue per minute is

$$\$1,264,958 \div 20,160 = \$63$$

White Star's business case was also based on reducing costs. A larger ship carries more passengers and has greater economies of scale. The projected costs from one round trip, as shown in Figure 1.5, assumed the following operating costs:

- The average crewmember's wage was $50 per trip, with around 900 crew members.

- Provisions, or meals, were $70 per trip per passenger/crew (averaged).

- Fuel or coal consumption was 825 tons, or $25, per trip per passenger/crew.

- Routine maintenance was $5,000 (200 staff at $25 per week).

Operating costs projected per trip		
Average cost per person	**Numbers**	**Cost**
Crew wage	$50	900	$45,000
Provisions	$70	3,547	$248,290
Fuel	$25	3,547	$88,675
Maintenance			$10,000
(routine)			
Gross costs per trip			$391,965

Figure 1.5: Operating costs projected per trip.

The solution investment costs per trip were as follows:

- Construction costs of one ship were $7.5 million; round to $9 million with interest.

- Amortize the construction costs over 36 months = $250,000.

- Depreciate at 10 percent per year, or $900,000; amortize over 12 months = $75,000.

Therefore, solution investment costs = $325,000 per month, or $162,500 per trip. Remember that

> Revenue > fixed costs + variable costs + solution investment costs
>   + total unavailability costs

However, White Star assumed 100 percent availability. Thus, unavailability costs would be zero, so per round trip:

> $1,264,958 > $394,165 + $162,500 + 0

A healthy profit! White Star completed a "profitability analysis" (discussed in appendix B) to mitigate the liner construction costs based on the total projected cash flow. The breakeven point was reached five years into the project, or at the end of two years of operation. However, a liner's life span was 20 to 30 years, so the investment was longer-term. In cost-justifying your on-line operation, the breakeven point will probably be reached within one to two years into the project. However, today's on-line operation lifespan is typically a short three to five years.

Calculating Titanic's Real Cost Benefits

Finally, and most important, let's look at the formula with the real unavailability costs factored in, assuming that revenue, operational costs, and solution investment costs are the same. The first outage minute—the first minute that the boat was incapacitated—was catastrophic. It had this tremendous effect on the calculation (allowing for creative math in which infinity is subtracted from a non-infinite number):

> If repercussion losses = infinity

> Then absence effect = infinity

> Then unavailability cost = infinity

> Then total costs = infinity

In this case, the formula

> Revenue > costs

is not true. Thus, White Star goes bankrupt! This did not happen, however, because White Star was bailed out by the government through the British Investigation. For pure business accounting, though, a government bailout is akin to total failure and bankruptcy.

In your on-line operation these costs may be prohibitive to even starting the project. Therefore, you need to ensure that you allocate some of your solution investment costs on risk mitigation (discussed in appendix D) to lower the probability of unavailability. The subsequent chapters will highlight where and how to focus these investments.

Availability of On-line Operations: It's How You Look at It

The following sections look at different aspects of availability in detail, so that you can competently navigate the business requirement process with your technical workers and vendors.

If you think "availability" is a simple term that is not open to interpretation, think again. Consider this scenario: An employee at a company complains of limited information access because the LAN is "always down." The LAN manager responds that the LAN is up 95 percent of the time.

This might sound impressive, but Table 1.3 shows how some percentages break down in a 40-hour work week, and over one year. Look at the second column of the last row! One percent downtime translates to 3.5 days! That certainly isn't what most people think of as good availability. Companies can't afford 1 percent downtime, much less 5 percent.

Table 1.3: Translating Percentage Uptime into Minutes

Outage Minutes per 40-hour Week					
% availability	90%	99%	99.9%	99.99%	99.999%	100%
Outage minutes	240	24	2.4	0.24	0.024	0

Outage Minutes per Year					
% availability	90%	99%	99.9%	99.99%	99.999%	100%
Annual outage minutes	50,000	5,000	500	50	5	0
Outage impact	35 days	3.5 days	8.3 hours	50 minutes	5 minutes	0 minutes

Why You Need to Avoid Percentages

Typically, IT management measures downtime as the total percentage of time the hardware environment is not available to provide the service. This is extremely misleading and completely unacceptable in today's business environment for the following reasons:

- It has no consideration for *critical periods*, when many customers require a service, such as ATM service during peak periods like Friday and Saturday.

- It only reflects the hardware delivering the business service. It does not address layers such as the software, process, or organization.

- Ninety percent availability translates into 50,000 minutes of outage, which is 35 outage days. Would customers accept five consecutive days of outage? No, but the figures allow for this.

- This is a view from the inside out, and not representative of the customer. A partial outage is not recognized by this approach, so the approach is flawed.

Availability has to be measured from a customer's perspective, that is, the point to which the service is delivered. Figure 1.6 illustrates the two measures or views of availability. The view on the left is the predominantly used technical view, where uptime percentage numbers are presented based on the availability of underlying servers (where the overall percentage is an aggregate of all the servers) or some other definition of percentage. The view on the right is a business view, where downtime is measured in User Outage Minutes (UOMs). This is a far more accurate and indicative way of representing availability. The views can be summarized as bottom-up or top-down.

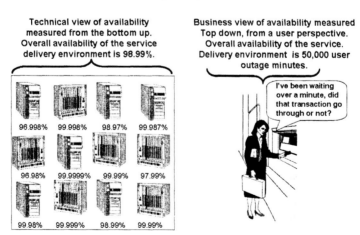

Figure 1.6: Two different views of availability. The right hand view is the more meaningful and preferred.

Unavailability of on-line business operations varies by industry, organization, and business. However, within financial institutions, 4,000 unscheduled outage minutes per year is common. This translates into 66.67 hours, or 10 days, of complete downtime. Organizations achieving 1,000 unscheduled outage minutes a year are doing really well.

User Outage Minutes

The recommended method for viewing your unavailability or downtime is to view it from the outside in, from the customer/user perspective. The recommended way to measure end-user service unavailability is by UOMs per year, assuming a 24-hour, seven-day, year-round clock. UOMs provide a more meaningful measure and baseline to organizations. UOMs should be continuously collected and recorded in a database, initially through manual processes, and then evolving to automated ones. The cause of each failure should be determined. Selected business users or client representatives should act as watchdogs to ensure that this is done diligently.

Table 1.4 illustrates one service measured in annual UOMs. The approach is useful, as it provides an accurate client view of unavailability. An organization needs to include planned outage minutes for the component, so that improvements can be made continuously.

Table 1.4: Annual User Outage Minutes (AOM)

Component Affected	AOM per Component	Total Components	Total AOM	Clients Affected	AOM Unplanned	AOM Planned
Application	600	1	600	2,000	1,200,000	100,000
Server	1,200	2	2,400	500	576,000	200,000
Network	600	1	600	2,000	1,200,000	500,000
LAN cards	240	100	24,000	20	480,000	100,000
Total	2,640	104	27,600	4,520	3,456,000	900,000

Table 1.5 illustrates how measuring availability has to move away from technology-centric measures to client-centric ones to be meaningful, with availability measured at a client touch point like an ATM, kiosk, Web site, or other channel. The numbers represent outage minutes. The goal is to reduce these to zero. The components making up the overall view of availability include everything from the hardware, system software, and application software, to the network, clients, staff, operating environment, and the processes and procedures that guide the staff.

Table 1.5: Moving the Availability View Out to the Client

UOMs	100,000	50,000	10,000	5,000	1,000	500
Client						
Hardware	➡➡➡➡	➡➡➡➡	➡➡➡➡			
Operating system	➡➡➡➡➡	➡➡➡➡➡				
Application software	➡➡➡➡					
Network						
Hardware	➡➡➡➡➡	➡➡➡➡➡	➡➡➡➡➡	➡➡➡➡➡		
Operating system	➡➡➡➡➡	➡➡➡➡➡	➡➡➡➡			
Application software	➡➡➡➡➡	➡➡➡➡➡				
Server						
Hardware	➡➡➡➡➡	➡➡➡➡➡	➡➡➡➡➡	➡➡➡➡➡	➡➡➡➡➡	
Operating system	➡➡➡➡➡	➡➡➡➡➡	➡➡➡➡➡	➡➡➡➡		
Application software	➡➡➡➡➡	➡➡➡➡➡	➡➡➡➡➡			

Industry Standards for Availability

It is generally accepted that reasonable industry-availability standards are 99.9 percent with a three-hour recovery time. However, this does not include planned downtime, nor does it specify whether this is top-down or bottom-up.

Environments that are continuously available give you a chance to distinguish your organization's customer service from that of your competitors. This is an increasingly important competitive edge in industries where pricing and quality differences are minimal. Customers want the freedom to conduct business at their convenience, from wherever they happen to be. Availability enables companies to deliver that level of service.

Some Industry Averages for the Cost of Downtime

To provide you some further insight into the cost of downtime, let's examine the banking industry. For every minute a critical business service is down, the organization loses over $1,000. For an organization achieving only 90 percent availability, this calculates to a loss of $50,000,000 per year. Even a figure of 99 percent, considered to be high and thus good, calculates to a $5,000,000 loss per year. When all factors are considered, the cross-industry average outage loss is $330,000. The average outage time is four hours.

Table 1.6 highlights outage costs by industry. These are minimums, reflecting only the more obvious losses. Not included are reactions by the marketplace and shareholders, or such things as service-level penalties.

Table 1.6: Outage Costs By Industry

Industry	Description	By Minute	By Hour
Package shipping	Like Fedex	$467	$28,000
Internet e-tailer (small)	Like CDNow	$750	$45,000
Computer vendor	Like Dell	$1,000	$60,000
Financial Institution	Like Citibank (credit/debit)	$1,300	$78,000
Retailer sales catalog	Like Sears	$1,500	$90,000
Internet e-tailer (large)	Like Amazon	$1,500	$90,000
Financial institution	Like Charles-Schwab (brokerage)	$1,500	$90,000
TV home shopping	Like The Shopping Channel	$1,550	$93,000
Telco	Like ATT	$2,000	$120,000
Pay-per-view	Cable provider, like Rogers	$2,500	$150,000
Network vendor	Like Cisco	$2,783	$167,000
Microchip manufacturer	Like Intel	$3,750	$225,000
Airline	Like Sabre	$36,000	$2,160,000

It is very easy to view your service and applications uniformly and look to applying high availability unvaryingly across applications, as shown in Table 1.7. However, this is a very expensive solution.

Table 1.7: Outage Costs by On-line Operation
(Source: "Five Ts of Database Availability," Standish Group Research, 1999.)

Application	Downtime Cost per Minute, Normal Load	Downtime Cost per Minute, Peak Load
Customer Relationship Management	$2,200	$2,500
Data Warehouse	$5,800	$6,300
Electronic Commerce	$2,500	$7,800
Enterprise Resource Planning	$6,400	$7,900
Supply Chain Management	$4,400	$6,600

Calculating downtime costs is critical. An honest evaluation of the real economic impact of unavailability is required to determine investments. Table 1.8 shows how an organization's business services are assessed for service availability, measured in dollars per hour. For some business units, like finance, the availability requirements vary greatly across the breadth of service offerings. The integration of services creates interdependencies and changes the status of these services.

Table 1.8 helps you determine what applications are critical to the revenue stream, and what you need to protect. However, you should take care. For many organizations, the dependence on some services like email has shifted from convenient to mission-critical. Determining investments is like a fire drill. You might have to leave some of your infrastructure and applications in the burning building. The question is, what can you afford to leave behind?

Table 1.8: Defining Degrees of Service Availability

Business Services (Value in Thousands of Dollars per Hour)	Can Tolerate Extended Loss	Can Tolerate Loss for a Day	Can Reenter Lost Work	Can Tolerate Loss for a Few Hours	Can Lose Inflight Transactions	50,000 AOM 9 a.m. To 5 p.m., Mon to Fri	25,000 AOM 8 a.m. To 2 p.m.	5,000 AOM 24/7	Zero AOM 24/7
HR	$5	$5	$10						
Financial		$7	$11	$15	$20	$25			
Administration			$12	$16	$20				
Communication				$20	$25	$29	$34	$39	
Business operation								$35	$40
External client									$50
External partner								$40	$45

Conclusion

The following sections summarize the major points of this chapter and how they relate to your business today. For more information on these concepts, search the Internet for these keywords and phrases: *Project Management Institute, financial business case, ROI and metrics, ROWI, downtime, service levels, outages,* and *outage metrics.*

Major Points, Considerations, and Titanic Lessons

- Under competitive pressure, White Star took advantage of new emerging technologies to create a bold and competitive business strategy to win the lucrative transatlantic trade for all three classes of passage, specifically the first-class nouveau riche.

- The strategy pushed the limits of emerging technology and created substantially larger ships. The strategy was based on luxury and comfort rather than speed.

- *Titanic*'s class segregation system is no different from today's business services, which cater to different customer segments with varying value to the organization.

- White Star's "profitability analysis" for the construction of the liners highlighted a breakeven point at the end of two years of operation.

Best Practices for Your Organization

- Outline a business case or cost-benefit analysis as the first step in the creation of your on-line operations.

- Determine the cost of unavailability, based on the potential number of customers/users affected.

- Determine which services are mission-critical to keep the business going.

- Understand the service/application integration and interdependencies, as some backend applications might be critical to other applications.

- Take a top-down view of availability from a business user perspective, rather than a bottom-up view from the technologies. That is, take a customer-centric rather than technology-centric view.

- Establish desirable service-level targets to guide the architect in subsequent phases in the project lifecycle. (This is discussed in more detail in chapters 2 and 3.)

- Avoid the misguided rush to acquiring solutions driven by a new emerging technology. Ensure due diligence by examining the business problem, articulating business requirements, defining the potential costs, and assessing the possible risks of the initiative.

- Bring in users to define the business requirements; avoid second-guessing them through IT representatives. This dramatically raises the likelihood of success.

Questions You Can Ask Today

At this stage in the project, you should expect back the following answers from IT:

An articulated business problem or opportunity:

- What are the changes affecting the organization? Are responses required? If so, what type of responses? What are the risks of responding and not responding?

- What are your desired capacities? What is the gap between your current and desired capabilities? How urgently is this needed?

A defined business solution to the problem:

- How can this problem be addressed? What is the approach?

- What type of solution is likely to address this problem? What are the choices? How are the choices ranked, and what are the criteria?

- What emerging technologies are available?

A specification of what the on-line operation is supposed to do:

- What is the expected output of the on-line operation?

- How does the new capability look?

A justification of the value of the on-line operation:

- What is the business rationale and justification for the on-line operation?

- How will an on-line operation benefit the organization? Who will it benefit most?

- How will an on-line operation affect other parts of the organization?

- What are the investment and operating costs? What is the ROI and breakeven period? What are the unavailability costs?

- What are the current levels of availability of other business services (Table 1.6)?

CHAPTER 2

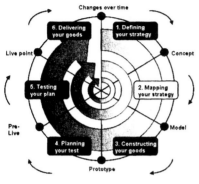

Mapping Your Strategy

Where we have mapped out a strategy and business architecture we have found that we can build the technology solution first time and get it right.

Richard J. Smith, C.A.,
14 years as CFO for
companies in the electronics sector

Chapter Objectives

When you are done with this chapter, you will be able to define the functional and non-functional requirements for your on-line operation. With these, you will be ready for chapter 3, in which you start to construct your on-line operation.

In this chapter, you learn how to look at the on-line operation and verify, or checkpoint, strategic elements of your plan. The existence of these elements will help you create the setting for granular decisions in chapter 3. The chapter ensures that the business view is etched into the design, and that the service-delivery environment can be built with the appropriate levels of availability to protect the on-line operation.

What Steps Do I Need to Follow?

You go through the following eight steps to checkpoint your plan's strategic elements:

1. Transfer the business into functional requirements.

2. Identify the existence of non-functional requirements.

3. Verify the logical storage and movement of key elements.

4. Plot the physical layout of the delivered goods.

5. Break the physical model into granular components.

6. Test the physical model for robustness in a typical operating environment.

7. Test the physical model for robustness in extenuating circumstances.

8. Guarantee the delivery of the required physical layout.

Transfer the Business into Functional Requirements

You need to transfer the business requirements into functional requirements to understand the main functions of the business entity and what it does. The White Star architects turned the business requirements into functional requirements, and defined the functionality of the ship. The main functions of the ship were transportation and hospitality. Likewise, your project must turn the stated business requirements, the reason for existence, into functional requirements. These are the main functions of the on-line operation, in the form of the application, and what it does through its interfaces, transactions, and information. For example, its main functions involve how it interfaces and communicates outside of itself, how it handles transactions and their processing, and how it maintains and exchanges information.

Titanic's functions and features were defined for the three passenger classes and crew, the equivalent of a small town. These included such day-to-day functions as hospitality in the form of accommodation, catering, recreation, and entertainment; internal communications; and external (wireless) communications. Likewise, your project's functions and the features are defined for user and customer segments. Your system must have certain user-system interface (*UI*) features, which can range from attractive to unsightly. UI elements such as user profiles and how the users will use the services become *scenarios* or *use cases*.

Identify the Existence of Non-functional Requirements

Non-functional requirements are incredibility important to a project, as this is where you could lose your shirt. It is necessary to identify non-functional requirements because they define the operational characteristics of a system. Non-functional requirements are the requirements outside of the main functions of an entity and what it does. For a ship like *Titanic*, these requirements related to safety, stability, security, maintainability, and environmental factors. For example, the hull had to be stable, with a correct draught and an even keel. These requirements had to be carefully considered, as every ongoing change to these had an effect on the weight and the center of gravity. They also affected functions like the overall number of cabins on the decks. Also, the loads on board had to remain within safe parameters, so that stability was always maintained no matter what the ship was carrying. Through the journey, water and fuel were used, shifting the center of gravity.

For an IT system, requirements related to non-functions include availability (similar to safety); security; and system management based on the *runtime properties*[1] of the system. A solution has to be stable and continuously available, so the requirements have to be carefully considered. Other requirements based on *non-runtime properties*[2] include scalability, portability, maintainability, environmental factors, and evolvability. A mistake in defining non-functional requirements can have a significant cost impact on the project budget, far more reaching than the equivalent mistake in functional requirements.

The non-functional requirements for ship performance and passenger capacity that defined the speed, power, and fuel consumption had a far-reaching impact. The hull form determined *Titanic*'s speed, which had to be able to sail at high speed using less than its full complement of engines, a concept known as *redundancy*. The ship's business requirements specified a luxurious ship of immense size. Speed was not as critical as space or comfort, which reduced the power requirements and engine size, providing even more space.

Likewise, the non-functional requirements for system performance and capacity have a far-reaching impact on operations. The system has to perform with redundancy. With on-line operations, speed or user response is absolutely critical.

The ship constraints started with defining size specifications like length, width, breadth, and draught. These were mandated by docking conditions. For example, length was dictated by the length of docks, while draught and width were dictated by entry into ports, canals, and channels. With on-line operations, the constraints must conform to the technical and business standards already in place (such as the standard operating environment and the geographic location).

For the ship, non-functional requirements also define service levels for runtime properties like performance, capacity, and safety, and set baseline targets for the speed of crossing and the service output. With on-line operations, non-functional requirements define the runtime properties for performance, capacity, and availability, and set baseline targets for service output. These are subsequently used for developing SLAs and SLOs.

Verify the Logical Storage and Movement of Key Elements

The White Star architects had to determine how and where passengers and crew would be accommodated within the living quarters, and how they would move about the ship. These factors dictated the physical layout of the ship. Driven by the business requirements, the

---

1. Functions that are dependent on the system running.
2. Functions that are not dependent on the system running.

ship's space was allocated to carry the optimum number of first-class passengers. Table 2.1 illustrates the space allocated to the three classes and crew. Third-class space per person was about 10 percent of the first-class space allocated.

Table 2.1: Number of Passengers and Crew

Class		Numbers	Allocated Space
First class	✝✝✝✝✝✝✝✝✝	905	60%
Second class	✝✝✝✝✝	564	28%
Third class	✝✝✝✝✝✝✝✝✝✝✝	1,134	7%
Crew	✝✝✝✝✝✝✝	944	5%
Total		**3,547**	**100%**

The logical architecture focused on the needs of the passengers and provided a detailed view of the principal functions of a ship. Since the principal business driver was luxury, the ship was architected to provide plenty of space for the first- and second-class passengers, along the lines of a luxury hotel (as shown in Figure 2.1). This was also reflected by the relatively high crew-to-passenger ratio.

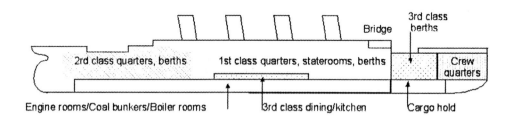

Figure 2.1: The logical architecture model for the ship laid out the space requirements for passengers and crew.

The completion of functional and non-functional requirements leads to the creation of the *logical architecture model* that shows the movement and storage of system data (crew) and business data (passengers). Your project needs a logical layout of the functions to determine what data should be stored where, and how it should be moved through transactions,[3] like *Titanic*'s passengers. The logical architecture model for an on-line operation is a box diagram representing all the major functions, as shown in Figure 2.2.

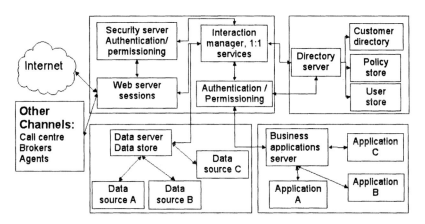

Figure 2.2: The logical architecture model for your on-line operation.

Similar to the way *Titanic*'s architects allocated space to the three-class system, many organizations recognize the need to move away from a "one service for all" approach to a *tiered*, or *segmented*, service structure, as shown in Figure 2.3. Typically, this is based on the relative value of customers to the organization and the needs of these customers. For example, service packages based on variant levels are mapped to customer segments determined by individual profitability and value. The pricing of services is also driven by the relative value of each segment and the choice of delivery channels available.

---

3. Use of e-business patterns greatly facilitates the creation of an architecture through asset re-use.

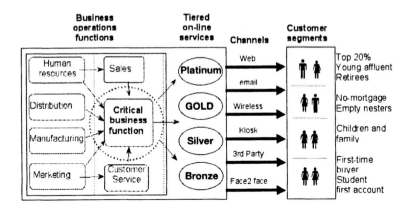

Figure 2.3: How an organization offers tiered business services, through channels, to a segmented customer base.

One important consideration is that a business service might need to be subdivided into levels of availability based on the service levels provided. For example, some customers might

- Not mind 20-second wait times and limited channels, and prefer electronic touch points.

- Demand 24/7 service guarantees regarding certain channels.

- Require a consistent experience and access to multiple channels.

Plot the Physical Layout of the Delivered Goods

The White Star architects had to define a physical layout for the ship, which would shape its construction. The *physical architecture model* in Figure 2.4 highlighted the physical layout of the ship, the detailed dimensions, the number of floors, and how the major functions would be allocated to the floors. It also illustrated how people would move around between floors and gain access between points, using elevators and staircases.

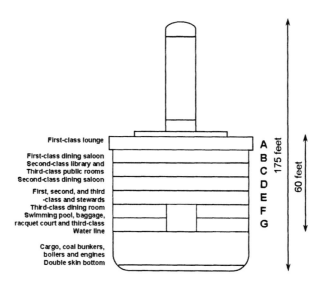

Figure 2.4: The physical architecture model, showing the physical layout of the floors.

Your project needs a physical architecture model like the one in Figure 2.5 to lay out the on-line operation and the surrounding service-delivery environment.[4] The physical architecture model determines the construction that needs to be undertaken and helps you visualize the integration requirements. It reflects the major physical or technological entities, such as the client, network, and server, that make up the overall service-delivery environment. It also provides a high-level view of the kind of availability that is built in at a technology level, such as where the fault-tolerant servers are, how resilient the network connections are to a single failure point, and where the redundancy is.

4. Assuming an existing service delivery environment to which you are adding an online operation.

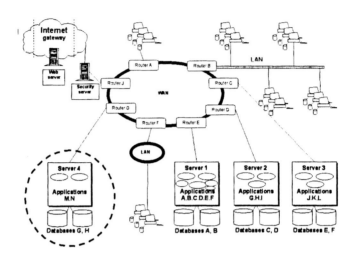

Figure 2.5: The physical architecture model commonly found in many IT departments, with the new on-line operation in the left corner.

Break the Physical Model into Granular Components

The White Star architects had to refine the physical layout of *Titanic* and break it down into granular components so that they would know what they needed to build or buy. The first step was to build a model to determine these components. This was the *general arrangement plan (GAP)*, or blueprint, for the ship. The GAP, shown in Figure 2.6, included the space layout for the ship and its main functions. It was driven by the economics of the business case in appendix C, and the segregation of the ship into three classes.

The GAP provides a detailed and granular view of the infrastructure and technology supporting the functions of the ship. It defined the layout of each of the floors in detail, e.g., the number of public rooms, staterooms, cabins, galleries, restaurants, and cargo areas required to meet the business, functional, and non-functional requirements.

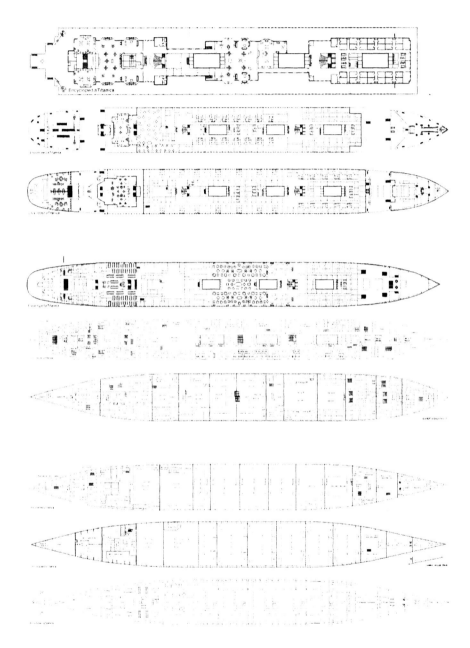

Figure 2.6: Titanic's general arrangement plan.

The Role of the Inventory Model

With your project, the *inventory model* shown in Figure 2.7 provides a more detailed view of the individual entities like the hardware, software, and technologies, so that you know what to buy. Related to the physical architecture model, the inventory model provides a framework for simplifying and understanding the complex structure of a service-delivery environment. It is an effective reference and diagnostic tool, so a lot of care and judgment should be taken over its details.

The inventory model includes the following major layers:

- *Applications* that deliver the business services.

- *Databases* that support the applications with data.

- *Middleware* that supports the applications and their intercommunication.

- *System utilities* that support the middleware.

- The *operating system* that provides the underlying software environment.

- *Hardware* such as servers, networks (access methods), and clients.

- The *environment* composed of physical elements like air conditioning and power.

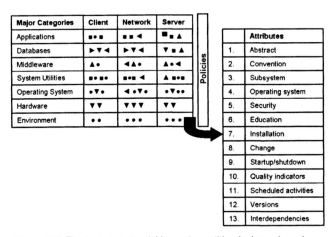

Figure 2.7: The inventory model by major entities (columns), and major categories (rows), with each component having a set of attributes defined according to the collected information available.

The *policies* of the inventory model refer to the specific guidelines for each major category. For example, the application policy contains guidelines for application development and support.

The *attributes* of the inventory model provide a detailed definition of all the activities associated with the component, e.g., potential states and interfaces. The inventory model provides a logical categorization of flow from the user (client) into the environment (host) through a network. Typically, the model is created in a relational database to map relationships and dependencies.

The Role of the Interdependency Model

The physical architecture (Figure 2.5) and inventory model (Figure 2.7) help determine the infrastructure and technologies in place. With the identification of applications in the inventory model, it is possible to map the business services and user populations to the physical architecture model, resulting in the *interdependency model* shown in Figure 2.8. This model readily identifies the principal technology entities/components that underpin each business service. From there, you can start to understand how the entities interrelate and interact, and their overall interdependencies.

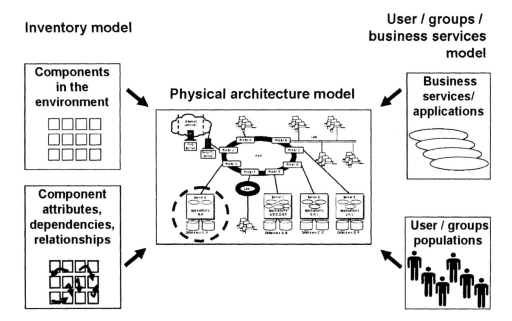

Figure 2.8: The interdependency model—similar to the physical architecture model, but overlayered with the business services from Table 2.2 and information from the inventory model.

Why is this important to understand? On-line operations drive the demands for instantaneous information and easy access to it. Typically, this means integrating back-end systems with front-end (e-commerce) platforms. However, in most organizations, legacy data is unwieldy because legacy systems and applications were never designed to share information with customers or suppliers. Many organizations can only provide access to legacy application information through convoluted application integration, i.e., access paths to information that are beyond the scope of the original architecture.

To create the interdependency model, user populations need to be defined at a granular level. You need to define which business units, departments, and groups require what type of access to what services, and where these users are located. Table 2.2 highlights how an organization's user populations map to its business services and applications.

Table 2.2: *User-Groups/Business-Service Model*

Business Unit	Group	Location	1 A	B	C	D	E	F	2 G	H	I	3 J	K	L	4 M	N
Finance	User group 1	Toronto	✓	✓	✓		✓	✓	✓	✓	✓	✓	✓	✓		
Sales	User group 2	New York	✓		✓	✓	✓	✓	✓	✓	✓	✓	✓			
Marketing	User group 3	Los Angeles							✓		✓	✓	✓	✓		
Manufacturing	User group 4	Mexico City							✓	✓	✓	✓	✓	✓		
Distribution	User group 5	Dallas							✓	✓	✓	✓		✓		
Customer Service	User group 6	Vancouver										✓	✓	✓	✓	✓
Customer access	External	Internet										✓	✓	✓	✓	✓

A common perception is that all users have to have access to all services. This ubiquitous access extends the user population for each service and carries a high cost.

Test the Physical Model in a Typical Operating Environment

The White Star architects had to test the models to determine how the logical and physical designs worked and their expected performance against plan. The objective was to identify vulnerabilities, to save costly mistakes later.

Models Used for Testing

Model testing, where the hydrodynamics of the ship was tested in water tanks with design models, was still a new field. David Watson Taylor, an American marine architect, built the first ship-model testing establishment at the Washington (D.C.) Navy Yard. In 1910, Taylor undertook experiments to discover what characteristics of a ship's hull governed its water resistance to ensure that its power could meet its speed. These experiments were also done to test the ocean equivalent of the ship's road-handling ability.

Prior to construction, a 30-foot model of *Titanic* was completed. As shown in Figure 2.9, it was accurate in detail and scale. It was useful in the initial study, as it provided both the qualitative and quantitative views required for design analysis. During the analysis, thousands of calculations were made by hand[5]. The output was significant, as it influenced areas such as the hull construction and bulkheads, and even the number and position of cabins. The shipbuilder's model also acted as a showcase for the builder for potential clients and investors.

Figure 2.9: The shipbuilder's model of Titanic, now on display in the Ulster Museum of Folk and Art.

---

5. Today's computers have dramatically improved this activity, thus allowing for complex modeling.

Flow Analysis for Titanic

The shipbuilder's model was used to provide a quasi-simulated environment for determining how the logical and physical designs worked, relative to the functionality of the ship. This was based on the *flow analysis*, a high-level trace of the passenger and crew navigation around the ship, focusing on ease of access and use of functions.

The approach determined the "passenger experience" taken from the view of the captain, who oversaw this and other "back-office" events. The passenger's experience was explored, particularly for the first class, from boarding to expected departure, from entering the great dining room via the grand staircase to using the recreational facilities like the swimming pool, Turkish bath, and squash courts. The analysis determined the passenger interaction with the ship's functions and measured the quality of service through the value to passengers, ease of use, and the overall standards of service onboard.

In completing the flow analysis, the crew navigation also had to be assessed. Consideration was made for horizontal access routes through the ship and the bulkheads. This was particularly important for the crew engineers and fire stokers. These groups operated the machinery, and therefore needed to rapidly move between the engine, boiler rooms, and coal bunkers, across all the compartments. These rooms supported the mechanical components and extended practically the full length of the ship, as shown in Figure 2.10.

In designing access and doorways, consideration had to be given to the different rates of flooding and how the doors would operate. For example, the circular hatches found on submarines were possibly too small and cumbersome to operate. Increasing the size of doors, however, limited how quickly they could be locked shut. The ship required doors that could be shut automatically and safely in a matter of seconds. Effectively, gravity-based drop-down doors could best meet these requirements.

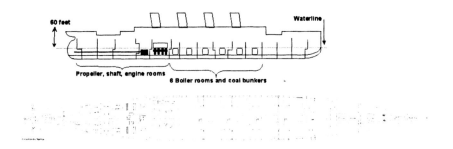

Figure 2.10: The access routes model, showing the layout of the mechanical components that the crew required for rapid access of operations.

In modeling failure scenarios, thought was given to the complete evacuation of the ship. At the time, lifeboats were considered ferrying vessels to move passengers to a rescue ship, rather than rescue vessels themselves. Therefore, consideration was made for the number of lifeboats required, along with their access and locations. As shown in Figure 2.11, lifeboats were traditionally located on the top decks, where they would be filled and carefully lowered the height of the ship. Ease of access depended on where you were on the ship. The lower down you were in the "bowels" of the ship, like third class, the more difficult the access.

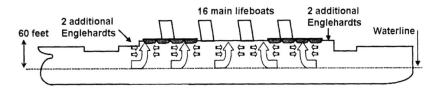

Figure 2.11: The flow analysis for evacuating and abandoning ship, with the location of the main lifeboats on the first-class deck.

Flow Analysis for Your On-line Operation

Your project needs to test whether the logical and physical designs work. The objective is to identify vulnerabilities and to save costly mistakes. The solution is to test the model in a simulated software environment.

The purpose of the flow analysis model is to provide a high-level trace of each critical business transaction as it traverses the end-to-end service-delivery environment. The activity reviews the new business service. The environmental considerations affecting the availability of transaction delivery are considered, such as the likelihood of hardware or software failure. The trace follows the progression of interactions on the critical business transaction. As shown in Figure 2.12, a transaction path is followed and monitored for its interactions with each function/component/element, as it snakes through the service-delivery environment based on the underpinning components. The integrity of each transaction is also measured. The flow analysis considers the whole business transaction path from entry to exit, detailing each interaction and every change of circumstances, and then examining every circumstance for high availability.

From this trace, each component on the business transaction path is identified and assessed for its availability. A what-if failure scenario is then determined for the impact of any of the components failing, and the likelihood of this Mean Time between Failure or to Recovery (*MTBF/MTTR*). This type of analysis depends on the identification of output from the architecture and availability models, and requires a lot of effort. It should be reserved for very specific, critical parts of the service-delivery environment.

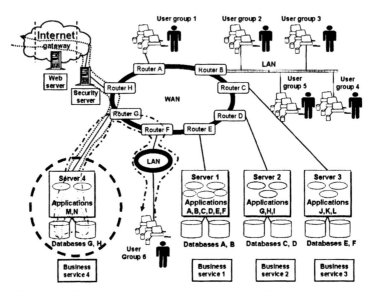

Figure 2.12: The flow analysis model for two critical business transactions.

Key components can be further reviewed for availability and reliability by using the questionnaire in appendix D. For example, determine whether the following components are in place:

- Multiple internal communication paths.

- Duplicate telecommunication lines.

- Contingency ports for lines.

- Redundant power supplies.

- Replication and redundancy in application servers.

- Automated backup or recovery processes.

Where a single point of failure is found, a business decision is required as to whether to provide a greater level of availability, or accept the risk-to-cost ratio. At each stage, "what-if" questions should be considered to cover less obvious eventualities, like where links exist to processes requiring human intervention. For example, groups of users might interact with a call center or over the phone to complete a transaction. The activity also includes examining data flows and the interdependencies of the various components in the environment.

The last part of the review examines the principal components underpinning the service and transactions, and determines the availability of all these delivery components. This involves examining an environment, including the network topology, for stress points and their bandwidth. The stress points identified include hardware, software, code, procedures, training, and maintenance. The review also identifies dependencies between components. From this, you can develop a selection strategy for the availability features for each of the components, as discussed in chapter 3.

Test the Physical Model in Extenuating Circumstances

The White Star architects had to consider worst-case scenarios in model testing, just as you will need to do in your project.

Test Titanic*'s Physical Model*

The following "what-if" failure scenarios were modeled to determine alternative safety features and their optimum implementation, i.e., size, scope, and numbers of.

Running Aground

In "what-if" failure scenarios for a ship running aground or beaching, the hull would sustain ruptured plates along the bottom, which would cause major flooding. Ruptures could extend the full length of the ship. A proven safety feature to mitigate this type of damage was a second hull or "tank top," shown in Figure 2.13, where the flooded ship would still remain afloat on the tank top. Consideration had to be given to the height of the gap between the bottom hull and the tank top. Ideally, this double skin would wrap around the ship to above the water line. In practice, however, this was a very expensive solution.

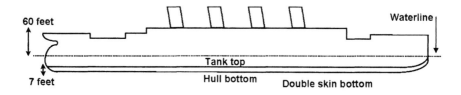

Figure 2.13: Hull ruptures to the double-skin bottom, which is well below the water line.

Collisions

Two types of "what-if" failure scenarios had to be considered for collisions, as shown in Figure 2.14. In the first, a front-end collision could cause massive damage to the ship, depending on speed and the type of object struck. Collisions with docks, other ships, rocks, and icebergs were well documented. In the second scenario, a side-impact collision to the ship could cause severe damage through a ruptured skin and flooding.

A proven safety feature to mitigate the damage from both these scenarios was to use bulk-head walls to divide a ship into watertight compartments. Consideration had to be given to the number of bulkheads and their height, which was dictated by the underlying threats and the length of this ship. For example, how many flooded compartments could the ship contain before the weight would pull the ship down?

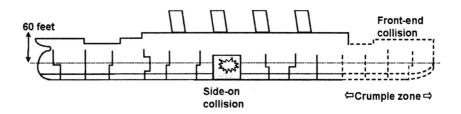

Figure 2.14: Withstanding collision scenarios with a crumple zone at the front for a front-end collision and sealed compartments to contain a side-on collision.

Your On-line Operation

Your project needs to consider worst-case scenarios in testing the physical and inventory models. The starting point is the interdependency model (Figure 2.8). The project architect must establish the critical parts of the service-delivery environment, and how the new on-line operation needs to be architected into the environment to meet its minimum availability requirements. This is done through four steps:

1. Identify critical areas.

2. Identify critical components.

3. Determine each component's availability and risk.

4. Model worst-case failure scenarios.

The analysis essentially is bottom-up. It models "what-if" failure scenarios by examining elements that affect the on-line operation and the service-delivery environment. These include primarily physical faults and environmental factors, and, to a lesser extent, design faults, operations errors, and reconfigurations. (These are further classified in appendix B.) For example, what is the impact of a poorly written software application, integration problems, or a defective server? Which user group or customer segment will it affect? What is the impact of a manmade or natural disaster?

Identify Critical Areas

At this point, the new business service shown in Figure 2.12 can be reviewed by identifying any critical areas of the service-delivery environment that require a higher degree of availability. This process also identifies component dependencies, such as from the application to the server, or between applications. With analysis, some of these critical areas will become apparent. For example, note that the single router G in Figure 2.12 supports access paths to databases G and H. If that router fails, how severe would the impact be?

Identify Critical Components

For an identified critical area, the next step is to complete a detailed assessment of the underlying critical components. The questionnaire in appendix D provides some starting points for collecting information on specific components. The interdependency model (Figure 2.8) highlights how the critical components relate to one another. Their availability can be readily identified and assessed, as follows:

- The implementation of the on-line operation opens the service-delivery environment to external Internet access and radically changes the availability requirements.

- The new application software has a number of single points of failure, and hence higher than normal risk.

The output of the assessment is a list of critical components.

Determine Individual Component Availability and Risk

The next step is to complete a high-availability risk assessment for all critical components. You need to identify the following:

- Bottlenecks, e.g., potential performance limitations of services over the LAN.

- Overall reliability based on aggregated MTBF figures if these are available.

- Dependencies and business-service overlaps that increase component criticality.

- Preventative facilities and capabilities required, i.e., spare/pair, mirroring, typical time to recover the service, data recovered, and planned versus unplanned downtime.

From this information, it is possible to create the critical component matrix shown in Table 2.3. The output of the matrix depends on the size and complexity of the service-delivery environment. Typically, the greater the complexity of the service-delivery environment, measured by the number of components, the lower the environmental availability and the higher the risk of failures.

Table 2.3: Critical Component Matrix

Priority	Component	Business Services	User Group	Users	Reliability	Comment	Availability Risk
1	WAN	All	All	1,800	3	Very unreliable	High
2	Database G	4	6,1	500	4	Reliable	Medium
3	Router G	1	6,1	500	2	Unreliable	Low
4	Application M	4	6,3	350	1	Unreliable	Low

Model Worst-Case Failure Scenarios

The objective of modeling worst-case failure scenarios is to determine, from the interdependency model in Figure 2.8 and the critical component matrix in Table 2.3, the worst-case scenarios for the failure of a single component, or for aggregate components. This analysis is completed at a high level. It identifies environmental weaknesses, for example:

- An access path failure to database G affects business service 4 and user groups 1 and 6.

- A failure of the WAN will affect all user groups. If this occurs in conjunction with problems in database G, there will be a prolonged outage of 2,000 UOMs.

This analysis provides a subjective view of both the technical and business risks. For example, if router G fails, databases G and H will be unavailable for two to four hours while awaiting a spare. This provides a much better understanding of the overall risk of that component: the combined availability risk and business risk equates to a large overall risk.

This worst-case failure is based only on the infrastructure and technology currently in place. At this point, the services' organization and processes have not been set up, so the operational risk for these are unknown. Nevertheless, this analysis identifies the "holes," from a technology point-of-view, that could be improved. Typically, further work is required at a transaction level to determine a suitable work-around.

Guarantee Delivery of the Required Physical Layout

The White Star owners needed to be assured that *Titanic* would be delivered according to specification, and would perform and be available under the necessary conditions. The answer was to set up a contract with the shipbuilder, with certain stipulations for conditions and requirements. Shipping lines were stringent over the terms of the contract. If contractual obligations were not met, ships were sent back to the builders. This happened with North German Lloyd's *Kaiser Friedrich* in 1898.

Likewise, your on-line operation needs to be delivered according to specifications and be available under all conditions. A solution is to set up stringent service-level agreements with the developer and other important parties, stipulating conditions and requirements.

Conclusion

The following sections summarize the major points of this chapter and how they relate to your business today. For more information on these concepts, search the Internet for these keywords and phrases: *runtime* and *non-runtime properties architecture, functional* and *non-functional requirements, service delivery, logical* and *physical architecture models, manageability, operability, reliability, redundancy, customer value management, impact component analysis,* and *e-business patterns.*

Major Points, Considerations, and Titanic Lessons

- The designers created a luxury ship with priority given to first-class accommodation and service.

- For the public, the lavish attention and investments paid to passenger comfort implied there was an equivalent investment in the safety and operations features.

- White Star made a large investment in a ship-builder's model and used early modeling techniques to test the designs and identify vulnerabilities.

- The shipbuilders relied heavily on flow analysis or static testing to review the ship's characteristics compared to expected attributes, experiences, and standards. This was a sound strategy considering the limited testing options available, in that it identified problems early, prior to construction.

Best Practices for Your Organization

- Determine who your customer or target audience is, define clear value propositions, identify customer segments, create profiles for each of these, and build scenarios.

- Define end-to-end availability as extending from the ISP (Internet Service Provider) through the back-end systems, along the paths of critical transactions.

- Complete the component impact analysis shown in Table 2.3.

- Invite suppliers and partners to collaborate in an overall mission-critical supply chain.

- Build environments and remove any single points of failure:

  - Avoid idle components in a standby mode.

  - Ensure automatic failover is in place.

  - Design proactive security-intrusion detection.

- Build security zones for Internet access into the service-delivery environment across the "Demilitarized Zone" (DMZ).

- Ensure that due diligence is paid by the team to granular decisions required, and that the appropriate escalation mechanism is in place a steering committee.

- Build the service-delivery environment geographically, to avoid local interruptions and cope with Internet congestion.

- Ensure that operations services complete the inventory model and familiarize themselves with the structure of the service-delivery environment.

- In building e-business solutions:

  - Avoid complexity, strive for simplicity, and hone in on the root cause of problems.

  - Anticipate future requirements.

  - Design for manageability, operability, and ease of use.

  - Design for mass customization.

  - Design "learning" into tools. Experienced users might not have time for training.

  - Design to support different types of users.

- Ensure your team goes through this stage with due diligence. Problems caught at this stage are significantly simpler and less expensive to fix than later in the project.

- Avoid underinvesting in non-functional requirements. A mistake in defining non-functional requirements is far more costly than in functional requirements.

- Avoid running one type of technology. Lack of technological diversity or wholesale standardization on one operating system makes your operation susceptible to a single Internet virus.

Questions You Can Ask Today

At this stage in the project, you should expect back the following answers from IT:

- A technical risk assessment by business service of how the environment is architected for high availability and a list of components that are high risk (Table 2.3).

- A technical risk assessment for each new business service, identifying size, probability, and financial cost (appendix C). This includes expectations for how the new solution is architected for availability, and an outline of the safety features for high availability.

C H A P T E R 3

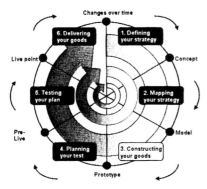

Constructing Your Goods

IT construction projects are normally complex, consisting of integrating subassemblies and components. The success of these projects will be determined by selecting the right team and having the business processes clearly defined.

John Keogh, CEO
Virtual Execs International, Inc.

Chapter Objectives

In this chapter, you learn about protecting critical areas and components by selecting from a comprehensive list of availability techniques (software and hardware). This includes looking at the advantages and disadvantages of high availability, the best circumstances for each technique, and—of course—the costs. When you are done with this chapter, you will be able to construct the solution for your on-line operation. With this, you will be ready for chapter 4, in which you start to plan your on-line operation for testing.

What Steps Do I Need to Follow?

In today's world, solution-construction consists mainly of integrating technologies, hardware, and software, and assembling off-the-shelf products and configurable modules.

You go through the following three steps to construct a solution:

1. Identify the required level of availability.

2. Determine the design specifications.

3. Proceed with construction steps.

Identify the Required Level of Availability

White Star was in the business of selling the cruise experience, not just a ship. The company planned to go through four years of extensive construction to create the most elaborate ship and hotel ever. But White Star had to assess availability (safety) features, make investment choices, and effectively select one of four levels of availability.

Your project, too, involves assessing the availability features, making investment choices, and selecting one of the four levels of availability. There are numerous techniques for improving the availability of a solution through software and hardware, and protecting against the five classes of outages (physical, design, operations, environmental, and reconfiguration). However, the business requirements and business case should be the principal contributing factors to determining the appropriate level of availability.

You need to differentiate the availability levels so that you can map them to your solution. The language of high availability can be confusing because there are many degrees assured by the technology employed. However, you can simplify the various degrees to four levels:

- Basic level of availability

- High level of availability

- Continuous level of availability

- Fault-tolerant level of availability

Let's walk through these four availability levels, using *Titanic* as the backdrop.

Basic Level of Availability for Titanic

The basic level was defined as having no safety features at all. The ship would perform its basic functions correctly, so long as no faults occurred. At this level, the ship had the characteristics of a closed rowing boat. It was good enough to operate across a small body of water, such as the English Channel. For any longer crossings, however, the risk substantially increased. Clearly, this level was the least expensive, but the one with the greatest risk.

Basic Level of Availability for your On-line Operation

For an on-line system, the basic level involves designing, implementing, and deploying sufficient components to satisfy the system's functional requirements and some nonfunctional requirements, and no more. Such a system will deliver the correct functionality so long as no faults occur and maintenance is performed. This availability level might be adequate for some noncritical aspects of the on-line operation, and where manual alternatives are readily available for a switch-over. In today's world, few systems can operate at this level. Clearly, it is the least expensive, but carries the most risk.

High Level of Availability for Titanic

A high level of availability was defined as having at least one safety feature. For example, the ship had the regulated number of lifeboats (Figure 3.1), as well as water pumps in the event of flooding. The ship had the characteristics of a sea-going vessel good enough to operate in major shipping channels within proximity of land. However, the risk was too great for transatlantic crossings.

Lifeboat technology was very well known, proven, reliable, easy to maintain, and simple to retrofit. However, lifeboats were slow to load and launch, and required a skilled crew.

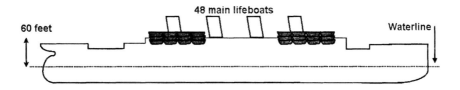

Figure 3.1: The lifeboats were located on the first-class deck. A total of 48 lifeboats could have been housed by triple-stacking.

The board of trade regulated the number of lifeboats on a ship based on the ship's cubic feet, not on the number of passengers. The regulations stipulated 16 lifeboats, as ships of *Titanic*'s size were not considered feasible. This was adequate for a 10,000-ton ship with enough room for 1,000 people, or 33 percent of *Titanic*'s capacity.

Water-pump technology was similarly well known and proven, and effective for flooding. It was reliable, required careful maintenance, and could be retrofitted. Water pumps rapidly stabilized flooding, so that repairs could be completed by patching the rupture.

At this availability level, the ship's safety features were cost-effective, but only within the numbers stipulated by the regulations and not even meeting the basic need of a lifeboat seat for each person.

High Level of Availability for Your On-line Operation

A high level of availability is defined as an on-line system that meets all of the basic availability requirements, and also has sufficient redundancy in components (hardware and software) to recover from the defined faults or unplanned outages shown in Table 3.1. The aim of a high-availability system is to recognize when the system goes down, and recover the application and the data as quickly as possible. High availability attempts to avoid single points of failures in the system by making them redundant.

This availability level is probably the most common for on-line operations. The system's availability features are cost-effective and offer some protection that lowers the overall risk. However, this level should not be used for mission-critical operations. If this is the only level available, then major enhancements are required to the processes and organization that support them.

Table 3.1: Features for High Level of Availability

Category	Techniques and Features	Potential Protection
Application	Instrumentation	Error messages are identified and converted into system-readable messages. This simplifies automating applications.
	On-line configuration	Software can be altered dynamically on-line, reducing planned downtime.
Database	Reconfiguration	Maintenance operations are performed on-line (backup and restore), improving integrity and failure rollback.
Middleware	Transaction monitoring	Facilities are included for monitoring and tracking mission-critical transactions.
	Two-phase commit	Transaction-processing software ensures all writes connected with a transaction occur or are backed out.
	Transaction auditing	Facilities for auditing transactions ensure complete interactions, improving integrity and failure rollback. (Transactions should never be found in an ambiguous state.)
	Load balance	Facilities are included for load-balancing resources in the environment.
	Shutdown and recovery	Automatic recovery of components is available in a shutdown situation.
	Automatic server fail-over	There is forced software fail-over to a backup server.
Operating system	Backup processes	Backup processes and resources are included, such as disk processes, applications, and software processes.
	Clustering	Two or more servers are connected, monitoring "I am alive" heartbeats. The servers can take over from each other.

Table 3.1: Features for High Level of Availability (continued)

Category	Techniques and Features	Potential Protection
WAN/LAN	Network management	There is automated management of network components.
	On-line reconfiguration	Software in the network can be dynamically altered on-line.
Server	Clustering servers	Two or more servers are hard-wired to take over from each other. In a *shared database cluster*, two servers are hard-wired to one disk, primary for one and backup to the other. In *hot standby*, primary and backup systems are networked, with database duplication software.
	Partition	This supports IP-address failover, and it is transparent to users. (*Failover* is the ability of a function to switch to an alternative location and continue to operate.)
	ECC (memory)	Error-checking and correction are built into the memory to help identify and recover errors.
	ECC (cache-protected)	Error-checking and correction are built into the cache memory.
	Hot plug cards	This technique allows for the dynamic removal of a failed card without having to power-down the server.
	I/O operation retry	This self-healing technique will retry an (I/O) operation until it restarts. However, it should monitor the total number of retries.
	SMART	This stands for "Self-monitoring, Analysis and Reporting Technology"; it is for controllers and disk arrays.
	Dual disk controllers	Two controllers are attached to two disks. This provides two separate paths to the disks.
Environment	Redundant fans	Spare redundant fans kick in when a failure occurs, to continue to provide cooling.
	Redundant power supplies	Spare power supplies can be brought on-line in a very short time.

Continuous Level of Availability for Titanic

For *Titanic*, a continuous level of availability level would be defined as having several safety features. For example, the ship would have a full compliment of lifeboats with seats for everyone, water pumps, double-hull construction, and water compartments. The ship would have the characteristics of an ocean-going vessel good enough to make transatlantic crossings at a much lower risk, but with some considerations.

The double hull, shown in Figure 3.2, consists of two watertight skins. The double hull is divided by longitudinals running across the width, as shown in Figure 3.3. These strengthen the ship by connecting the two skins and creating 73 watertight compartments. This technology was well-known, reliable, proven in running aground, and required little maintenance. However, it increased the ship's size and weight, and had to be incorporated at the design stage; otherwise, the retrofit was very expensive.

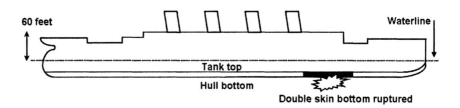

Figure 3.2: The double hull contains flooding from a rupture to the bottom, like running aground. The ship continues to float on the tank top as sections of the double-skin fill with water.

At this availability level, the ship's safety features become a significant and important investment. They clearly are well advanced for their time and appropriate for a transatlantic liner.

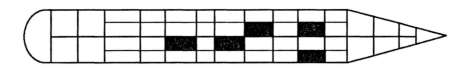

Figure 3.3: The top view of the ship and the individual watertight compartments sandwiched between the tank top and hull bottom. The ship continues to float as individual cells flood.

Continuous Level of Availability for Your On-line Operation

The continuous level of availability extends the high-availability definition to include planned outages, like upgrades, backups, and location changes. It is approaching the premium availability level, with features to handle unplanned outages, as shown in Table 3.2. This level is common to on-line operations and is a starting point for mission-critical operations. This level requires enhancements to the processes and organization that support them

Table 3.2: Features for Continuous Level of Availability

Category	Techniques, Products, and Features	Potential Protection
Application	Disaster recovery	The environment can be recovered to a remote site.
WAN/LAN	Automatic recovery	Network components can recovery automatically.
	Multiples	There is duplicity in paths and redundancy.
	Network topology	The network is distributed for resource sharing and redundancy.
	Dual paths	Telecommunications, links, and routers have automatic rerouting.
	Intelligent routers	Workloads are moved from to server to server.
Server	Redundancy in sites	Redundant physical site are made up of servers and devices to support cross-site failover.
	Redundancy in servers	Multiple single servers are used with a "load balancer"[1] to improve availability in an intelligent three-tier architecture.
	Spraying technology	A sprayer directs Web traffic to a target Web server.
	Mirrored-disk RAID[2] 1	Mission-critical data is protected by being written twice to primary and backup disks.
	Mirrored disk RAID 3/5	As above, except RAID 3/5 writes records across several drives, plus an additional ECC (error-correction and checking) drive.
Environment	Uninterruptible power	There is an intelligent power supply with a two-hour battery backup.

At this level, the system's availability features are becoming a significant and important investment. This level offers a good degree of protection that lowers the risk for mission-critical operations, but it requires a lot of risk planning and assessment.

Fault-Tolerant Level of Availability for Titanic

For *Titanic*, a fault-tolerant level of availability would be defined as having a comprehensive set of safety features. For example, the ship would have more than a full complement of lifeboats with an excess of seats, water pumps, a double hull, water compartments, sealed

1. Hardware-based load balances according to least used connection method. Software-based load balances using application logic. Done without end-user knowledge, it reduces Internet traffic jams.
2. RAID – Redundant Array of Inexpensive Disks.

bulkheads, electric doors, a collision ram, and pressurized air. The ship not only would have the characteristics of an ocean-going vessel, but would likely be the flagship of a fleet, good enough to make transatlantic crossings at full speed, with reduced risk.

As shown in Figure 3.4, the 15 self-sealing bulkheads contained 16 compartments within the interior hull. Bulkhead technology was well-known and proven for ruptures. It could contain the flooding from a rupture to two adjacent compartments. It was reliable and required little maintenance, but it had to be incorporated at the design stage and could not be retrofitted.

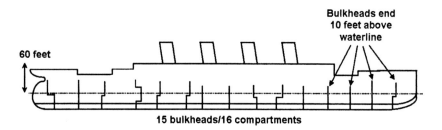

Figure 3.4: The bulkhead walls built did not reach the upper decks.

Electric doors (shown in Figure 3.5) could be built into the bulkhead walls. They could be rapidly closed in the event of flooding, either automatically using a float, or from the bridge using an electric switch. This feature gave the officers a greater sense of control. This technology was ahead of its time, could be rapidly deployed, and was automated. However, it was complex, unproven, required a lot of maintenance, and had to be incorporated at the design stage.

Other technologies that were considered but not implemented. For example, in the event of a collision or beaching, if water was detected in the ruptured compartments, pressurized air could be forced in. This would slow down the flooding, so that emergency repairs could be made. Similarly, in a front-end collision, a ram at the front of the ship would absorb the shock of impact above the waterline and preserve the structure of the hull.

Clearly, this availability level had the highest cost of all four levels. However, the level of investment had to be in line with the protection offered, since if the ship foundered, the shipping company risked bankruptcy.

Fault-Tolerant Level of Availability for Your On-line Operation

The fault-tolerant level of availability is defined as a system where the objective is to prevent the mission-critical operation from coming down in the first place, at any cost.

Initially, fault-tolerant applications were found in do-or-die situations, like NASA mission computers. Today, they are not only found in every industry, from stock-trading to shop-floor manufacturing, but also in organizations that are putting operations on-line. You might decide that this level is irrelevant to your business, but you have to first review it carefully. Every on-line operation is likely to have a mission-critical segment or "moment." For example, month-end or year-end processing might be critical. You need to find these moments in your operation. This availability level, described in Table 3.3, is not common for on-line operations, but it is essential for mission-critical operations.

Figure 3.5: The electrically operated watertight doors could be lowered from the bridge by an electrical switch, or through automated water sensors. The electric switch released a clutch, and the door would descend under its own weight. A ratchet and hydraulic arrestors were installed to control the rate of descent and protect against a falling door.

At this level, some enhancements are required to the processes and organization. One significant approach at this level is *tiering* which enables "sideways scalability" of selected components. This allows for the elimination of single points of failure through replication and redundancy, failover links, and independent scaling. The approach re-architects the environment into a three-tier architecture, as shown in Figure 3.6, where each tier can be geographically dispersed across data centers to avoid local disruptions and cope with Internet congestion. Single server failures are then accommodated, as transaction requests are redistributed. Tiering is no small task and should be considered as part of a larger strategy to reduce UOMs.

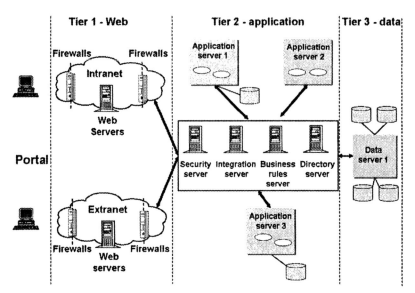

Figure 3.6: *The three-tier architecture of Web/application/data services created for high availability. Web services manage the site (portal) and the on-line operation interaction. Application services manage the applications, and include security (authentication and permissioning), integration, business rules, and directory services. Data services act as an intermediary for data access.*

The system's availability features are a significant investment and offer the best protection available with the lowest risk. These incorporate all the techniques of the previous level, plus the features shown in Table 3.3.

Table 3.3: Features for Fault-Tolerant Level of Availability

Category	Techniques, Products, and Features	Potential Protection
All	User-context persistence	This ensures users do not reauthenticate in an outage. Elements are synchronized for failover or fail-back.
Application	Check-pointing	Applications self-check at critical points, improving integrity and failure rollback.
	Topology	Applications are partitioned into presentation, business, and data layers, increasing reliability and testability.
Server	Additional fault-tolerant components	For example, adding parallel processors, LANs, and controllers offers a very high degree of protection.

What Was the Availability Outcome for Titanic?

White Star did go through due diligence, and reviewed all the levels of availability for *Titanic*. However, both the builders and the passengers were overconfident in *Titanic*'s safety.

Passenger Overconfidence in *Titanic's* Safety

Harland and Wolff were the most expensive builders in Europe; the quality of their craftsmanship was unmatched. Lavish attention was paid to every detail of passenger comfort. This contributed to the impression that *Titanic* was the greatest ship there ever was. It is not surprising that the visible investments in passenger comfort implied there was an equivalent investment in the ship's safety and operations features. In other words, passengers assumed they were getting the highest level of availability possible.

Builder Overconfidence in *Titanic's* Safety

White Star's architects made a number of assumptions through the availability selection process, which led them to conclude that *Titanic* was practically unsinkable:

- *Enormous size—Titanic* had increased ship size by 50 percent, which led to the perception that nothing in the natural world could affect its sheer monstrous size.

- *Bulkheads*—If the ship struck anything in a head-on collision, it would be protected by the bulkheads. The ruptured compartment would contain the water, so it would not fill adjacent compartments.

- *Electric doors*—If the ship was in any danger, the doors were designed to seal the bulkheads through a switching mechanism in the bridge, operated quickly and efficiently.

- *Double-skin hull and compartments*—These were a very innovative feature that protected the ship from running aground and from ruptures.

All of these led to a general acceptance that the ship was a giant lifeboat.

From the final designs of *Titanic*, it is apparent that a lot of thought was put into the ship's safety. White Star had indeed put investment dollars into the implementation of innovative availability features for the time. White Star's architects perceived that *Titanic* was unsinkable because of its design and use of the latest availability technologies. This led to a general overconfidence that nothing could go wrong. As a result, the directors made a number of decisions that compromised the fault-tolerant level of availability:

- The bulkhead walls did not reach the full height of the hull, as originally intended. Instead, they were only 10 feet above the water line, to make room for spacious staterooms.

- The double-skin bottom was only continued seven feet up. It remained well under the water line.

- Considerations were made to increase the number of lifeboats from 16 to 48,' but in the end this was deemed unnecessary because of all the other safety features, and because the incapacitated ship would be able to float while the ship's lifeboats would ferry passengers to the nearest ship answering the distress. Therefore, only enough lifeboats were installed to cover one-third of the passengers.

In hindsight, the lifeboat legislation of 1912 was grossly inadequate. It is a good example of how rapid technological change can outpace legislation. However, it was well within White Star's authority to go beyond the legislation to meet the business requirements.

In summary, *Titanic* was presented as being at fault-tolerant level of safety, but passengers actually purchased only the high availability level.

Availability Outcome for Your On-line Operation

For your operation to achieve maximum availability, availability techniques must be introduced into the application during construction. However, this is much more expensive than creating regular applications.

Off-the-shelf software packages might not have the adequate level of availability built in. It is possible to improve this by introducing high-availability components, mainly hardware and some software. However, introducing high-availability features retroactively into applications is very expensive and difficult. This accounts for the popularity of off-the-shelf mission-critical solutions, or tiering the environment for availability.

Many organizations invest in high availability technology as the primary safety feature. However, many fail to realign the organization and processes to take advantage of this feature. The most common cause of unplanned downtime is operator error. Similarly, in the airline industry, pilot error is the most common cause airline disasters.

Determine the Design Specifications

The construction phase commences by creating and rationalizing design specifications. These are the details the builders require to begin construction.

For Titanic

The first step of construction takes the output from the previous phase and creates and rationalizes a set of design specifications, both external and internal.

External Specifications

The design specifications for the exterior had to present *Titanic* as the world's leading luxury liner, from the hull shape to the number of smoke stacks. Hence, the owners made significant investments to gain competitive advantage. For example, they wanted to create a feeling of space on the deck outside the first-class cabins. This was another factor in reducing the triple-stacked lifeboats to a single ring, to improve the look of the decks.

Internal Specifications

The design specifications for the interior had to meet the expectations of the passengers, specifically in first class. The public areas had to be very carefully designed, as each inch of space was at a premium. The designs followed themes, and were important for creating an ambiance that helped determine the aspiration levels of passengers. In fact, the designs focused on far exceeding the expected levels of first-class service.

The main difference between first- and third-class quarters was that the ship looked like a ship in third class, with no effort to hide its interior infrastructure. In first class, a concerted effort was made to disguise the ship's structure, through paneling and tapestries. The bulk of resources was put into first-class accommodations. For example, the Turkish bath was half again as large as the third-class galley, the former holding a dozen passengers, and the latter around a thousand. The difference in cost of passage was $4,350 for first class, compared to $30 for third.

For Your On-line Operation

Your project has to create and rationalize external, internal, and manual design specifications, as shown in Figure 3.7. The objective is to create output that can be readily converted into something tangible at the end of the construction, with a recognizable "look and feel," like a model of the user interface. An alternative is to create a small-scale version of the end solution, with limited functionality.

This step crystallizes the overall objective of the project and influences the project team through the construction stage. Its output might be as simple as an electronic presentation (storyboard) containing a hierarchical screen structure, with screen images and high-level navigation flows.

External Specifications

The external design specifications include external system interfaces, transaction descriptions, physical equipment configuration, data sources, and operational and security requirements. Effectively, an external description is made of the system for the end-to-end processing.

Internal Specifications

The internal design specifications are the heart of the application, and for "white box" or custom application development, these involve dividing the software into program modules and describing the internal logic, flow, and structures for each module, as well as the test plans. The logic flows define all branch points, processing iterations, entry points, recovery logic, and external storage and usage. These specifications also include physical database schemas and key data structures.

Manual Specifications

The manual specifications plan for training, user support, a users' manual, and an application operations manual. A table of contents briefly describes each chapter of the manuals, along with the estimated length and number of illustrations.

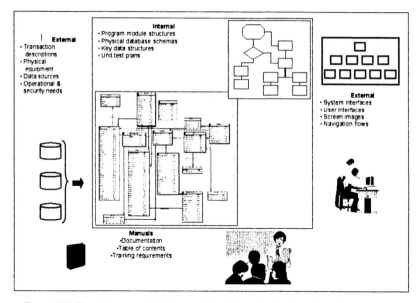

Figure 3.7: The design specifications include internal and external design specifications, and documentation specifications.

Proceed with Construction Steps

You go through the following five steps for construction:

1. Define the building blocks.

2. Procure, collect, and stage materials.

3. Lay in the main pieces.

4. Lay in the filler pieces.

5. Lay in the cosmetic pieces.

The priorities of *Titanic*'s construction were defined as follows:

- Build the most luxurious ship possible and set new standards for comfort at all levels, where speed is less important than luxury and capacity.

- Engineer a ship that would use the latest technology to provide safety features, in support of the first objective.

Your on-line operation needs to transition from the design specifications to the functioning solution by following the same logical process. The priorities of your project are by your business requirements.

Define the Building Blocks

The White Star architects had to determine at what level they were going to proceed with construction. For example, they could start at a base level with iron plates and girders, or they could purchase prefabricated components. In the early twentieth century, ship-building firms like Harland and Wolff chose to assemble at a granular level. Today's architects have a greater choice. They construct from large prefabricated assemblies, like the complete cross-section of a ship.

The scope and cost of construction projects has changed dramatically in the last 20 years. This has been driven by the increasing scope and complexity of the business problems re-solved, the rising costs of labor, the dropping costs of technology, and the continuous im-provement of processes and methods (such as project management and quality control).

Construction projects have seen a rapid growth in the use of automation tools (like fourth-generation languages, object-oriented code, and automated operators) and frame-works (like the public-domain software development lifecycle, or SDLC). This has reduced the size of project-development staff. In addition, software standardization has led to an in-crease in off-the-shelf software modules that can be readily integrated into the solution package. Versatile database-management software and nonprocedural programming lan-guages further enhance these packages. All these improvements have reduced solution-development time, but their overall affect has not been dramatic, as the complexity of solu-tions has risen in parallel. You need to decide at what level you are going to make your purchases, whether in basic blocks or fully integrated solutions, as described in Table 3.4, and the overall approach to construction.

Table 3.4: Alternatives for Construction

Alternatives	Description	Pros	Cons
Custom application development	A developer or team creates the design and codes of the solutions. This approach is used in traditional (legacy) environments.	Very flexible, closely matches business problem, and addresses the idiosyncrasies of the organization.	High cost, large teams, and lengthy overall construction time.
Custom packaged solution	A developer can modify the design and code of the solution (the white box).	Flexible, but within an existing framework.	Relatively high cost, but major pieces are pre-built.
Configurable solution	A developer can modify the solution (the black box) indirectly, through a configuration language.	Easier to configure than a custom package.	Limitations of working around the black box. Costs are reasonable.
Off-the-shelf solution	Minimal configuration is required through parameter changes within the solution (the black box).	Construction time is short; extremely easy to configure. Hardware and software products are the most integrated.	Might not closely match the business problem. Lowest costs, but limited flexibility.

In making the selection, the solution should readily integrate with existing and installed solutions and environments, and leverage the minimum number of vendors. Also, it should have suppliers with good geographic coverage, technical support, and reputation in the marketplace, and have additional and future capabilities. Large, custom application development is available today through software houses. However, most have a secondary objective: to convert the custom solution into an off-the-shelf package, to provide a better return on investment.

Procure, Collect, and Stage Materials

The White Star architects had a major logistical challenge in constructing at a granular level. Materials had to be procured, collected, and staged well in advance to ensure the huge workforce of 15,000 was fully occupied and continuously engaged.

Once you have established the building blocks for purchase, you need to go through a procurement process to collect and stage the materials. Generally, you should consider as many sources and perspectives as relevant to the design specifications in the allowable time, and follow these steps:

1. Review and set up policies for vendor preferences (i.e., rules for qualification).

2. Define vendor-evaluation criteria based on design specifications, ability to support, local presence, financial strength, and a weighted scoring method.

3. Define policies to use vendors' services to maximum advantage, e.g., product presentations and references for visits. From these, collect the needs to explore.

4. Set up an audit trail for the evaluations.

Lay in the Main Pieces

To begin construction of *Titanic*, the ship's "lines" were taken, from either the shipbuilder's model or general arrangement plans, and used to make full-size patterns. The "lofting" process involved drawing out the designer's lines full size on a huge lofting floor. The general construction process of building iron ships was the same as for wooden ships. The ship was constructed on a building berth, in huge outdoor gantries. The construction officially started with the "keel laying" of the ship's backbone, a main structural element, made up of flat plates (shown in Figure 3.8). To this, backbone ribs were attached on each side of the hull from stem to stern, along with posts.

Figure 3.8: The construction of the ship's keel involved flat iron plates.

Unlike *Titanic*, you cannot wait for a four-year completion. The construction of your project is completed in short iterative cycles that deliver ever-increasing levels of functionality. This approach is taken from a method known as Rapid Application Development (discussed in appendix E). These cycles evolve as follows:

- Demo—A model, possibly generic, that illustrates a particular technical solution or combination of tools.

- Prototype/proof of concept—A disposable model to verify functional and technical availability assumptions, or facilitate user feedback.

- Pilot—The initial fully operational solution, limited in scope, but used for rapid development.

- Scale-up—An expansion of the pilot cycle to a fully operational solution.

At this stage, your project should be configuring and validating the selected physical products, which together satisfy the design specification. In laying the main pieces of hardware and software, or *macro design*, the demo and prototype are delivered first. The "solution" prototype consists of technical and user-interface prototypes. These are typically evolutionary, or even throwaway, to gain early feedback from users.

Lay in the Filler Pieces

In the next step of *Titanic*'s construction, beams were hung from the ribs and ribbands (long pieces of iron), which held the whole framed structure together. The skeleton floors were laid in place, and plating was added. The work to be done was started by calculating the loading (weights) that the different parts of the ship had to support. Pillars spread the weight of each floor, from the top to the bottom of the hull. The double hull was, in fact, a giant box girder.

The steel plates for the hull were sand-blasted, painted, and then riveted together by hand, an enormous job that required "squads" of men. The plates were laid out in a mosaic and fitted like a jigsaw as part of the general arrangement plan.

The ship had three engines: a low-pressure turbine for the center screw and two expansion engines for the wing propellers. The ship used a gearbox to maximize the efficiency of the engine propulsion and provide the necessary extra power for bad weather. Once the engines and gearbox were installed, work started on implementing the long propeller and shaft (shown in Figure 3.9), which required close alignment.

Figure 3.9: The propulsion shaft assembly required close alignment.

The propeller construction determined how well the ship ran, being the only external moving component. It was under tremendous stress at high revolutions, which could cause vibration. If unbalanced, it could drop off, leaving the ship in a precarious position. Therefore, much attention was paid to its qualitative construction and balancing.

For Your On-line Operation

For your project, laying in the second pieces of hardware and software, or *micro design*, delivers a pilot or scale-up solution. The pilot creates a physical solution that can be implemented into production.

Program Modules

The activity develops individual program modules in accordance with the design specifications. The program modules are quality-assured through a process of visual inspection, where the code is compared to the logical flows from the design, and through a peer walk-through of the documentation. This approach is also known as *static testing*. Identifying potential problems at this point in the project is far more cost-effective than identifying them during full testing, discussed in chapter 5.

Unit Testing

The first level of testing for a solution is unit testing. This activity tests all of the program modules individually, in accordance with the functional requirements and design specifications. The focus is not on nonfunctional requirements at this point in the project. Each program module is unit-tested before broader and more complex testing is conducted (discussed in chapters 4 and 5).

Unit testing includes testing paths, conditions, exceptions, and error-handling. The testers are concerned with the execution of all possible paths of control flow through the program, and its logic. This is similar to *white-box testing*, which takes an inside view and looks at "how it is done" rather than "what is done." The latter is part of *black-box testing*.

Application Modules

The activity integrates individual program modules, in accordance with the design specifications, so that they interact and work together cohesively. Regardless of which approach you have selected, you will need to integrate the solution with its environment and with other solutions, including many independent, discrete, and complex pieces of technology, modules, and components (hardware and software). This requires careful consideration in the selection process. It is necessary and unavoidable. The scope and breadth requires many partners to collaborate, with a *prime* manager who takes responsibility and ownership, evaluating the risks and managing them accordingly. Do not take a gamble by working without a prime.

The complexity of systems integration and its importance in e-business has given rise to the emergence of *Enterprise Application Integration (EAI)*, which brings disparate systems together and links front-end to back-office applications. EAI has a common language and rules for implementing meaningful communication and the interoperability of various technologies. Its functions include security management, protocol management, and data mapping.

EAI introduces the concept of *integration servers* that include packaged connectors to major business applications. Integration servers shorten integration time and investment for implementing new business processes by using pre-built connections. These can eliminate 75 percent of integration work done by custom programming. Additionally, they go beyond point-to-point integration to allow for a spoke-and-hub model.

Lay in the Cosmetic Pieces

With the propulsion system installed, *Titanic*'s completed structure was "floated out." The final phase involved finishing other decks and turning the huge steel skeleton into a hotel. A starting point for the internal construction was the galley (kitchen), a very important area of the ship. *Titanic*'s galley was very large, since it was the heart of its hospitality operations. Other important areas were the staterooms, restaurants, and dining areas.

The interior included novelties such as Turkish and swimming baths, a gymnasium, and a squash court. A swimming bath was difficult to construct, as the amount of water carried was a danger to the ship's stability. All this luxury is difficult to attain even by today's standards. The bridge, the nerve center of the ship, was the last part completed.

For Your On-line Operation

For your project, the cosmetic pieces are peripheral to the primary hardware and software, but absolutely critical to the output.

Documentation

The activity completes the documentation for the users' and operations manuals, with a full description of each chapter, including illustrations. The user manual describes the use of all menus and screens, but not the specific business uses. The operations manual describes the application software and the information required for its support and operation, including how to install, start, stop, and operate it.

Release Management

This stage is the start of a release-management process, as the tested deliverables are propagated to the source code, object code, and document libraries through a configuration tool. Version control is critical in today's complex service-delivery environments. It ensures stability, as introducing the wrong version of software can be catastrophic.

Conclusion

The following sections summarize the major points of this chapter and how they relate to your business today. For more information on these concepts, search the Internet for these keywords and phrases: *high availability, fault tolerance, tiered availability,* DMZ, *check-pointing, scalability, programmatic recovery, redundancy, failover, design specifications, software enterprise application integration, development lifecycle, custom application development, rapid application development,* and *off-the-shelf solution.*

Major Points, Considerations, and Titanic *Lessons*

- The designers had an array of investment choices in safety features, from the lifeboats to the relatively new technology of bulkheads and electric doors.

- Safety regulations and guidelines, specifically for lifeboats, were hopelessly outdated and made redundant by advances in ship-building technology.

- In selecting the availability level, a number of assumptions were made, which led to overconfidence in the safety of the ship through construction.

- No *Titanic* construction dollars were diverted from meeting basic safety requirements to enhancing the luxurious surroundings of the first class. Investment dollars were put into expensive safety features based on new technologies like bulkheads, a double-skin hull, and electric doors, in preference to lifeboats. As a result, a perception developed that *Titanic* was unsinkable.

- Aesthetic factors like the need for spacious public areas compromised safety features like the height of the bulkheads, which carried only 10 feet above the waterline.

- The visible investments in passenger comfort implied there was an equivalent investment in the ship's safety and operations features.

- *Titanic* was presented as being at fault-tolerant level, but in terms of passenger safety, it was actually only at the high availability level.

- The expensive construction effort was very misdirected. It incorporated into the structure the mistakes made earlier, in the requirements and design stages.

Best Practices for Your Organization

- Identify the building blocks (components versus prefabricated) and all the alternatives for solution construction (build versus buy).

- Identify availability alternatives for incorporating into the solutions.

- Build in cycles. Start small (with demos and prototypes), and scale rapidly.

- Tier the environment and functions using a three-tier server architecture. Each tier can be scaled independently to allow for backups and failovers. Create redundant sites that support cross-site failover, and ensure that sideways scalability is in place.

- In construction of robust, mission-critical solutions, keep the following in mind:

  - Avoid complexity and strive towards simplicity.
  - Use generic components or building blocks with minimal exceptions.
  - Leverage components that can be portable between environments in their execution, and are linearly scalable.
  - Reengineer business processes, rather than construct complex extensions.
  - Use open systems, industry standards, open interfaces, and interoperability.
  - Determine a maximum lifespan.
  - Anticipate future requirements.

- Integrate solutions internally first, before external integration, as the latter requires additional complexities such as transaction integrity, security, and route management.

- Use release management and configuration tools for version control and propagation into production.

- In comparison to *Titanic*, the rate of technological change in today's world is much faster, more pervasive, and has greater impact at more levels. It is extremely difficult for governments to effectively track and modify legislature. The emergence and growth in e-commerce, e-retail, and the Internet are having profound effects. Practically every industry has redundant or inadequate legislation. Review all regulations and guidelines that might effect the on-line operation, and then plan accordingly.

- Ensure that the differences between a project that involves off-the-shelf software implementation versus one that requires custom application development are highlighted and well-understood.

- Avoid IT projects that do not involve the business side. The business manager needs to be part of the project throughout the construction, through steering committees.

- Chapter 2 touched on the problem of "design driven by technology" and its disadvantages. Very often, projects begin with construction. (For more information, see the case study in appendix A.)

- Problems caught at this stage are significantly simpler and less expensive to fix than further on in the main testing (discussed in chapter 5).

Questions You Can Ask Today

At this stage in the project lifecycle, you should expect the following information from IT:

- A risk assessment of the solution, identifying size, probability of success, and financial cost.

- An assessment of the availability level.

- A list of availability features.

- An assessment of the construction.

C H A P T E R 4

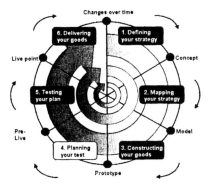

Planning Your Test

Testing plans provide the assurance that all key functionality is verified prior to production. It is always beneficial to revisit the business case or objectives/strategies to ensure that the testing plan takes into consideration not only the performance of the current application, but also what the original desired outcome was.

Christopher Misener, Sr.
Internet Manager, Amicus Bank

Chapter Objectives

When you are done with this chapter, you will be able to complete the plan for the test of your on-line operation. With this, you will be ready for chapter 5, in which you start to test your on-line operation for robustness.

In this chapter, you learn how to get ready to test your solution for the characteristics that you find important. This includes planning for the level of dynamic testing required, selecting the right kind of tests, and preparing the test environment. You will be planning to test either a new isolated solution, a new solution that is integrated with an existing solution, or a new solution that is replacing an existing solution.

What Steps Do I Need to Follow?

You go through the change management process in three major steps:

1. Go through planning.

2. Complete the first-stage test.

3. Complete the final-stage test.

This chapter addresses the first step, while chapter 5 addresses the other two.

Why Is Testing Such a Challenge?

Testing can be a challenge for many organizations because many spend little time, effort, or resources planning for it. As you prepare to roll out the concepts in this chapter, be prepared for some resistance to your efforts, for the following reasons:

- Testing is not considered important, based on an unclear understanding of it, its purpose, and its impact on availability.

- No budget is allocated for testing, as it was not considered up-front in the investment evaluation and planning.

- The scale or scope of the testing is deemed too large.

- The right skill sets for testing are unavailable.

- There is a lack of appreciation of what kind of testing needs to be done.

- Testing is considered part of another group's mandate, such as operations services.

- There is no time to test because you are under too much pressure to launch.

If you run into one of these perceptions, use these counterarguments:

- Budget should have been allocated to this stage at the project outset.

- Catching problems costs a factor of ten less in this stage than in production.

- Testing identifies impending problems and allows corrective actions to be taken.

- This is the last stop before delivering services to the customer.

- Testing helps determine the state of readiness of the operation going on-line.

- Testing provides a vehicle for ascertaining the risk of implementing the solution into the surrounding service-delivery environment, and the potential impacts to it.

In fact, the planning and testing stages (discussed in chapters 4 and 5) should be as comprehensive as possible. They will probably take as long as the strategy and construction stages (discussed in chapters 2 and 3).

What Is the Purpose of Planning?

The objective of this stage is to plan, prepare, and select tests that help determine whether the end product meets the design according to specifications defined by the business, and particularly the nonfunctional requirements. This is akin to *black-box testing*, which takes an outside view and looks at what is done, the output, but specifically the impact on the service-delivery environment. This stage also plans for dynamically testing the critical components and areas identified in chapter 2.

The Need for Models

Typically, testing in service-delivery environments is complex and requires simplification. The approach to testing can be considerably facilitated by using a model to answer the questions around where to start and what to test. At this point, it is essential to start with a very high-level view of the service-delivery environment and determine all the elements required for testing. A tried and tested model comes from the engineering world of finely balanced systems, which has been around for over 200 years.

The Fishbone

The model consists of *transformation processes* that transform raw materials and resources into useful products and services using machinery, equipment, labor, resources, processes, and buildings, as shown in Figure 4.1. In economics, this is referred to as the *factors of service* or the *six M's model*: machines, man, materials, management, methods, and money.

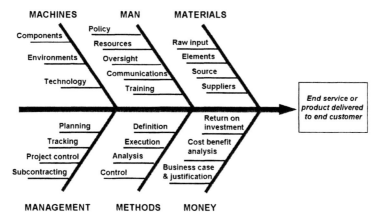

Figure 4.1: The fishbone, or "six M's," model transforms raw materials and resources into useful products and services.

This well-established model can also readily be applied to an on-line operation within a service-delivery environment. Table 4.1 explores how.

Table 4.1: Fishbone Mapped to Titanic and a Service-delivery Environment

Elements	Titanic	Service-delivery Environment
Machines	The technologies that help deliver the service, like propulsion systems, heating, electricity, lighting, etc.	The environment technologies, like servers, networks, and clients, which deliver the on-line operation and business services.
Man	The crew who run the ship's operation and the overall services: the officers, cabin staff, caterers, engine-room engineers and stokers, and other specialists.	The people required to run the on-line operation smoothly, like the IT staff, business staff, call-center agents, and client representatives.
Materials	The basic resources, like fuel, water, and food, which provide the basis for the ship's operation.	The software, applications, and delivery information required for processing and running the on-line operation smoothly.
Management	The project techniques to plan, direct, and manage changes in a controlled way for the ship's operation, to maintain services across the three classes.	The project techniques to plan, direct, and manage a new solution introduced into a balanced service-delivery environment in a controlled way.
Methods (Process)	The methods, processes, and procedures that surround the ship's operation and protect it from service disruptions.	The methods, processes, and procedures that surround the service-delivery environment. These help run and operate it while avoiding downtime.
Money	The financing and asset utilization of the ship's operation. This requires a fine balance in achieving the desired level of service.	The financing and budgets required to create and run the on-line operation smoothly in the service-delivery environment.

The fishbone model is useful for planning the tests, as it provides a macro view that can be readily dissected into a detailed view. The macro view ensures testing is evenly distributed across the elements. For example, a single technology change might affect several elements simultaneously, like requirements for training, new processes, and documentation. Having end-to-end coverage is vital, especially with e-business and complex service-delivery environments.

Go through Planning

The first task is to outline a plan for testing your on-line operation. The objective of testing is to provide a degree of assurance that the change will not disrupt your service-delivery environment or its mission-critical areas, or alter the delivery of business services.

Rationale for Testing Titanic

As a ship nears completion, a number of tests are planned by the shipbuilder before it is passed over to the new owner. The Harland and Wolff shipbuilders needed to be assured that *Titanic* would meet the conditions and requirements laid out in the contract. Failure to meet the obligations could lead to an embarrassing situation, where the ship could be sent back to the shipbuilders.[1] Testing gave the shipbuilder an opportunity to make any necessary adjustments and avoid the risk of financial penalties.

Titanic was operationally tested for seaworthiness, checked for stability, and carefully assessed for weight and loading particulars. One test was the "incline test," which checked the ship's weight and center of gravity, obtained from a simple inclining experiment. It also provided a check on calculations. Other tests included the dockside trials, which were held for the preliminary testing of main and auxiliary machinery.

Formal speed trials were normally necessary to fulfill contract terms. These required achieving a certain speed under specific conditions of draft and deadweight. This was done by making runs over a measured course, where the ship's performance was measured and evaluated over a range of speeds to provide a yardstick for performance delivery in service. The sea trials were done in a controlled environment with an adequate depth of water, no sea traffic, good weather conditions, and non-exposed waters, to well-marked distance posts.

Rationale for Testing Your On-line Operation

A basic requirement of this stage is to plan the testing of all the availability features built into the on-line operation and the service-delivery environment. Testing is an activity that should be driven by very specific objectives and test criteria, and signed off by an acceptance group. It raises the confidence of an organization delivering services. However, very few organizations adequately complete testing. Many organizations actually launch the on-line operation with the view that any problems will be flushed out by the user or client in the short term. In today's world, this is an extremely risky approach that might put the business in serious jeopardy. It could open the door to potential competition and cause dissatisfied users and clients to switch services.

Many organizations test effectively at the unit level (as shown in Figure 4.6). However, adequate testing is not done at the macro level partly because organizations perceive that a simulated service-delivery environment cannot be adequately replicated, is too expensive to set up, and is difficult to fund. Therefore, only partial testing is ever completed, which

---

1.   This happened with North German Lloyd's *Kaiser Friedrich* in 1898.

lowers confidence for a successful launch. The first function of the change-management process includes the three activities shown in Figure 4.2.

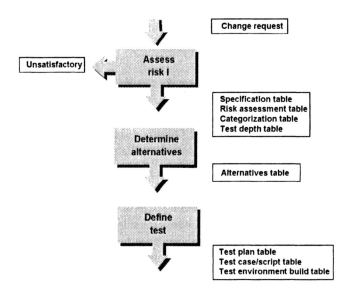

Figure 4.2: The planning phase for the change-management process.

Assess the Risk for Titanic

In assessing the potential risks to *Titanic*, the ship owners were likely very influenced by *Olympic*, which was launched on October 10, 1910. *Olympic*'s story involves three significant events.

Olympic's Collision with the Tug Hallenbeck

On June 21, 1911, *Olympic*'s maiden voyage to New York was completed uneventfully under Captain Smith, one of the most experienced Atlantic captains. *Olympic* was pulled up the North River by 12 tugs and maneuvered into Pier 59 for mooring. The tug *Hallenbeck* was standing by at the stern of the liner, when a sudden reverse of *Olympic*'s starboard propeller drew *Hallenbeck* in. *Olympic*'s propeller cut off *Hallenbeck*'s stern frame, rudder, and wheel shaft. Captain Smith was ultimately deemed responsible for this. The owners of the tug sued White Star for $10,000, a small fortune at the time. White Star countersued but both cases were dismissed for lack of evidence.

Olympic's Collision with HMS *Hawke*

On a later crossing in the afternoon of September 20, 1911, *Olympic* was involved in another collision while sailing out of the Solent at the start of her sixth voyage. She was traveling in parallel to the Royal Navy cruiser HMS *Hawke*, in a narrow channel called the Spithead off the Isle of Wight. The two ships were 200 yards apart and traveling at about 15 knots. In broad daylight, on calm water in the middle of the day, *Olympic* was overtaking *Hawke*, when *Hawke* suddenly turned hard and collided with *Olympic*, as shown in Figure 4.3. *Hawke* hit the starboard quarter of *Olympic*, just below her main mast, head-on, and pierced the outer skin. The damage was considerable: a gaping triangular hole, around 15 feet high, 10 feet across, 10 feet deep, and 6 feet above the watermark, as shown in Figure 4.4. Two of the largest watertight compartments rapidly filled with water, so all the watertight doors were closed. Captain Smith knew that even with any two compartments open to the sea, the ship would not sink.

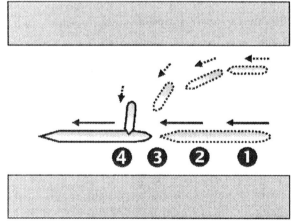

Figure 4.3: This figure illustrates the collision: ❶ Olympic and HMS Hawke are sailing approximately 15 knots around 200 yards apart. ❷ As Olympic edges ahead, Hawke begins to turn hard toward it. ❸ Olympic is not sailing fast enough to outpace Hawke, and in the narrow channel, collision is inevitable. ❹ Hawke slams hard head-on into Olympic and causes considerable damage.

Incredibly, no one was hurt. The second-class cabins that were sliced open happened to be empty. All the passengers were lunching in the dining room on the floor above. *Hawke* was equipped with a ram that absorbed the shock of impact above the water level, and there was little damage below. The naval cruiser narrowly avoided sinking, as all her watertight doors were closed in time.

Olympic unloaded her 1,300 passengers to shore and was out of service for six weeks in the Belfast dry dock, as plating was replaced. At the accident inquiry, Royal Navy experts put the blame on the powerful forces of suction exerted by *Olympic*. Physicists know this as Bernoulli's Principle. *Olympic* was seven times heavier than *Hawke*. This incident is significant because *Titanic* had a very near collision on leaving Southampton in 1912. What is even more significant is the fact that Captain Smith, First Officer Murdoch, and Second Officer Lightoller, were part of the ship's crew on both voyages. In fact, White Star promoted Captain Smith to command the flagship of the fleet as a show of confidence. The incident haunted Captain Smith, however; he continued to claim innocence, in that *Hawke* had struck *Olympic*, and so the collision was the fault of *Hawke*'s captain.

Figure 4.4: The damage caused by Olympic's collision with HMS Hawke. A warning sign for Titanic?

Olympic Loses a Propeller Blade

On a later crossing in February 1911, *Olympic* lost a propeller blade and had to return immediately to Belfast for repairs. *Titanic* had to vacate her graving dock to accommodate this.

Conclusions to Assessing the Risk

It is very likely that, with *Olympic* in service, White Star deemed *Titanic*'s maiden voyage a low risk. After all, the two ships were nearly identical, and the ship's owners and crew were very confident in *Titanic*. However, no two ships have identical handling characteristics. So, were any of *Olympic*'s lessons or experiences transferred to *Titanic*? Yes, in that the crew on *Titanic*'s maiden voyage included *Olympic*'s captain and senior officers.

Assess Risk for Your On-line Operations

The input to this activity is a change request, as signed by a requesting sponsor. The outputs to this activity include a specification of the change and an assessment of the business risk (and to a lesser extent the technical risk) of an impending launch. The groups involved in this activity are the business manager, users, and IT, including solution, technical, and operations services. Table 4.2 lists some of the change questions that need to be asked as part of the specification process.

Table 4.2: Specification Table

Specification	Change Questions
Change to the business operation, function, process, or workflow	What type of change is requested?
Urgency of change	How soon does the change need to be deployed? Is it an emergency?
Change requestor	Who is making the request? What are their positions and authority in the organization?
Reason(s) and rationale	What are the business drivers and justification? Are there technical reasons for the change? What about the competition?
Size of change	Is the change small, medium, or large?
Potential impact	Who will be affected? Business operations, user population, customers? What are the dependencies on process, organization, and technology?
Estimated costs	What are the likely costs, in terms of resources, time, and materials?
Alternatives	Should we even go through with the change?

The priority and importance of the risk assessment should be based on the organization's track record of successful changes to the service-delivery environment. The following questions should be asked in a business assessment of the on-line operation project:

- Is there a business rationale and justification for the change?

- Is there a change sponsor?

- Could the change have a negative impact on current business operations, groups, and processes?

- Could the change have a negative impact on the organization's customers?

For a technical assessment of the on-line operation project, these questions should be asked:

- Is there a strong technical rationale for the change?

- What is the scope and complexity of the change?

- Could the change adversely affect the service-delivery environment?

For a new on-line operation solution, these questions should be asked:

- How sound is the technical solution? Is the software already written? Is it proved?

- Are there delivery dates for any major components, such as hardware and communications?

- Does the change integrate into current systems?

- Does the change involve unproven or unknown products?

- What are customer expectations for availability, performance, security, and scalability?

- Are there any guarantees for factors like performance or security?

- What is the required live date? Is this reasonable?

- What are the major risks (discussed in appendix D) that could make this launch unsuccessful?

- What are the five most important post-launch risks?

Tables to Simplify Risk Assessment

Answering these questions allows your team to complete a simple risk-assessment table, shown in Table 4.3, designed to quickly hone in on any apparent risk. This table also simplifies the decision-making process by determining the likely compliance with the change requested and the requestor's cooperation level.

Table 4.3: Change Risk-Assessment Table

Business	Technical	Project	Compliance	Change requestor	Overall Risk	Code
High	High	High	Non-compliant	Overconfident, not supportive	High risk	Red—Very serious, must correct
Medium	Medium	Medium	Non-compliant	Insistent, inflexible	Medium risk	Yellow—Serious, should correct
Low	Low	Low	Somewhat compliant	Indifferent	Low risk	Blue—Minor, fix if time
Low	Low	Low	Compliant	Helpful, flexible	Very little	Green—Good

Further risk assessments should be on-going and performed as required. The deliverables o this activity include the Categorization table shown in Table 4.4. This table defines change to the service-delivery environment (operating system, base products, configurations, third-parties products, and tools) as small, medium, or large.

Table 4.4: Categorization Table

Change	Definition	Size
New isolated solution	Requires no integration into the service-delivery environment.	S, M, L
New integrated solution	Requires integration into the service-delivery environment.	S, M, L
Solution replacement	Requires integration into the service-delivery environment.	S, M, L
Solution modification	Changes the functionality of a solution.	S, M, L
Solution bug-fix	Requires a fix or patch to a solution, typically a technical driver.	S, M, L
Application	Could be third-party or in-house applications.	S, M, L
Product	Could be a business product related to the applications.	S, M, L
Tool or utility	Could be a tool related to the operating system.	S, M, L
Business processes	Falls under the auspices of change management.	S, M, L

The Test Depth table in Table 4.5 shows the cost justification, schedules, and the change process. This table is vital to review the fishbone model and agree on the elements that require change.

Table 4.5: Test Depth Table

Factors to Consider	Definition
Test environment(s)	The extensiveness of the simulated test environment required.
Cost justifications	Based on business drivers, some associated financial metrics.
Test plan	The types of and increasing levels of testing. For new solutions, this is an iterative process, progressing through the following levels: unit, integration, system, systems integration, user acceptance, and operability.
Business impact of change	The business operations or functions affected.
Deadlines	The hard and soft dates for the change.
Schedules	Any external project dependencies that might exist.
Resources	The test team's organization, skill level, and time requirements.
Expected results	The outcome of the tests and how the test is measured.
Change strategies	Small, medium, large, or emergency changes.

All Changes Are Potential Threats

All incoming service-delivery environment changes need to be considered as potential threats to stability. The number of changes is likely to increase over time, and the procedures need to adjust to allow for this. The only feasible way of coping with the volume of incoming changes is to establish very clear and flexible change strategies that can scale. This kind of approach can provide the following benefits:

- Improved quality of service delivered to the client.

- Reduced overall cost of operations.

- Appropriate level of resourcing applied, according to priority.

- Greater efficiency and effectiveness.

The Test Depth table defines the change objectives and strategies required at different levels. For example, with a small change, the development group might actually implement the change directly into the live environment, under the minimum auspices of the operations services. An emergency change, on the other hand, requires a more rigorous and rapid strategy, where due diligence and speed are critical.

Comprehensive change strategies ensure quality and stability in the service-delivery environment, balanced with getting new solutions and functions to the user. Many problems occur when unplanned changes are launched without going through a process, or where the level of rigor is lower. This situation arises during a scheduled outage window or an unplanned outage, when there is little time to do comprehensive testing. In contrast, a small change might not require extensive work, so a judgment has to be made as to what degree of planning and testing is required. You need to evaluate and categorize the incoming change and select a suitable change strategy to cover small, medium, large, and emergency changes.

In many organizations, it is often unclear whether change strategies really exist. Typically, a rigorous change strategy should exist for all new solutions or major enhancements. However, this is not always the case for small and medium changes. Therefore, the size of the incoming change should determine the level of rigor applied.

Determine Alternatives for Titanic

The following alternatives were available prior to *Titanic's* maiden voyage:

- Postpone the trip and remain in Southampton.

- Proceed back to the shipyard in Belfast, as *Olympic* did after her collision with *Hawke*.

- Complete the crossing with known faults.

As a contingency, on the maiden voyage *Titanic* carried eight engineers from Harland and Wolff. The engineers' roles were to look for defects and note them for repair. Most notable among the engineers was Thomas Andrews, the chief architect. He knew every detail of the ship and was the most experienced person in *Titanic*'s construction.

Determine Alternatives for Your On-line Operations

The groups usually involved in this activity are IT staff, including solution, technical, and operations services. The groups usually determine two to three alternatives open to the test team. The deliverable of this activity is an Alternatives table, as shown in Table 4.6. An Alternatives table is drawn up to offer some alternatives for use in the incremental launch. For example, if after reassessing the risk (discussed in chapter 5), the change is deemed too risky to go live, its alternatives should be assessed. Some changes are driven directly by customers, so client-management input needs to be solicited as part of the process.

In many organizations, this is the point in the launch when the technical support and operations teams first get involved. Typically, however, this is too late in the process.

Table 4.6: Alternatives Table

Alternatives	Definition
Invoke "backout" plan	Go back to planning and re-plan the testing.
Do nothing	Maintain the current service-delivery environment and do not implement the change.
Implement with minor faults	Risky, but well controlled; remain live until the next planned window.
Implement with major faults	Risky; prepare for Potential Problem Analysis (a technique for analyzing potential problems).

Define Tests for Titanic

Titanic was a copy of an existing ship already in service, *Olympic*, which launched 19 months earlier. White Star might have deemed *Olympic*'s track record adequate for launching an almost identical sister ship straight into service. However, that decision only involved comparing the physical structures of the two ships, and not looking at the readiness of the crew (people) or procedures (processes). The fact that *Olympic* had been in operation for 13 months probably further enforced the ship owner's perception that *Titanic* was mission-ready, together with the belief that the ship was practically unsinkable.

Define Tests for Your On-line Operations

Defining tests uses the Test Depth table to determine the tests required. The deliverables of this activity include a Test Plan table (Table 4.7), a Test Case or Test Script table (Table 4.8), and a Test Environment Build table (Table 4.9). The IT groups usually involved in this activity are solutions, technical, and operations services. The Test Plan table is the main document for testing. It outlines why the test is being undertaken, along with its objectives, overall strategy, and documentation.

Table 4.7: Test Plan Table	
Factors to Consider	**Definition**
Purpose and objectives of testing	Scope and summary. How broad, deep, and long?
Documents related to the test	Documents associated with the change, like descriptions, references, and links to other locations.
Test concepts (overall strategy and approach)	Test philosophy for incoming change; verification methods; test levels and extensiveness; organizational roles (who carries out the tests).
Verification requirements	Test criteria, personnel, and verification standards.
Requirements/test summary	Expectations for testing, output, and variances.
Types of testing	The battery of tests, such as unit, integration, and stress.
Verification testing	Verification personnel and standards. (This should never be left to the developers.)
Acceptance testing	Acceptance personnel and criteria.
Control/reporting procedures	How the results will be communicated.

Based on the predefined change strategy, the extensive tests performed could include stress, performance, regression, security, and operational tests, shown in Figures 4.5 through 4.24. The Test Case/Script table outlines test cases for each testing objective: what is being tested, how it is tested, with what data, the expected outcome, and the results.

Table 4.8: Test Case/Script Table	
Case/script	**Definition**
Integration	Test the integration of applications, modules, and components.
Operator interface and acceptance	Have operators test the operational interface and functions.
Security	Test the integrity of the front-end, based on a hostile attack.
Stress	Test the module against a peak load of transactions.
Heterogeneous systems	Test the impact of the change on the heterogeneity of the environment.

A test script is a sequence of actions that executes a test case and includes detailed instructions for setting up and executing the test, and then evaluating the results.

The test environment is usually a simulated environment. The test system does not necessarily have to be similar in size to the service-delivery environment (except, usually, for the number of disk drives). A standard testing environment could be enhanced through tools that allow for the simulation of complex environments and the combinations of events. The Test Environment Build table (Table 4.9) outlines how the physical environment is built and assembled.

Table 4.9: Test Environment Build Table

Factors to Consider	Definition
Scope of the environment	The size of the simulated environment, based on the type of tests.
Simulated components	The types of simulated applications and software, extracted portions of live files and data, where confidential fields are encrypted.
Transaction engines	The types of simulated transactions or simulated user populations.

Release Management

With the environment outlined, the right components need to be identified from the object libraries and assembled into the test environment. This requires defining a baseline for levels, versions, and locations of components. The release-management process, through a configuration tool, assures that the correct versions of the components are removed from the library. It also provides an audit trail for propagating components. The components are compiled, installed, and packaged for promotion into the test environment.

Who Should Do the Testing?

An independent group, not directly involved in the project to date, should always do the testing. This is the only way to ensure that an objective, scrutinized, and diligent approach to testing is taken. The group needs a clear mandate with the authority to make go/no-go decisions. Effectively, this requires strong support from executives and business managers. Sponsors might be involved as observers, to increase their buy-in.

Environments Used for Testing

In most organizations, there is a strong case for establishing an alternative to a live environment for all testing, particularly Operational testing (Figure 4.14). However, many organizations are restricted to testing only in a live environment by the availability of test facilities. For example, testing is squeezed into a timeframe when these facilities are available but underutilized.

Many organizations use their existing development environments as a simulated testing environment. This typically requires some modifications, like an increase in the size of the environment and adjustments in using it in nonoffice hours. This approach creates many organizational headaches, like the challenge of rapidly switching environments at short notice and the introduction of work shifts. On the plus side, it seems to be an inexpensive option. The cost of the investment technology has already been justified, and the development staff can act as the testers. However, there are many risks in this approach. The development environment is typically used for constructing or enhancing business applications. Software code is developed and evolved, so it is a service-delivery environment in its own right. Likewise, the development staff is there to deliver a full-time development function, which might have some testing of its own.[2]

The risk of taking this approach is high. The development environment contains all sorts of tools, like compilers, interpreters, and debuggers, which could be triggered accidentally and might corrupt the incoming change. For example, objects could be recompiled or put out of service.

Types of Testing Required

The approach to testing defines that any failures identified in this phase means the test was successful. The various types of testing should be able to test the each aspect of the service-delivery environment and the incoming solution, described below as an *element*. The following tests should be carefully reviewed and selected to fit in with the change strategy:

- In the simulation test (Figure 4.5), a test environment is set up to replicate a live service-delivery environment, partly and wholly. Ideally, this environment is used specifically for all the testing described below. Typically, this is a partial representation in size, so various techniques are required to simulate the full service-delivery environment. For example, transaction engines might simulate hits on a Web site. Once it is set up, the environment needs to be tested itself, so its limitations are known.

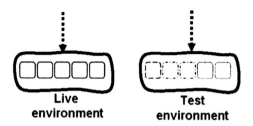

Live environment   **Test environment**

Figure 4.5: The simulation test.

---

2. Typically, the unit testing of modules in accordance with functional requirements and design specifications (refer to Chapter 3).

- In the unit "black box" test (Figure 4.6), the new element that will be implemented into the test environment is tested standalone, as a black box. This test highlights whether the element meets its acceptance criteria, requirements from a nonfunctional perspective, and overall robustness to stand alone without failure. This is a continuation of the unit test in chapter 3, which focuses on testing the functional requirements.

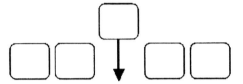

Figure 4.6: The unit "black box" test.

- In the function test (Figure 4.7), the test environment, with the new element, is tested for the effectiveness of the functions of the overall solution and whether they work together as a whole. The functionality of the new service or enhancement is assessed against the functional requirements, design specifications, and expectations. Does the environment, with the implemented new element, deliver the service it was designed for? The end user should take part in this test. This is one of the functional requirement tests.

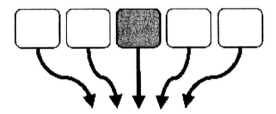

Figure 4.7: The function test.

- In the user-readiness test (Figure 4.8), the test environment, with the new element, is tested for its business user-effectiveness. This includes testing the impact of the element on the day-to-day operations and procedures, as well as subjective testing, which is the difference between a deliverable (output) and the expectations of its users. It also examines the users' readiness to use the solution.

This test takes a close look at the infrastructure (man, methods, and materials, as shown in Figure 4.1). For example, will the incoming service expose back-room operations to the customer? What is the impact on business processes, and will new ones be required? What design documentation is available (refer to Chapter 2), and does it adequately describe the new element? How effective is the business user interface (usability) for performing day-to-day operations?

Another area for exploration is user education and training, usually accompanying a major service change. Poor delivery of any of these things can reduce the chance of satisfaction and user acceptance. Business users need to have a high level of confidence in the incoming element. This is one of the functional requirement tests.

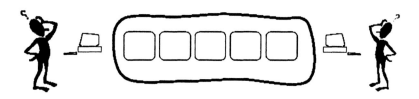

Figure 4.8: The user-readiness test.

- As Web sites have evolved from simple on-line brochures to complex e-business sites, so has user experience testing (Figure 4.9). This type of testing determines the kind of experience a customer has with a site or on-line experience. Specifically, this testing is done with a new solution or change that affects a Web site. Testing is completed in three main areas: performance, navigation, and content. It is evaluated over the entire transaction, from logon to when the transaction is completed.

Performance testing determines overall how well the site interacts with the user, in terms of things like wait time for page loads and the return of information. The user experience should pre-set user tolerance levels for this. For example, if completing the entire transaction takes a lot of steps and is longer than 15 minutes, it is likely the user will just give up.

Navigation testing determines how intuitive the site is. Is the home page clear? How does the site flow? Can the user get lost? Is known and captured data automatically populated into screens? Can the user lose the main site in URL transfers? Broken links and crashes are still the biggest source of user frustration.

Content testing determines whether the users are presented the correct content, and how well the content is integrated. What is the look and feel of the site? Is branding consistent across the site? Is the content self-serving? What if the user branches to another site?

In many ways, user-experience testing is the ultimate test, as it measures the kind of experience a user has and the quality of that service. This is one of the functional requirement tests.

Figure 4.9: The user-experience test.

- In the integration and regression test (Figure 4.10), the element is introduced into the test environment, and all the elements are tested together. This tests the level of integration, the interaction of elements, and how well the elements are integrated together. This is a very significant test, as it reveals the way the test environment reacts to the change. This test follows the unit "black box" test, a necessary prerequisite that the individual element must satisfy. Interlinked into this is regression testing, which tests the element against previous versions of the environment and verifies that no unwanted changes were introduced to one part of the environment as a result of making changes to another part. The integration and regression test highlights inconsistencies between the elements, the existence of integration bugs, the weaknesses in the integration links, and flaws in the external interfaces, interoperability, and stability.

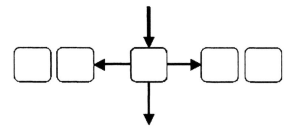

Figure 4.10: The integration and regression test.

- In the unknown-element test (Figure 4.11), a bug is deliberately planted into the element, which is then implemented into the test environment. This test highlights the test environment's ability to detect the bug, determine its impact, and take any required actions. This test determines the robustness of the overall environment.

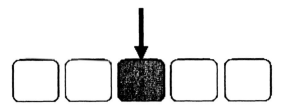

Figure 4.11: The unknown-element test.

- In the load test (Figure 4.12), the test environment, with the new element integrated, is tested for total throughput, by placing increasing volumes of transactions against the whole environment. This test pushes the environment to its limit and is typically beyond the perceived worst-case volume scenario. It demonstrates the resilience of the environment to the change and the ability to handle large volumes of transactions. It also highlights any bottlenecks in the environment and potential weak points under loads.

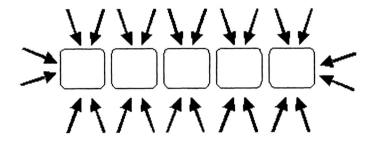

Figure 4.12: The load test.

- In the stress test (Figure 4.13), the test environment, with the new element, is tested by running varying volumes of transactions against a specific part of the environment, single components, or functions. For example, there might be a specific new function or element that has much higher usage and interaction, or that might be deemed critical to the operation. This test determines the resilience of this element. This test is useful for investigating and pinpointing suspect parts of the environment.

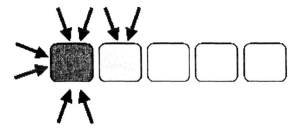

Figure 4.13: The stress test.

- In the operational test (Figure 4.14), the test environment, with the new element, is tested for its operational effectiveness and operability. This includes the operational impact of the element on the day-to-day operations and procedures, and the operational readiness of staff running the environment to interact with the client.

  This test takes a close look at the infrastructure. For example, does documentation for the new element adequately describe it? How effective is the human (operator) interface (text, graphics, audio, and video) for command and control, network management, problem management, and automation? Bad design can increase the chance of human error in routine maintenance.

  Operations services are invited in during the design phase to "swarm" over the element to spot problems. Operations services need to have a high level of confidence in the incoming element. At this point, the organizational structure can also be evaluated to determine whether it is adequate to support the change.

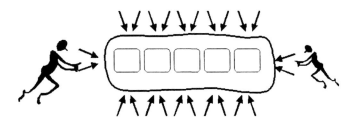

Figure 4.14: The operational test.

- In the change-implementation test (Figure 4.15), the test environment is tested for its ability to absorb the implementation of a change or new incoming elements. The change could be as small as a parameter change or as large as a solution replacement. The following questions should be asked: What is the overall effect of the change? Does it affect stability in any way?

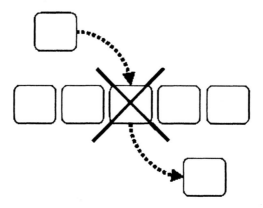

Figure 4.15: The change-implementation test.

- In the automated-operations test (Figure 4.16), the test environment is tested to see the effects of the automated operator on the changed environment. The automated operator is scrutinized to determine whether it sees the interactions of the element as hostile to the stability of the environment. How will it interact with the new element, its outputs, and its actions? It is certainly feasible that the automated operator could try to "fix" actions taken by the element, so it needs to be fully tested.

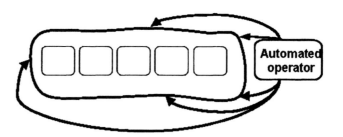

Figure 4.16: The automated-operations test.

- In the configuration test (Figure 4.17), the test environment, with the new element, is tested to see the reaction of the element to its own assignments. The test changes the configuration parameter and measures the impact of this change.

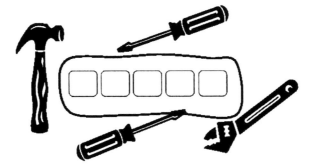

Figure 4.17: The configuration test.

- In the environment test (Figure 4.18), the test environment, with the new element, is tested in varying environmental conditions, such as variations in temperature, humidity, and pressure, and fluctuations in power. This might seem somewhat absurd in the context of a machine room, but consider the decentralization of servers to different locations, and the diversity of devices interacting with a service-delivery environment. For example, a new element might include handheld devices, which could be exposed to a wide variety of conditions.

Figure 4.18: The environment test.

■ In the parallel and switchover test (Figure 4.19), the new solution is tested alongside the original solution. This type of testing is extremely common because it provides a baseline, and hence a very high degree of assurance in a cut or switchover. The input and output of the two solutions can be monitored and compared in parallel. Adjustments are made until the output is identical. However, one limiting factor is the lifespan of the replaced system. Effectively, as soon as it is decommissioned, the test environment is limited; further changes cannot be adequately tested.

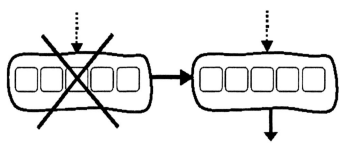

Figure 4.19: The parallel and switch-over test.

■ In the degradation test (Figure 4.20), the test environment, with the new element, is degraded by gradually shutting down individual components. The effect of each component on the service output is measured, as is the overall environment.

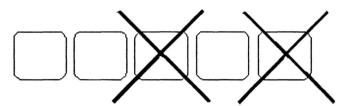

Figure 4.20: The degradation test.

■ In the recovery test (Figure 4.21), the test environment, with the new element, is tested against a series of impacts. For example, a component or element is shut down or stalled. This test highlights and measures the environment's ability to recover against these impacts. It might not be possible to fix these impacts, but it will allow a risk assessment and provide a foundation for risk-mitigation strategies.

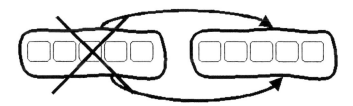

Figure 4.21: The recovery test.

- In the shutdown and startup test (Figure 4.22), the test environment is completely shut down, and then measured to see how successfully the shutdown completes. This test reviews the startup, the completeness of the environment, and the state of all the components. The test also reviews the overall time required, and whether this falls within permissible requirements of the SLAs.

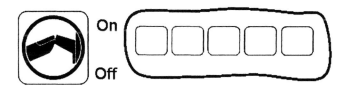

Figure 4.22: The shutdown and startup test.

- In the security test (Figure 4.23), the test environment is tested for integrity against any form of hostile attack. Most people would visualize hackers trying to break through with a PC and modem. However, sabotage takes various forms, such as reading transactions or files undetected, compromising transactions, overloading the system to cause crashes, modifying environmental operations, and mimicking users.

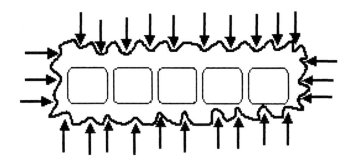

Figure 4.23: The security test.

- The denial-of-service test (Figure 4.23) is based on trends in the Internet world that indicate a coordinated effort in sabotaging systems. Saboteurs, using servers, pose as Internet users innocently accessing an organization's Web site (e.g., querying information). However, these attacks typically harness great numbers of distributed servers around the world, coordinated to flood the organization's Web server with automated requests or queries for information. Some attacks have involved thousands of servers sending millions of queries in a matter of minutes. Effectively, distributed denial-of-service attacks can severely limit the ability of an organization to conduct normal business on the Internet. The denial-of-service test should test for the effectiveness of the environment and element to withstand these attacks. It should look for security practices and for identifying elements like *source-address spoofing*, used by intruders to conceal their location.

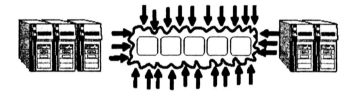

Figure 4.24: The denial-of-service test.

Conclusion

The following sections summarize the major points of this chapter and how they relate to your business today. For more information on these concepts, search the Internet for these keywords and phrases: *software planning and testing, change management, software bugs, release management, integration and regression testing*, and *denial-of-service attacks*.

Major Points, Considerations, and Titanic Lessons

- *Olympic* was used as a test bed or yardstick for *Titanic*. However, it is debatable how well the experiences learned from *Olympic* were applied to *Titanic*.

- The business pressures for *Titanic* to go live were enormous and understandable, considering the large investments tied up in its four-year construction. In addition, *Olympic* had been out of service in dry dock for repair because of the collision with HMS *Hawke*. This further delayed work on *Titanic*, moving the maiden voyage back from March to April 1912. The lesson from this is to move into launch according to pre-agreed plans and to assess business changes through a change-management process.

- The pressure was on to get *Titanic* into operation, so extensive sea trials and testing were likely not considered critical. In part, this was because *Olympic* was established in service. Also, formalized change management and control theory had not been established. Much faith was put in the track record of *Olympic*.

Best Practices for Your Organization

- "If you fail to plan, plan to fail." Include planning for the level of testing required, and be sure to select the right kind of tests.

- Follow a change-management process. This is fundamental to a well-run service-delivery environment.

- Assign the operations services group full ownership of and control over the change-management process.

- Use risk assessments (business, technical, and project) throughout the change-management process.

- Ensure that nonfunctional testing is a priority over functional testing.

- Use a release-management process with version control to assure that the correct components are used from the library.

- Define alternatives to launch (e.g., withdrawal), including back-out plans.

- Create a test environment that is separate from, but mirrors as closely as possible, the service-delivery environment, so that operability and other testing can be completed.

- Select from a broad array of available tests that test the availability of a solution.

- Ensure that all software bug-fixes go through extensive integration and regression testing.

- Realize that the dynamic nature of e-business and the Internet increases the frequency of changes required. This can make testing a challenge for many organizations.

- Use computer simulations and models to reduce testing time, complexity, and cost.

- Ensure the solution is implemented into a test environment first, and run in parallel to the service-delivery environment.

- Ensure an independent test group performs the testing.

- Ensure the testing is not just based on application or function testing, but is open to other types of possible testing.

- Avoid simply discussing this stage, without completing it.

- Avoid change-management processes that are missing or lacking.

Questions You Can Ask Today

- Are small changes implemented without going through change management?

- Once a project is underway, is it possible to stop it from within the organization?

- Which group leads all major implementation projects?

- What is the role of that group? Scheduling the launch? Coordinating, testing, and informing all the parties of the results?

At this stage in the project, you should expect back the following answers from IT:

- A process risk assessment of the overall change-management processes (discussed in appendix D). This should address ownership and the power to stop the launch.

- A definition (specification) of the change going in (Table 4.2).

- A risk assessment of the change, identifying compliance and risk (Table 4.3).

- The categorization of the change (Table 4.4).

- The depth of the testing required (Table 4.5), including the kind of testing, who is going to complete it, and the expected results.

- A definition of alternatives for change (Table 4.6).

- A cost associated with the testing.

C H A P T E R 5

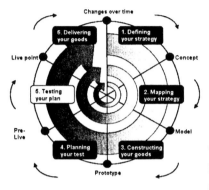

Testing Your Plan

Testing is the crux of any project that will make or break it. You get real-time feedback on your logic and the strength of your idea, as we experienced in the Harvard Student Registration Project. This is certainly the high-profile stage or, as I like to call it, "the afternoon of business-building opportunities."

Ken Ledeen, Chief Executive Officer,
Nevo Technologies, Inc.

Chapter Objectives

When you are done with this chapter, you will be able to complete the test of your on-line operation. With this, you will be ready for Chapter 6, in which you run your on-line operation.

In this chapter you learn how to test your plan. This stage integrates your on-line operation, or solution, into a test environment. Through extensive testing, you determine its overall integrity and availability, as well as its potential impact on the surrounding service-delivery environment. Once all the tests are passed, the stage prepares to *go live*, which delivers a fully working and tested solution into the live service-delivery environment. The testing stage is a critical part of the project lifecycle. Typically, this is where any warning signs of a potential failure start to become visible.

What Steps Do I Need to Follow?

You go through the change-management process, shown in Table 5.1, in three major steps:
- Go through the planning.
- Complete the first-stage test.
- Complete the final-stage test.

Chapter 4 addresses the first function, which involves determining what you need to test for and creating your test plan. This chapter addresses the last two steps, which establish the success criteria, complete the testing on the test plan, and if satisfactory, commence with going live.

Why Do Organizations Resist Change?

Many organizations are reticent to introduce any new changes into their live service-delivery environment because of the perceived risks. To maintain the integrity of your service-delivery environment, each change must be carefully assessed for its impact and risk. Hence, you can cost-justify the depth of testing and make a business decision on the level of testing required. Locking up the service-delivery environment using the "Berlin Wall" approach, where no change can get through, is not realistic in today's world.

A major challenge for your organization is to find a balance in which changes are made rapidly, but do not compromise the business. For example, large Web sites with thousands of pages require daily content changes that could affect user experience and therefore need some degree of testing. Other situations require an emergency change, like a software fix, when there is little time for testing. In all of these cases, the business manager needs to be part of the decision process in assessing the changes.

Your on-line operation will probably be one of the following:

- A new isolated solution

- A new solution that is integrated with an existing solution

- A new solution that is replacing an existing solution

Each has its set of advantages and disadvantages in testing. For example, a new isolated solution has the least impact on the service-delivery environment, whereas the latter two have the most impact because of the interdependencies they each have. (Refer to chapter 2 for more details on these interdependencies.)

Table 5.1: Change-Management Process

Functions	Comments
Complete first-stage test	*Testing phase in test environment.*
Complete tests.	Conduct and complete the battery and levels of tests, incrementally.
Review results.	Review the results of the tests.
Assess risk.	Assess the risk to the business, and the technical risk of the solution.
Complete final-stage test	*Testing phase in live environment.*
Load in increments.	Move/migrate the change incrementally, in predetermined stages, into the live service-delivery environment.
Test each increment.	Check the basic functionality of each solution increment to determine its impacts.
Monitor increments.	Monitor incremental stages holistically for environmental anomalies.

The pressure is on moving new services and functions into the live environment rapidly, to provide a fast return on investment and to stay competitive.

Success Criteria for Titanic's Sailing

In preparation for the maiden trip, *Titanic*'s shipbuilders defined the success criteria as follows:

- Successfully deliver a ship meeting the shipping company's acceptance criteria and contractual obligations. For example, the ship shows stability in all conditions, without any listing to port or starboard.

- Successfully complete the maiden voyage and deliver the expected levels of business service to meet customer satisfaction, like the duration of crossing (average speed), and the shipping company's acceptance criteria.

Success Criteria for Your Live On-line Operation

Your project also has to define the success criteria for going live, for example:

- Integrate your service-delivery environment without disrupting existing business services and provide a continuum of operation for a fixed, designated period.

- Meet the expected levels of business services through collected and measured feedback.

From the success criteria, you can identify risk factors and use these in the second risk assessment and to establish service levels.

Complete First-Stage Test

Completing the first-stage test is the middle phase of the change-management process (a continuation of Figure 4.2). It includes the three major activities shown in Figure 5.1.

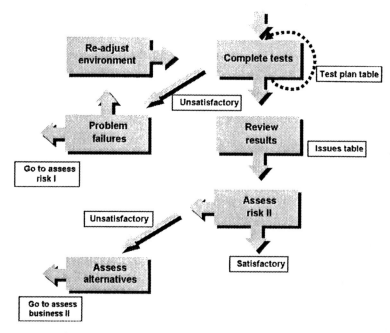

Figure 5.1: The first-stage test involves three major activities.

Complete Titanic's *Tests*

The construction of *Titanic* took four years. The business pressures to go into service were enormous. This is understandable, considering the huge amounts of capital that had been invested and sat tied up during construction. The business opportunity was there for another ship, and White Star's overall objective was to have two luxury liners crossing paths on the Atlantic on a scheduled weekly basis. In addition, *Olympic* had been twice unexpectedly out of service for about eight weeks. As a result, White Star's director, Bruce Ismay, was anxious to see *Titanic* move into service as quickly as possible.

Titanic underwent one day of sea trials in March 1912, precisely one month before her maiden voyage (Figure 5.2). The crew was eager to compare the new ship's speed to *Olympic*. *Olympic* underwent two days of sea trials that included actual engine tests and adjustments to her compasses. All expectations were exceeded by *Olympic*, which was able to maintain a speed well above her designed 21 knots.

Because *Titanic* was very similar to *Olympic*, and *Olympic* had been in service for a while, the testing was less comprehensive. *Titanic* reached a top speed of 23.5 knots[1] and then turned, making a circle 3,850 feet in diameter. A liner the size of *Titanic* had a stopping distance of several miles because of its overall mass, but was halted in less than half a mile from 20.5 knots with the engines reversed. However, in these trials, *Titanic* was not put through handling maneuvers like "S-turns" (used to get around hazards in an emergency). Therefore, the officers had very little time to acclimatize to the handling of the ship.

Complete Your On-line Operations Tests

Your project has to include extensive testing of your on-line operation. This activity completes the building of the test environment and checks its adequacy. For extensive testing, the test environment should closely simulate the live service-delivery environment. Typically, the test environment uses extracted portions of live environment files and data, with confidential fields encrypted.

The build strategy assembles the physical components incrementally into the test environment according to the change strategy and the levels of progressive testing required, as defined by Table 4.5. Testing is conducted at increasing levels of detail, where components are unit tested, then assembled and integrated, and tested again (a continuation of the unit testing in Chapter 3). This scales up to the next level of integration, as application subsystems are integrated and tested, and then the applications are integrated and tested themselves. The test environment is continually adjusted through incremental builds. The testing closely tracks the plan (Table 4.7), executes the battery of selected tests, and follows the predefined test scripts. The groups usually involved in this activity are an independent test group made up of the business managers and users, and IT (including technical and operations services).

---

1. Source: "Triumph & Tragedy," Eaton and Hass, page 45.

Figure 5.2: Titanic underwent one day of sea trails outside of Belfast. Was this enough testing?

The test team tracks the results from the progressive levels of testing to determine what parts have been successfully tested, how many variances were detected, and the variances' overall impact. The output of the testing is a set of results, a pass or a fail. The test plan defines the pass or fail criteria for the selected tests. If any fail, the *problem failures* activity is invoked. The library is notified of the failed test, and the components are removed or marked accordingly. Based on the severity of the failure, the activity either passes the problem to the first risk-assessment activity for a re-review, or re-tests.

For a re-review, the decision criteria for passing are based on the confidence of the test team in the Test Plan table. The team goes through the first three activities and reevaluates all the tables. If valid, the change is then re-tested. For a re-test, the test environment is re-adjusted and the tests are re-run as described above.

Review of Titanic's *Results*

Titanic passed her speed trials successfully, so, as far as Harland and Wolff were concerned, she was ready for her maiden voyage. In addition, *Olympic*'s track record was viewed positively. There is no question that White Star was convinced that *Titanic* was ready, and so Director Bruce Ismay pushed the sailing date forward. However, to ensure a smooth transfer of ownership, he was onboard for the maiden voyage with Harland and Wolff's chief architect and key engineers.

Review of Your On-line Operation Results

In your project, you must review and assess the results of the tests for any unexpected issues that might have arisen. For example, the results might have passed all the criteria, but all expectations might not have been met. Unexpected performance degradation might be an issue. The output of the activity is Table 5.2, which outlines the types of issues uncovered.

Table 5.2: Issues Table

Issues	Definition
A new solution startup requires further configuration.	Startup abruptly stops and needs manual intervention.
Host links require balancing and tuning.	Bottlenecks occur on 20 percent of the lines driving resource utilization, thus causing resource conflicts.
An integration bug was discovered	An integration bug might have a serous impact on UOM.

The impact of any identified issues should be assessed by performing a "try and see" approach, based on intuition and some guesswork. This should be done by members of the project team, namely operations services. Technical services should be brought into the process one week before testing. At this point in the process, solution services should be brought in to determine some of the alternatives to going live. Depending on the success, business users should be brought in for reviews, transfer, and acceptance.

Reassess Titanic's Risk

In assessing the potential risks to *Titanic* for a second time, the ship owners were very much aware of the pressing economic need to move *Titanic* into service. At this point, *Olympic*'s track record was significant in creating a sense of security that *Titanic* could be pressed quickly into service. *Titanic* had passed her trials and was deemed ready for sailing. White Star liners traditionally had their maiden sailing in June (according to *The Only Way to Cross*), when indeed *Olympic* sailed. The tradition was broken for *Titanic* in order to capture the trade that White Star had lost when *Olympic* was tied up in dry-dock for repairs because of the collision with HMS *Hawke*.

Titanic's April sailing date carried risks. The winter of 1912 was unseasonably mild, creating a lot of icebergs in the North Atlantic. White Star was very much aware of this condition, and as a precaution, moved *Titanic*'s sailing path 10 miles due south, as shown in Figure 5.3, to avoid "iceberg alley."

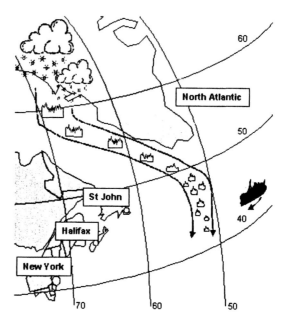

Figure 5.3: Icebergs break away from the polar caps. The Labrador currents (dotted lines) carry these south, into the shipping lanes. This is known as "iceberg alley." Seldom do more than two percent make it as far south as latitude 48 North.

Reassess Your On-line Operation Risk

Your project has a second opportunity to reassess the risk. In this activity, you evaluate Table 5.2, determine whether the issues justify the incoming change, and then decide whether to proceed with the change-management process. The groups usually involved in this activity are business (managers and users) and IT (including solution, technical, and operations services). The output is either satisfactory or unsatisfactory. An unsatisfactory output invokes a review of the Alternatives table and a step back to testing or a branch into the "withdrawal" activity (complete back-out of the process). A satisfactory output continues to the final-stage test.

The reassessment activity is critical, as it might be the last opportunity to stop a risky implementation. This activity is particularly important because it is a business and not a technical assessment. So, the change has to be ranked according to the impact on the business. You need to answer the following questions:

- Is there still a business rationale and justification for the change?

- Could the change adversely affect the existing Service Level Agreements (SLAs)?

- Could the change have a negative impact on current business operations, business groups, business processes, or customers?

Finally, the activity has to be signed off by a business manager who is evaluating whether all the acceptance criteria have been met, as set out in the Test Plan table. This also includes reviewing the testing success criteria.

The complete change package requires careful and controlled deployment from the test environment into the live environment. It should be checked again, for example, for approved versions of components like certain levels of software. The baseline for levels, versions, and locations of components is updated as part of the configuration tool, so that the integrity of the library is maintained.

Complete Final-Stage Test

The last phase of the change-management process, completing the final-stage test, includes the three major activities that are part of the loop shown in Figure 5.4 (a continuation of Figure 5.1).

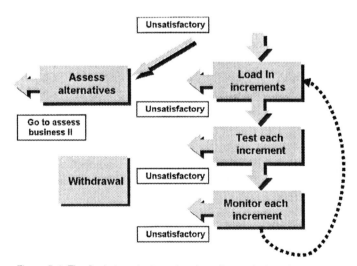

Figure 5.4: The final-stage test can be viewed as a single or incremental load, depending on the type of project.

Titanic's Loading

In this final phase, *Titanic* was prepared for sailing. The preparation was incremental, as all the major pieces were carefully assembled. The logistics of getting *Titanic* ready and the scale of preparation were enormous. The required cargo, provisions, foodstuffs, fuel, water, medical stores, and other necessities for a luxurious ship/hotel included the following:

- For provisions, the list of foods required for the maiden voyage included, among other things, 75,000 pounds of fresh meat, 35,000 fresh eggs, 40 tons of potatoes, 1,000 bottles of wine, and 15,000 bottles of beer

- For fuel, a total of 6,500 tons of coal were required for the trip. At the time, Southampton had been hit by a coal strike, which severely affected the transatlantic business. To acquire this amount of coal, *Oceania* and *Adriatic* schedules were canceled, and passengers were offered a passage on *Titanic* instead. *Olympic* had brought back extra coal from New York, but the amount of coal was still perilously close to the minimum required for the crossing.

- For fresh water, a total of 206,800 gallons was required for the journey, held in seven tanks. Fresh water was also distilled through apparatus on the ship.

- For the ship's hotel facilities, 12,000 dinner plates, 1,000 oyster forks, 15,000 champagne glasses, 40,000 towels of different sorts, and 45,000 table napkins were required.

Incremental Loading of On-line Operations

This activity involves invoking the release-management process. It is performed only on a satisfactory outcome of the risk reassessment discussed earlier in this chapter. The activity commences with release management, which might involve a series of actions like building a database, transferring data, and setting up applications and tools. The main deliverable from this activity is an incremental "build" and testing in the live service-delivery environment.

This activity is usually performed by technical and operations services during the weekly or monthly planned outage window. Typically, the testing window is on a Sunday morning from 2:00 to 6:00 A.M.

Care must be taken when making multiple changes. For example, are there any dependencies between the two changes being tested? These dependencies need to be carefully reviewed as part of the risk reassessment activity. If the build fails for some reason against preset measures, the testing activity can branch into assessing alternatives, with the assumption that this is completed within the planned outage window.

Test Each of Titanic*'s Increments*

It took the experienced dockers of Southampton almost a week to load the ship with supplies and cargo, to make her ready for her maiden voyage. The officers onboard kept a running checklist of the load, to ensure the whole operation was ready for sailing. It was rather like today's flight crews going through extensive preflight checks.

As the coal was loaded into the bunkers, officers checked it, and calculations were carefully drawn up to ensure the minimum amount was loaded to make the crossing. Similarly, as goods and provisions were loaded, officers checked that everything was ready for the ship's operation. At any point in this checklist process, the captain and officers had the option of delaying the sailing, if something was not right.

The officers kept an official record of all the crew and passenger boardings. *Titanic*'s crew of 900 was recruited in Southampton. This included 290 stewards and stewardesses. Around 340 of the crew worked below-deck, including engineers, stokers, trimmers, and firemen. Most of the crew embarked on sailing day.

Titanic's passengers also embarked on sailing day. A large number of passengers traveled to Southampton from London, and the advanced rail network transported them right up to the liner. *Titanic* was certified to carry a total of 3,547 people: 905 in first class, 564 in second, 1,134 in third, and 944 crew. On the maiden voyage, about 2,223 people sailed: 329 in first class, 285 in second class, 710 in third class, and 899 crew, as shown in Table 5.3. The ship was only 62 percent full, which is somewhat low, considering the passengers transferred from other ships cancelled to provide coal for *Titanic*.

Table 5.3: Passenger and Crew Capacity

	Capacity	Sailed
Crew members	944	899
First-class passengers	905	329
Second-class passengers	564	285
Third-class passengers	1134	710
Total	**3547**	**2223**

The passenger list was a "who's who" of public life, with 300 very famous people, collectively worth of over $500 million. This underlined the public confidence in the ship. Even the richest man alive, J.P. Morgan, was registered on the maiden voyage, illustrating the tremendous prestige of the maiden crossing (although he canceled at the last minute). White Star had done a very effective job in selling the service.

Test Each of Your Increments

Your project needs to go through some basic testing of the on-line operation in the live service-delivery environment. For example, the major categories of the on-line operation—application, database, etc.—are individually tested. This should not replace the testing activity. The groups usually involved in this activity are technical and operations services, as well as the user.

In many organizations, this is the most comprehensive testing of the entire cycle. The type of testing that is completed is usually functional. The deliverable to this activity is a pass or fail. If the live basic test fails for some reason against the preset measures, the activity can branch into the "withdrawal," activity, where the back-out plan is invoked. This is a difficult situation, as it would typically affect the business environment and the business.

In a withdrawal situation, an assessment is required of how quickly the change needs to be withdrawn. In other words, can the change remain in the live service-delivery environment until the next planned outage window? Also, the business manager needs to be notified at this point.

The final step is to update the inventory model. The degree of detail depends on the information available and the relevance of the change.

Monitor All of Titanic's Increments

The monitoring activity looks across all the increments to ensure consistency of the incremental loads and the officers' and crews' readiness to deliver the ship's operation. Before *Titanic* began the main leg of her maiden voyage across the Atlantic, she visited the ports of Cherbourg and Queenstown to pick up passengers. This gave the crew a brief day to get better accustomed to the ship's operation.

As *Titanic* was leaving the Southampton, her wash dragged the parked steamer ship *New York*, about half its size. All six retaining ropes to the jetty snapped, to the consternation of hundreds of passengers on deck. *New York* went adrift and moved toward the side of *Titanic*.[2] Only the tug *Vulcan* and the quick action of *Titanic's* Captain Smith, who used the starboard engines to force the steamer away, prevented a major collision. Eyewitnesses reported *New York* was within four feet of colliding with *Titanic* side-on, as shown in Figure 5.5. This was a very similar incident to *Olympic's* collision with *Hawke*.

---

2. In physics this effect is known as Bernoulli's principle, in which a large moving ship close to another ship creates low pressure between the two. The smaller ship is literally "sucked" towards the larger.

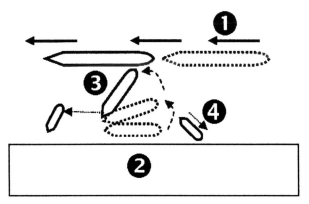

Figure 5.5: The ships Titanic and New York nearly collide.
Titanic ❶ drags New York ❷ off its mooring, breaking
retaining ropes. New York ❸ comes within four feet of
colliding with Titanic. The tug Vulcan ❹ prevents a major
collision by restraining New York.

The *New York* incident exemplified that *Titanic* was pressed quickly into service, and the crew was unprepared for the maiden voyage. The crew was not familiar with their responsibilities, with the ship, or with each other. The ship's monstrous size required days to get used to. For example, Second Officer Lightoller later testified that it took him three days to become familiar with getting around the ship—and Lightoller was a very experienced officer who had sailed on *Olympic*. This fact was later noticed by a number of passengers. Overall, *Titanic* was in a state of poor operational readiness.

At the outset of the main Atlantic crossing, the Board of Trade inspectors inspected *Titanic* in Queenstown, Ireland. As part of the inspection, officers determined the seaworthiness of the vessel, checking the hull, boilers, and machinery. They also checked for provisions, water, fuel, and medical stores. They looked over steerage compartments for light and air, and inspected the health of both the crew and steerage passengers.

An important part of the inspection was safety. A lifeboat drill was performed in front of inspectors to determine the readiness of the crew. During the drill, only two lifeboats were lowered, but they did not reach the water, so the test was not fully completed. The drill outlined that it took eight to ten well-trained men to prepare and lower a lifeboat. The test failed to highlight that the crew was not very well prepared to handle a disaster requiring the launch of all 16 lifeboats. There were only 83 mariners in a crew of 900. Following the inspection, *Titanic* received a report of "seaworthy and ready to sail" from the Queenstown Board of Trade.

Monitor the Created Whole

Your project needs to monitor all incremental stages holistically for environmental anomalies or glitches, and certify the readiness for a live operation. Look for any discrepancies in the service-delivery environment over a predefined length. If none exist, the change activities are seen as complete. The withdrawal activity is available at any point. The group usually involved in this activity is operations services.

The monitoring activity should be continued as part of the standard day-to-day functions of operations services. However, it needs to be balanced, with no specific part of the environment taking priority, so that any anomalies or inconsistencies are quickly spotted. For example, a busy period that has a major impact on the environment might appear only at the end of the month.

Are You Meeting Your Contractual Obligations?

Harland and Wolff had fulfilled all the preliminary contractual obligations for White Star. White Star representatives accompanied *Titanic* on her maiden voyage to ensure that the remaining contractual obligations were fulfilled. White Star also had contractual obligations in the form of *Service Level Agreements*, or *SLAs*, with its passengers. These covered the following:

- Level of luxury expected with a $4,350 first-class ticket.

- Crossing times set out in a published schedule.

- Safety of passage guaranteed.

- Limit to the number of passengers carried.

As your organization goes live, it also needs to establish SLAs with its customers. The demand for SLAs for business services has helped draw attention to the criticality of business services. This is reflective of user pressure for better service availability. SLAs attach a financial commitment to providing the desired level of availability. However, very few organizations define SLAs for all of their on-line operations.

What Makes a Good SLA?

A service level agreement is, simply, a formal written contract signed by all involved parties. An effective SLA contains the following elements:

- The identification of the contracting parties.

- A description of the work processed, including type, volume, mix, and time of arrival.

- The service levels to be provided, including response time, turnaround time, deadlines, accuracy, and availability.

- A performance and reporting procedure, detailing the frequency and type of reports to be provided to users and management.

- Penalties for noncompliance.

- Provisions for modifying the agreement.

- An expiration date.

Organizations need to consider SLAs for customers and for outside vendors, such as Internet service providers (*ISPs*) or application service providers (*ASPs*). This requires the tools to measure adherence.

Service Level Objectives (SLOs)

All your service levels should be measured and reported in customer-perceived terms. There is no sense agreeing to any service level if there is no way to determine if the level has been achieved or consistently met. SLOs outline the criteria by which the service is measured. They typically include service times, response times (not only for the application, but also for vendor responses to problems), exclusions, and penalties to be paid when the objectives are not met. Measurements against these objectives define an outage in the environment.

Examples of SLOs include the following:

- Times of service—Availability is specified for each phase of each service and/or application.

- Critical times for a service—These might occur in a specific hour, day, week, month, or year. Outages are weighted depending on the time of failure.

- Response time—Guaranteed levels are usually expressed in terms of average and maximum response times allowed, e.g., mean time to action is two minutes.

- Batch processing and other processing found to be a key part of the service.

Let's return to the *Titanic* to examine this further. With crossing times, captains were expected by the paying passengers and public to press on and meet the published schedule, very much like airlines today. However, Bruce Ismay took this a step further. He was determined to show that *Titanic* was an improvement over *Olympic* by beating *Olympic*'s best crossing time. Before *Titanic*'s maiden voyage, he published a shipping announcement in the *New York Times* that *Titanic* would arrive a day early to White Star's published schedule. Effectively, he was writing out a new SLO for *Titanic* that proved to be fateful in pushing the ship to its operational limits.

In truth, there were no improvements to *Titanic*'s power output, and therefore speed, over *Olympic*. He risked the ship's safety by forcing the ship to race across the Atlantic at maximum speed and beat *Olympic*'s best time, which was set over the course of 11 months of passage.

Important End-User Measures

The areas of service that are most important to end-users are typically response time and availability. The response time for on-line solutions is usually defined in seconds. If a transaction is designed and implemented to provide a 1.5 second average response time, the SLA would likely define the response time as 1.5 seconds for 95 percent of the transactions processed, and no transactions responding in more than 10 seconds. This would allow for varying arrival rates and queuing conditions.

If a user is unable to initiate a request for whatever reason, the service is considered unavailable. Long response times, exceeding the attention span of the end-user, should be considered an outage. For example, an ATM transaction spanning more than two minutes would equate to an outage for that customer.

Exclusions to SLAs

There are some exclusions to the SLA criteria. These fall into three major classes:

- Natural events, such as storms, floods, or other disasters

- Events outside of the organization's control, like the loss of power from the power company or failures in external telecommunications facilities

- Malicious acts, such as those committed by a disgruntled employee

Outages caused by these events, while affecting measurement of availability, are typically not counted against any penalties within Service Level Agreements.

Measuring SLAs with Performance Reports

A performance report compares planned versus actual workload characteristics and service levels obtained during a reporting period. By comparing both workload and service, it becomes easy to determine if missed service levels were due to excess work or inadequate performance on any part of the system. Performance reports provide the opportunity for identifying potential problems and eliminating the availability impact. (Chapter 8 has more information on metrics and reporting.)

Policies

Policies are one way for your organization to achieve its business service-level goals. Policies might state things like who is notified when an outage occurs, and that post-incident analysis must start no later than 24 hours after the resolution of the incident. Policies are most effective for ensuring simplicity through standardization, as shown in Table 5.4. They also provide an audit trail of changes.

Table 5.4: Policy Content Checklist for Monitoring and Updating Policies

Policy	Policy Description	Creation Date	Reason	Creator	Last Review	Comments
Disaster	Contingency	Nov 00	Audit report advice	SL	May 25	Mgmt direction
Security	Environmental security	Nov 01	Hackers	NJ	Sep 09	Mgmt direction
Outages	Outage analysis	Dec 01	Outage Apr 01	MP	Jul 29	IT lead
Equipment procurement	Purchase	Sep 02	Increase availability	JM	Nov 20	Business-unit need

Very often, policies are confused with SLAs. Policies are conventions or guidelines that organizations follow to accomplish goals. The SLAs should define the deliverables or goals, and not how they are accomplished. Many policies have never been written or approved; a common response is "well, that's the way we have always done it." Many organizations have an auditing group that sets, manages, and enforces policies. This group is critical when changes are being evaluated.

The final step is to begin to tie your team and individual job performance to SLAs. This involves creating reward or incentive programs and systems that drive the right behaviors, change direction, and refocus staff. The programs need to collect metrics to ensure staff are measured appropriately and subsequently rewarded.

Factors Affecting SLAs

The following factors should be carefully considered when you create SLAs:

- *Maintenance windows*—Most environments still require a maintenance window. This should be included in the SLA, clearly stating when, the duration, the notification procedure, and a contact name. Some criteria need to be established to clearly determine when the services are considered back on-line. Typically, a representative of the user community should accept this.

- *Correcting failed components*—Component failures are inevitable, so redundancy is built into the overall environment to improve availability. If a backed-up component fails, the service should not be affected, but the risk of service interruption is higher because there is no longer a backup component. The SLA should define an acceptable period of time to correct the failed component and reintegrate it. These components include such things as data files, application processes, network lines, and processors.

- *Batch processing*—Batch windows need to be considered separately in the SLA. An organization with a dependency on the batch processing should clearly define the batch-window begin and end times. It should also identify the critical processing that makes up the batch stream.

Conclusion

The following sections summarize the major points of this chapter and how they relate to your business today. For more information on these concepts, search the Internet for these keywords and phrases: *software testing methods*, *release management*, *test teams*, *implementation*, *service level agreements*, and *objectives*.

Major Points, Considerations, and Titanic Lessons

- On leaving port, *Titanic* had a near collision with the steamer *New York*. Eyewitnesses reported *New York* was within four feet of colliding with *Titanic*. This indicates the challenges the crew faced in operating the very large ship.

- Only one lifeboat drill was performed, and the crew was not well prepared to handle a disaster requiring the launch of all the lifeboats. The lesson from this is that the objective of testing is to bring to light major flaws missed in the requirements, design, and construction stages.

- The ship owners were very much driven by the pressing economic need to move *Titanic* into service. In reality, *Titanic*'s testing consisted of the maiden voyage across the Atlantic fully loaded with passengers.

- Director Bruce Ismay wrote out a new SLO for *Titanic* that proved to be fateful in pushing the ship to its operational limits.

Best Practices for Your Organization

- Carefully undertake business and technical risk assessments.

- Set up separate and independent test teams that have strong incentives to test objectively.

- Ensure users are involved in testing changes to the live environment, to guarantee that testing meets objectives.

- Establish the ability to stop an implementation into the live environment if the testing fails or is badly flawed.

- Ensure that major testing, once under way, can be halted when there are serious misgivings.

- Avoid bringing in operations services too late in the process, where changes are introduced "blindly" into the service-delivery environment.

- Avoid a change-management process that lacks the political support in the organization at a senior level and the "teeth" to be effective.

- Avoid giving developers any testing or deployment access rights to the live environment. In fact, this right should be reserved for one group only: operations services.

- Avoid testing in a development environment, as typically only the simplest configurations can be simulated. The resources available in a development environment are generally insufficient to simulate the live environment. The testing that is completed is basic application-function testing, and not the all-important nonfunctional testing.

Questions You Can Ask Today

At this stage in the project, you should expect back the following answers from IT:

- A risk assessment of the overall change-management processes in place. (For more information, see appendix D.)

- Testing success criteria.

- A summary of the results from testing.

- Results of the risk reassessment.

- Recommendations on whether to move the new element into the live environment.

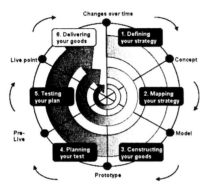

C H A P T E R **6**

Delivering Your Goods

You can get noticed for innovation, but a real success is built on delivering the goods day in and day out. This is where professionalism and dedication to the job really shine.

Dr. Prasuna Dornadula,
Senior Vice President, Chief Technology Officer,
CareTouch, Inc.

Chapter Objectives

When you are done with this chapter, you will be able to run your on-line operation. With this, you will complete the last project stage for your on-line operation.

In this chapter, you learn how to set up your organization and processes to deliver the on-line operation and service-delivery environment. This not only allows you to monitor and maintain your environment, but to improve the required levels of service and availability.

What Steps Do I Need to Follow?

Delivering your on-line operation involves three steps:

1. *Set up the delivery.* To maintain the integrity of your service-delivery environment, you need to set up an effective organizational support structure, taking into account centralized and automated operations.

2. *Determine actions to take when problems interfere with the delivery.* To minimize the impact of a service outage, you need to recover the service-delivery environment as quickly and accurately as possible. This is when further mistakes can compound a failure further by introducing more problems. The recov-

ery clock introduced in this chapter helps to focus the organization and align the processes for speed of recovery.

3. *Proactively maintain the delivery.* To maintain the integrity of your service-delivery environment and proactively prevent failures, you need to eliminate and reduce potential problems and their impact. The cost of preventing a problem is significantly lower than reacting to a problem. However, problem prevention is an up-front cost, which inhibits some organizations from implementing it.

Objectives for Your On-line Operation

Your on-line operation is now running live. You need to maintain the following:

- Deliver the level of service as defined by service-level agreements that provide the guidelines to follow. (Refer to chapter 5 for more details.)

- Prevent problems from occurring that could disrupt this level of service.

- Recover the service-delivery environment from an outage or problem in the shortest time possible, through rapid problem management, and restore the on-line operation to the agreed level of service.

To ensure that your service-delivery environment continuously delivers the newly implemented on-line operation, you need to look at the organization and activities required to support and maintain it. These activities include successfully maintaining the stability of the service-delivery environment, preventing disruptions from occurring, or minimizing these disruptions through a quick recovery method. This is based on a rapid and accurate problem-management process oriented around the recovery clock, as shown in Figure 6.1.

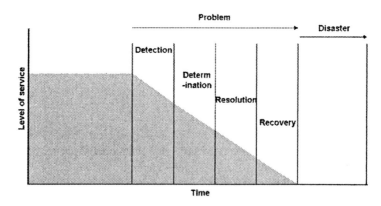

Figure 6.1: Recovering the service back to normal involves outlining the deterioration of a service mapped against time, and the steps taken to return to normal.

Set Up the Delivery

Service-delivery environments can be extremely complex and are susceptible to failures. To eliminate and reduce potential problems and their impact, you need to set up the following:

- An organizational support structure

- Centralized operations

- Automated operations

How to Organize a Support Structure

Titanic's organizational support structure consisted of a four-level support hierarchy. Your support organization, focused on continuous availability of the service-delivery environment, has a lot in common with *Titanic*'s operation.

First-level Support

Frontline support functions involve those staff who are monitoring, operating, and controlling an environment. On *Titanic*, this included the lookouts in the crow's nest, the on-duty officers, and the crew on the bridge. The radio operators in the wireless room could be considered as a help desk, communicating with the outside world, controlling the flow of information to and from the ship, and sending and receiving messages for passengers.

In your organization, frontline support is traditionally attributed to the operators (operations services), and is usually fronted using a help desk. The help desk provides a single point of contact for all problems, and it is responsible for all customer or user (problem originator) communications throughout the life of the problem. The help desk should be centralized, dedicated to all services available and through all service times. All problems are logged through the help desk, where a problem ticket is allocated, escalated, and tracked through to resolution and recovery. The problem status is communicated to the customer at designated intervals. The help desk is responsible for closing the problem ticket, with customer agreement, and for reporting any customer training needs to the business units. The help-desk function is enhanced by a problem-management system to assist the logging, tracking, and routing, with built-in timers for timestamping. It should have a common problem repository or database.

Typically, operators are generalists who have a high level knowledge of the service-delivery environment. Their primary role is to maintain this environment and monitor its general health. Operators need to see the bigger picture, and be sensitive to environmental changes and their associated impacts, with the ability to quickly drill down and investigate a situation and its causes.

The concept of the recovery clock is fundamental to running a successful environment and meeting service levels. The functions performed by front-level support are usually problem prevention, detection, and determination.

Second-level Support

The second-level functions support the front line, providing backup support and more specialized functions. The staff on *Titanic* at this level included the following:

- Safety officer (plotting positions of icebergs, currents, and weather systems)

- Navigation officer (plotting the position of the ship and maintaining the course)

- Specialized technical positions (like the carpenter and ship's doctor)

In your organization, this function is attributed to a specialist role, like a technical-support group called in to resolve and recover a problem and provide backup on problem prevention, detection, and possibly determination. A common way to map the specialist expertise is to follow the layers of an inventory model end-to-end (Figure 2.7).

Second-level support is also responsible for these management functions:

- *Performance management* measures how well your service-delivery environment is performing and meeting user expectations for service-response time and performance levels. Realtime monitoring tools help identify bottlenecks that might affect performance. The use of performance alerts is essential in determining environmental degradation and taking appropriate actions to prevent downtime. It is important to collect metrics that can break down "round-trip time" into back-end processing time, and the client's "browser render" time. This helps isolate the problem domains.

- *Security management* determines violations of security against your service-delivery environment that could interfere with the overall service delivery. This is becoming an increasingly complex function, with the broadening of communications through the Internet and all its associated risks, like hacking, viruses, and deliberate sabotage. On-line security alerts are important in detecting potential problems.

- *Capacity management* determines the throughput capacity of the service-delivery environment based on likely utilization, establishing the likely current and maximum levels. From this, the risk-benefit analysis of additional capacity investments can be determined.

Third-level Support

The third-level functions include supporting the second line. On *Titanic*, this level of backup support was provided through first and second officers and the captain.

In your organization, this group is called in to resolve and recover a very specific problem requiring specialists and expertise skills, like someone in solution services, development support, or even development. This is the last stop before the request goes outside of the organization.

The third-level support group is also responsible for application management, which requires detailed knowledge of the workings of the application or solution. Sometimes, it might also cross over into the underpinning levels of support (second and possibly first), depending on an organization's size.

Supporting applications over the Internet is vastly more complicated than traditional support because of application interdependencies and the 24/7 window. This inhibits quick problem-source identification. Application support needs to be organized along end-to-end flows of transactions, across applications and technologies. (Refer to chapter 2 for more details.)

Fourth-level Support

The fourth-level support function is a very specialist role, for someone with a high degree of knowledge in a specific area. This function is external to the organization. It involves a third party, consulting organization, or vendor. For example, *Titanic*'s architect would qualify for this role.

Avoid the Organizational Pitfalls

Many organizations fail to view the service-delivery environment holistically, as a well-balanced dynamic entity. Instead, they look at each element separately. For example, you might organize the technology infrastructure according to the principal technology entities of clients, networks, and servers. The support organization overlays this, with individual groups holding responsibility for specific technologies, such as network operations, client support, and server operations. Procedures are then developed and overlaid on this structure by the staff holding these responsibilities.

Organizations compartmentalized along these lines run into a lot of issues over responsibility. The infrastructures are prone to areas of uncertainty over technology, in terms of who owns what. This phenomenon is typified by the way problems occur in the service-delivery environment. For example, several problems might develop in various parts of the environment. These might be classified as technology problems and deemed unrelated. However, by "helicoptering up" and looking at the service-delivery environment holistically, you can correlate these problems. You might discover that they relate to the gray areas of responsibility attributed to poor change-control or inadequate problem-management.

Gray Areas

Often, there is a gray area between the first and second level of support that can lead to confusion over functions, as shown in Figure 6.2. The introduction of automated operations has seen a shift in functions, in which operations services have taken on more activities traditionally performed by the technical services groups, with hybrid positions like operations analyst evolving.

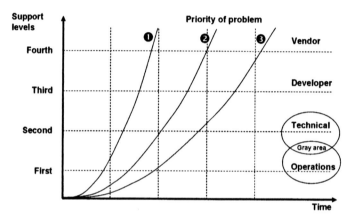

Figure 6.2: Escalating problems through the organization outlines the relationship between transitioning the problem through the support structure over time. Problem 1 is the highest priority, and therefore its escalation is accelerated.

How to Centralize Operations through a Bridge

Titanic's organizational support structure consisted of a multilayered hierarchy, which lent itself to centralized operations. The *bridge*, shown in Figure 6.3, is traditionally the command and control center of a ship. The engine room might be the heart of the ship, but the bridge is the place for decision-making. It has all the main controls, like the steering wheel and the engine room telegraphs that control the speed and direction of the ship. It also has the main navigation equipment, like the compass and sextants. The captain's and officers' quarters are connected to the bridge to allow for rapid access, even when off-duty.

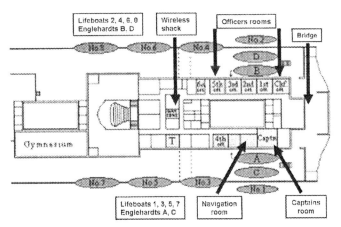

Figure 6.3: In this layout of Titanic's top deck and bridge, note the ease of access to the bridge or control center from the captain's and officers' quarters. The navigation room is next to the captain's quarters.

In the early days of mainframe computing, all operations functions were centralized like *Titanic*'s bridge. However, with the advent of distributed computing and networks, operations services became decentralized, and operators were relocated to business units and departments close to the business. The advent of automated operations and distributed systems management (remotely operated technology) has created a shift back to centralized operations based on rationalizing costs, although up-front investments are relatively high. Effectively, remote sites are run "lights out," with no local operators.

Centralized operations consist of a single command and control center in a service-delivery environment. Organizational support can be improved dramatically by centralizing activities to a single focal point. Centralizing operations allows the organization to better meet business and IT requirements through better visibility, command, and control. It requires a separate and independent system, or part of a segregated existing system. A strategy of implementing the operations tools on a separate system helps ensure the integrity of the environment. For example, where environmental degradation becomes critical, isolated operations tools and resources are better able to react and access the service-delivery environment to perform a recovery.

Centralizing operations is cost-justified in the time and resource savings from a more secure service-delivery environment. A centralized support center also reduces the number of operators (first-level support) needed on-site. Other considerations include the following:

- There must be a contingency for centralized operations, namely the failure of the central site.
- Automating the environment enables centralized operations and allows for "dark site" operations.

How to Use Automated Operations

The history of automation can be traced back to the Industrial Revolution. The field of automation evolved with the development of feedback systems, where systems were able to self-regulate and adjust. The first step in automating a system is to introduce a feedback loop, so that it can monitor its own output and compare that with a set of rules or standards stored in a table. If there is a match, then an instruction is invoked, as a control program, which adjusts the output and the performance accordingly. *Titanic* did make some limited use of automation, with things like the bulkhead doors that could be triggered automatically by a float.

The first step in automating a service-delivery environment is creating a *flight clock*, shown in Figure 6.4. The flight clock outlines the manual operations routines performed through a 24-hour period. Typically, routine activities performed by front-level support throughout the day would be documented in an *operations run book*. In today's environments, all functions are being automated. The operations services group needs a level of contact with the environment. With automated operations, however, this group loses direct interaction and skills in responding to abnormal states. This fact needs to be taken into consideration as part of the automation strategy.

Automated operations or computer automation is a significant topic because of its major prevalence and impact on today's organization. It is an important part of a recovery clock and is used to rapidly resolve, recover, and restore problems. Effectively, it provides a foundation for self-regulating, self-adjusting, and self-healing service-delivery environments.

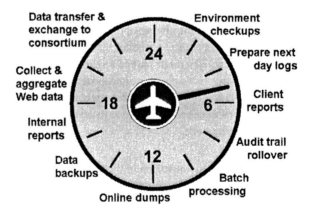

Figure 6.4: The flight clock outlines the manual operations routinely performed through a 24-hour period.

Automated Operator Functions

The automated operator is a function or system used in the automation of a service-delivery environment. It has the following components:

- *Sensing mechanisms, driven by Boolean logic*—This is essentially the part of the feedback loop that measures the output from the environment, which might come in different formats. One common output is a stream of either warning or error messages. Sensing error messages can become a very complex function because much information is monitored from various unrelated parts of the service-delivery environment.

- *Decision element to determine abnormal states*—This element compares the error messages from the sensing element to a rules base and generates the appropriate commands to activate the control element. This can become very complex as sequences of error messages are combined. Building the rules base to successfully match error messages to a course of action is a long, painstaking process that might take years to complete.

- *Control element to recover the components*—The control element reacts to the trigger passed by the decision element and invokes instructions or control programs. This becomes complex, as one program instigates many actions across the whole service-delivery environment.

As a product, the automated operator can take many different forms in the environment. For example, it can be part of the host server or it can stand alone.

The Pros and Cons of Using an Automated Operator

When a service-delivery environment is operating properly, an automated operator is able to regulate behavior in a wide variety of circumstances that need not have been foreseen or predicted in detail. An airplane autopilot is a classic example of a self-regulating device. It uses information from flight instruments to make continuous adjustments to the controls, staying on a preset course. Likewise, an automated operator can heal problems as they occur, contain their impact, reduce the environmental exposure, and, very importantly, reduce recovery time.

Automated recovery has evolved the function of operations services to more sophisticated levels, where recovery is completed at the highest level of the inventory model possible, at the service/business-function level rather than the component level. This explains its popularity. Over time, however, the automation process becomes more complicated. As a result, there are many downsides to automated operations:

- It is resource-intensive and can rapidly consume system resources when, for example, it gets caught in a loop. (For more detail, refer to the case study in appendix A.)

- It is likely to hide problems occurring and reoccurring from operations staff and therefore reduce visibility.

- It can remove the operators from the environment, reducing their effectiveness and eroding their skills.

- As the environment becomes more automated, the dependency on it greatly increases. It is a single point of failure, and if it fails, a backup or contingency is required.

- The increasing complexity of automated operations requires investments indirectly proportional to the benefit, as shown in Figure 6.5.

Effectively, automating operations can be an arduous process, requiring large investments in resources. These investments are typically measured in years, not months.

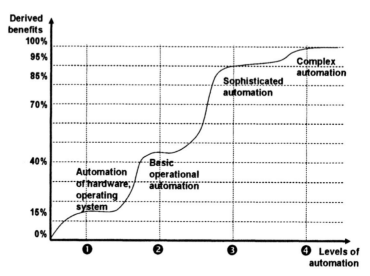

Figure 6.5: Automated operations proceed through four levels. The initial automation of simple hardware and operating system (1) accounts for a 10 percent return in derived benefits. Increasing levels of automated operations (2, 3, and 4) have limited payback until a sophisticated level is achieved.

Many IT departments view automated operations as a simple answer to reducing costs, improving the recovery clock, and meeting SLAs. Many organizations are trying to completely eliminate the role of first-level support through these technologies, which provide automated monitoring, alerts, and recovery. However, there are a lot of unforeseen risks, like the magnitude of complexity created, the investment to set it up, and the dedicated staff with the right skills to maintain and continuously enhance it. Without a well thought-out operations strategy and a solid foundation, automation can be a very costly exercise. In short, great care has to be taken in implementing an automated operator, and with approaches to automation in general.

Actions to Take When Problems Interfere with Your Delivery

There are many proven ways to organize your staff into an effective support organization. However, for service-delivery environments driven by availability of service, the speed of service recovery and accuracy are absolutely critical when problems interfere with your delivery. Therefore, the principal objective is to reduce the overall outage time by improving the mean time to recovery through rapid and accurate problem management.

How to Use a Recovery Clock

The recovery clock shown in Figure 6.6 measures the overall time taken from the occurrence of the failure to the recovery of the service-delivery environment to its normal condition. The use of metrics is essential for all aspects of support, as it provides a method for calculating and measuring improvements against SLAs. The recovery clock provides a logical breakdown of all the steps required for a full recovery. It should be one of the underlying models used to outline the operational functions in a support organization.

The four quadrants of the recovery clock are as follows:

1. Detect anomalies and issues, and verify that a problem actually exists.

2. Determine how broad the problem is, whether it is continuous or intermittent, and its impact on day-to-day operations.

3. Resolve the problem and take the approach necessary to repair it.

4. Recover the service-delivery environment and provide on-going monitoring to determine the success of the recovery.

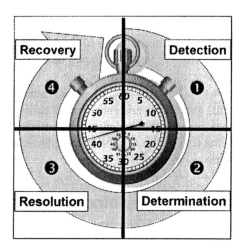

Figure 6.6: Breaking down the recovery clock into four logical time phases provides a consistent way of measuring and improving the overall time spent in each quadrant.

Detection on Titanic

The first quadrant of the recovery clock is associated with the speed with which a problem is detected. However, it is not always obvious that a problem is occurring. Pieces of intelligence must be collected that might, when put together, indicate a problem or issue.

Titanic had some built-in feedback mechanisms for warning the officers and crew (operations services) of changes in the surrounding environment. These included:

- Ships sending Marconigrams in the vicinity

- Visual monitoring from the crow's nest and bridge

Feedback mechanisms are essential in the creation and operation of automated operators and Early Warning Systems (EWS). This is discussed in more detail later in this chapter.

Ignored Ice Warnings at 00:00, April 13th

Over a two-day period, *Titanic* received at least eight ice warnings through wireless messages from other ships reporting ice, icebergs, and icefloes. The arrival of *Titanic* was a great social event in the port of destination, and the wealthy first-class passengers used the wireless to send personal messages to friends. Because of this flood of outgoing commercial radio messages, the radio operators only sporadically relayed the important ice-warning messages from the radio room back to the bridge.

In one unconfirmed story, a Mrs. Ryerson was concerned over getting to New York one day early and finding a hotel room. She asked Director Bruce Ismay if the ship would be slowed down as it coursed through the ice field. Ismay is said to have replied, "Oh no, we will put on more boilers to get out of it." Ismay denied the story at the U. S. inquiry hearing, but Fireman Frederick Barrett disclosed that on April 14, three additional boilers had been lit, more than at any other time in the journey, and the ship reached its peak speed.

On the night of the April 12, the ship *California* was north of *Titanic*, bound for Boston. After a near-fatal collision with an ice shelf, Captain Stanley Lord decided against proceeding forward and pulled up for the night. Surrounded by pack ice but in no danger, Radio Operator Evans, under orders from the captain, sent an ice warning to *Titanic*'s radio operators, who had been working a 14-hour day sending and receiving commercial traffic. The *Titanic* responded with the now infamous, "Shut up, shut up, I am busy. I am working Cape Race and you are jamming me." This last warning was not passed back to the bridge because of the message overload. The procedure for passing messages back to the bridge was confusing at best. Evans did not try again after being snubbed. He turned off his wireless and went to bed.

Signal-to-Noise Ratio

Finding the meaningful information in a sea of "noise," or redundant information, is invaluable. If someone had pieced together all the information from all the ice-warning telegrams, it would have indicated a giant ice field, around 80 miles wide, directly in front of the ship. Effectively, there was no macro view of the entire environment.

Any experienced mariner would recognize sea conditions that are indicative of ice fields. The sea is calmer, as the ice floes and pack ice dampen water movement. The seawater also takes on an oily appearance as it approaches freezing point. It was so cold that officers instructed the carpenter to prevent the fresh-water pipes from freezing.

Monitoring Visibility Affected by Cold at 22:00, April 14

The overall visible distance that objects could be seen from the ship was thought to be beyond the norm. This gave the crew a high level of confidence, possibly instilling overconfidence in being able to spot all hazards. However, although stars brightly illuminated the sky, and the sea was incredibly calm, there was a haze on the horizon created by the cold weather. This made it difficult to outline the horizon as it merged with the sky.

Titanic had some built-in visual monitoring through the crow's nest and the bridge. Beyond the two lookouts in the crow's nest, Officer Lightoller maintained a lookout himself from the bridge. *Titanic* carried six specialist lookouts, and the next shift change was due to start at 00:00. A question remains why no extra lookouts were on duty, considering all the warning signs. It was typical to post extra lookouts on the bow of the ship, to which a telephone link ran from the bridge. This is another example of the overconfidence of the officers.

In addition, the lookouts were missing binoculars, which was very unusual. It was customary to always have at least one pair in the crow's nest. The lookouts had repeatedly reported this problem, since the time the ship left Southampton. They were undoubtedly resentful of not having the binoculars, since these were their tools of the trade required to make them effective. (Explanations offered for the missing binoculars include that they were transferred to the officers on the bridge, or that someone stowed them away and was unable to locate them because of the immense size of the ship.)

No attempt was made to slow the ship down, despite all the aforementioned warnings. In hindsight, the captain and officers should have done more to clarify the scope of anomalies brought to their attention, investigate them more closely, and piece together all the intelligence. However, no one expected icebergs to be directly in the path of the ship so soon in the voyage, as icebergs did not usually drift down as far south as *Titanic*'s course. The officers must have perceived that anything would be seen well in time with such "excellent" visibility.

Detection in Your On-line Operation

In your on-line operation, specific steps and functions must be undertaken by first-level support (operations) in the first quadrant of the recovery clock. These include monitoring the environment and clarifying a problem that is detected.

Monitoring

In the early days of computer operations, each business unit paid for a single operator to sit in front of a screen, monitor the business unit's applications and services, and take actions on any problems detected. Operators worked as individuals, responsible for their own realm, and literal walls separated them.

Today's service-delivery environment is vastly more complicated. Applications and databases are interdependent and interrelated, and monitoring is completed in many ways by the various support levels. Sophisticated and automated monitoring tools further augment this, proactively monitoring for anomalies/inconsistencies and attracting the operator's attention at preset thresholds. Irrespective of how sophisticated the environment is, however, there are a number of important monitoring concepts to review:

- *Feedback mechanisms*—These provide information that can be used to measure how well a function is being delivered against a baseline, which is essential in tracking the service-delivery environment against SLAs. For example, feedback mechanisms highlight deviations from a set norm, and ensure that service levels' targets and objectives are on track.

- *Principles of good visibility*—In many service-delivery environments, operators have only a partial view because of the environment's complexity. It is difficult to visualize everything, see what is going on, and determine the impact of a problem and its effect.

- *Automated alerts*—This concept relates to providing an immediate warning to operators when something starts to go wrong and a problem is occurring. Alerts are usually integrated with a notification system that can dispatch first-level support. The objective is to act quickly and focus on determining the problem.

- *Collecting from the environment-monitoring information*—This information is classified as first and second line; the former is used for decisions regarding the existence of the problem, and the latter substantiates this decision and provides more detail.

- *Object state monitoring*—This monitors only the components that have been carefully identified as critical. Trying to monitor all environmental components is expensive and unnecessary. Each component has one of three states: *up*, *down*, or *pending*. These are represented through a "state diagram" or a hierarchy of importance. Tools for automatically monitoring components like network devices can adapt to the specific usage and traffic patterns of each service-delivery environment and assist in the data collection and analysis that helps in the prediction and prevention of failures.

One of the best sources of first-line information is an error message. However, hundreds or thousands of error messages are generated per hour. They have to be synthesized to a level where they carry a meaning and value, so that actions can be taken. It is essential to eliminate "noise" at the source; otherwise, important signals will be lost. This is a continuous process for operators who are aware of the ever-changing environment. Improving the signal-to-noise ratio is a key factor in improving the recovery clock.

Many service-delivery environments are swamped by poor and somewhat meaningless error messages, churned out relentlessly. For example, a component that is in an abnormal state will periodically send a message until it is corrected. Often, a single problem occurring in a service-delivery environment can create a domino effect on other components that react in a cascade, sending out even more messages related to the same problem. These duplicate messages further complicate the picture through noise pollution. An example of the impact is:

- A distributor (a software process that distributes error messages like a traffic cop) is overwhelmed by reading messages from the error-message log, and ends up consuming resources. This affects the host server and its ability to process other activities. (For more details, see the case study in appendix A.)

- A filter (a software process that filters out preset or preconfigured information) has little or no intelligence for handling incoming information, so it processes the messages on an equal priority and vital signals are lost. The solution involves embedding intelligence in the applications putting out messages, or invoking a "rules base" application for further support.

Clarification

Operators need to clarify the scope of anomalies brought to their attention by investigating the following questions:

- What is and is not an anomaly? In other words, what symptoms are exhibited?

- Where is it, geographically, related to the environment?

- When was it first noticed, and how does it occur (intermittently, solidly, cyclically)?

- What is the extent of it? Is it getting worse or more frequent?

- What is affected? The number of services, applications, systems, or users?

In certain situations, operators may request the originator or owner (if one exists) for a detailed description of the problem and supporting evidence. The problem is then moved into the determination quadrant, and a problem ticket is assigned and timestamped.

Problem Determination on Titanic

The second quadrant of the clock is associated with the speed with which a problem is determined and understood.

"Iceberg Right Ahead" at 23:40, April 14

At around 23:30, one of the lookouts, Fredrick Fleet, spotted a shape looming on the horizon. Because of the band of haze, however, he was not certain what it was. As the ship steamed ahead, the lookouts recognized it as a "black iceberg or growler." The sea was still and with no breakers to illuminate its base, the growler was practically invisible. The lookouts were trained to report but not to analyze. At around 23:40, they reacted by ringing the bell three times and calling to the bridge, "Iceberg right ahead."

The ship was heading in a westerly direction, traveling at 22 knots.[1] On the bridge, the sixth officer replied "Thank you" to Fleet, and repeated the warning to Officer Murdoch, who might have hesitated so that he could sight the iceberg before he ordered Hitchin, at the steering wheel, to turn "hard-a-starboard." He then ordered, "Stop. Full speed ahead,"[2] which effectively cut off the power to the propeller (Figure 6.7). *Titanic* had a very large

---

1. 27-30 miles per hour or half a mile per minute where 1 mile is 1600 meters or 5000 feet.

turning radius and could not turn quickly. The ship then steered "hard-a-port" in an attempt to dodge the iceberg and decelerate the ship through a port-around or "S turn." Murdoch threw the electric switch controlling all the watertight doors between all the bulkheads.

Collision with the Ice Shelf

The time to impact took 37 seconds. The lookouts braced themselves for a head-on collision, but instead of crashing to a halt, the ship slowed down with a grinding sound akin to running aground over an iceberg shelf.[3]

It was likely that the officers on the bridge were confident that a major disaster had been averted; the impact seemed minor. Murdoch's successful port-around (shown in Figure 6.7) meant the ship had decelerated enough to have a small impact, a tremble that barely rattled the breakfast cutlery in the first-class dining saloon. With all the electric bulkhead doors closed, any flooding would be contained within the ship's compartments.

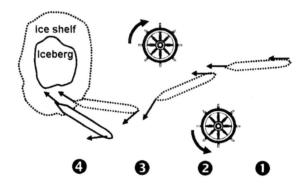

Figure 6.7: Murdoch's course of action was to port around the iceberg. At ❶, Murdoch throws the wheel hard to starboard, moving the ship left. At ❷, the bow slowly reacts and moves left, while the stern continues forward. At ❸, Murdoch throws the wheel hard to port, moving the wheel right. At ❹, the bow slowly reacts and moves right while the stern continues moving left, away from the iceberg. The bow runs aground on the underwater ice shelf and the ship grinds to a halt.

2. "Last log of *Titanic*" speculates the command was misrepresented at the inquiry and in fact was "ahead" not "astern." Murdoch knew putting the engines in reverse would cause a "emergency stop," throwing everything forward, and injuring and killing many people on board. In addition, a reversing propeller would chop up the water, affect the rudder, and give the ship limited control.
3. The iceberg was around 50 to 60 feet above the water, but with 80 percent of it below the water, it was massive. It probably weighed around 500,000 tons, well over 10 times the weight of *Titanic*.

Ignoring the Glance

Most of the passengers slept though the incident, and those awake ignored it as insignificant. They were confident in the safety of the ship. The real extent of the damage was unknown to the majority of passengers. Some ventured out onto the main deck, but saw no visible damage. In the boiler rooms, the water pumps slowed down the flooding.

Captain Smith, awakened by the collision, immediately came to the bridge to assess the situation. The most visible impact from the collision was a set of buckled plates and sprung seams to the starboard side of the ship's hull, above the double bottom but below the waterline in the first six primary compartments. Smith ordered "all hands on deck" and then reconnaissance and surveillance reports. Two groups surveyed the ship.

Problem Determination in Your On-line Operation

For your on-line operation, the second quadrant of the recovery clock is associated with the speed with which a problem is determined. This translates into understanding what the problem is and assessing its impact on day-to-day business operations and business users completing tasks. Once its scope is understood, it is categorized with a severity code (1, 2, or 3) based on its impact.

Similar to *Titanic's* assessment, the problem is then routed to the next level of support. Second-level support sets a priority for the problem (either high, medium, or low) based on other problems in the queue. High priority is allocated to the problems with the greatest impact on UOMs and SLAs. Second-level support might also request additional resources required for the determination and resolution quadrants. First-level support continues to interface with the business user and set expectations on priority, and likely time to determine, resolve, and possibly recover the problem. This includes notifying all business users affected.

Second-level support continues to assess the problem's cause and whether it is likely to reoccur. If time permits, second-level support also recreates the problem in a simulated test environment, and tests root-cause assumptions. When the root cause of the problem is determined, it is moved into the resolution quadrant and the problem ticket is timestamped.

Resolution on Titanic

The third quadrant of the problem cycle is associated with finding a resolution to the problem.

Assessment Reports

The first group, led by Officer Boxhall, returned quickly at 23:50 with an inaccurate report of no major damage. In fact, they had descended only a few decks—not low enough to make an accurate assessment. At this point, Bruce Ismay, awakened by the collision, joined the bridge. He thought the ship had dropped a propeller.

Rash Actions Sink the Ship

At this point, the pumps were able to keep up with the flooding. The collision seemed relatively minor; nobody had been killed or even injured. The damage seemed slight and controllable. All the evidence indicated the ship had ground to a halt on the ice shelf as shown in Figure 6.8, and the double-hull had done what it was supposed to do: protect the ship.

There were several options available for recovery. The first was to remain static and put out a distress call for a rescue ship. The second was to restart the engines and limp back to Halifax. However, the former would have a major impact from a credibility standpoint, as a distress call from *Titanic* would not go unmissed by the world's media. Before the architect came back, it is likely that the director took the decision to sail off.

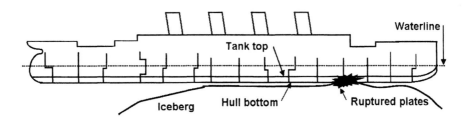

Figure 6.8: Titanic grinds to a stop on the iceberg shelf, which had ruptured the hull bottom and tank top. The flooding was contained by the water pumps.

Resolution in Your On-line Operation

For your on-line operation, the third quadrant of the recovery clock is associated with finding a resolution to the problem. This means determining a roadmap of actions for putting the service-delivery environment back into a normal state. At this point, the root cause of the problem is known, and a plan for preventative measures is drawn up to prevent the problem from reoccurring. Second-level support might notify third-level support to clarify root causes and help determine potential fixes.

Temporary Patch or Permanent Fix?

In keeping with the philosophy of speed of recovery, there are few options for a fix. Either a temporary patch or a permanent fix could be implemented, based on the impact of the problem. The former is applied if a very quick fix is required, the problem is known, or it needs to be contained. The latter is planned for a new release of the software or application.

This approach is very common, as there should be no further disruption until the next planned downtime window.

Link Back to Change-Management Process

At this point, the fix needs to be tested in a test environment under simulated conditions. This should be done in accordance with the change-management process discussed in chapter 4, which is interlinked to problem management. If this is successful, the problem is moved into the recovery quadrant and the problem ticket is timestamped. Otherwise, the problem is returned to the determination quadrant.

Recovery on Titanic

The fourth quadrant of the recovery clock involves recovering from the problem. On *Titanic*, the crew was ordered by the captain and director to restart the engines and float off slowly, with the hope of limping back to Halifax. This also happened to be in the direction of *California*. Telegrams were sent to the White Star offices in New York outlining the plan and course of actions.

Recovery in Your On-line Operation

For your on-line operation, the fourth quadrant is associated with recovering from the problem. Typically, this means implementing the roadmap of actions for putting the service-delivery environment back into a normal state. If the problem cannot be fixed and service restored to a normal condition, then alternatives need to be determined. This might mean implementing a disaster-recovery plan.

Temporary Patch or Permanent Fix?

Based on the impact of the problem and the priority of recovery, either a temporary patch or permanent fix is implemented. The problem is passed to operations and into the change-management process, as discussed in chapter 4. If a permanent fix is applied, the problem ticket is closed. Otherwise, for a temporary patch, the problem ticket changes status and remains open until a permanent fix is found.

Reducing Startup Time

Another aspect of problem recovery is that the service-delivery environment might need to shut down so that the fixes can be applied. In these situations, the actual startup time of the service-delivery environment needs to be minimized, in accordance with the recovery clock and to minimize UOMs. This requires reviewing each system and determining how dependencies in and between them can be removed, so as much as possible can be started in parallel. Likewise, in multiprocessor servers, processes are started in parallel. Typically, startup time can then be increased by factors of 60 percent.

Proactively Maintain the Delivery

Service-delivery environments can be extremely complex and susceptible to failure when they incur problems. To further eliminate and reduce potential problems and their impact, you need to examine a step before the first quadrant: problem avoidance, or preventative action. The recovery clock is essentially a reactive process, but it is possible to evolve it based on recognizing that problem avoidance, a proactive process, is really the first step.

Preventative Actions on Titanic

Some preventative actions were taken prior and during the voyage. The winter of 1912 had been exceptionally mild, and many icebergs had broken loose. White Star had known this, so as a precaution, the ship was rerouted a further 10 miles south. In addition, during the voyage, Captain Smith delayed the mid-Atlantic turn by 30 minutes, to take a more southerly course. However, this did not prevent the ship from proceeding full steam ahead through the ice field. The ship's captain and officers were fully aware of the iceberg dangers ahead.

The temperature of water is a very accurate guide to the proximity of ice in the water. Normally, when entering ice fields, tests were taken by drawing seawater from over the side of the ship through a canvas bucket, and then placing a thermometer in the bucket. Repeated every two hours, these tests were probably the most accurate indicator of the proximity of large ice floes.

The temperature of the water at the time of the collision was 31 degrees Fahrenheit, or just below 0 Centigrade. However, one of the passengers noticed a sailor filling the ice bucket with tap water because the rope was not long enough to reach the sea. This is a good example of a feedback mechanism gone drastically wrong. Rather than reporting the problem with the rope, the mariner deliberately falsified data to cover up the problem with the equipment.

Preventative Actions in Your On-line Operation

The recovery clock can be further enhanced by the introduction of an *EWS* (Early Warning System), which provides an alerting mechanism to a problem likely to happen. The earlier the warning, the more valuable the time to take actions to prevent or limit the extent of the failure, as shown in Figure 6.9. This is an extremely important mechanism for problem avoidance. The prediction of systems behavior is based on good historical feedback data. Hence, collecting statistics on this information can help build up accurate profiles of how the system is behaving over time. This information is analogous to a heartbeat, and this feedback is best illustrated through graphs. Over time, the predictive accuracy of the statistical models improves.

As part of the EWS, error-message information needs to be continuously collected and aggregated, preferably through a statistical package. This allows for comparative views using hourly, daily, weekly, monthly, and yearly baselines. This also needs to be done for the more granular performance information, which requires more aggregation and effort.

Operations alerted by an EWS need to see quickly into any part of the environment, at any time, and from any location. The reaction time to a deteriorating situation such as an emerging problem is very small, measured in seconds or minutes. Good visibility to individual environmental components through a monitoring facility is vitally important.

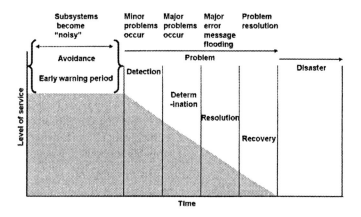

Figure 6.9: The first period in the graph is an early warning period. This is an extremely important mechanism for problem avoidance.

The final capability is command and control, the ability to take corrective actions based on the information provided through a monitoring facility and thus avoid a major outage. This is done in a proactive mode prior to the problem occurring.

Conclusion

The following sections summarize the major points of this chapter and how they relate to your business today. For more information on these concepts, search the Internet for these keywords and phrases: *availability, problem management, problem recovery clock, automated operations, centralized operations, dark-site operations, monitoring operations, operational metrics, risk management, PMBOK (Project Management Book of Knowledge),* and *autonomic computing.*

Major Points, Considerations, and Titanic *Lessons*

- Operators overloaded by commercial traffic (noise) did not pass the ice warnings (signal) along in a timely fashion.

- The officers, through arrogance, kept the binoculars and did not share them with the lookouts, limiting the ability of operations to provide any early warning.

- *Titanic* had a number of built-in feedback mechanisms that were discounted, fudged, or just ignored.

- Ice-warning information that was eventually communicated through the hierarchy to Captain Smith wasn't adequately acted on.

- The captain was an old mariner and very resistant to technology. He relied on "gut" feel and experience. Marconigrams were a new technology, and hence he potentially undermined the significance of this information.

- The captain succumbed to the director's pressure to sail at full speed through the danger area.

- The most significant lesson is that business pressure on *Titanic* overrode the mandate of operations services. Stringent guidelines were in place, but they were broken, putting the whole operation in jeopardy.

Best Practices for Your Organization

- Assign the operations services group sole responsibility for service-delivery environment support to cut across organizational technology "silos."

- Structure the support organization using a holistic customer view of the service-delivery environment (top-down), rather than using principal technology silos (bottom-up).

- Ensure the business and operations services develop SLAs, and that these are adhered to.

- The basis for continuous availability is through a comprehensive approach to organization, processes, and tools, as defined by the fishbone model in chapter 4 and a carefully laid-out operations plan.

- Build a problem-management process based on the speed of recovery of the four quadrants of the recovery clock.

- Create a problem-management system for logging, tracking, and routing problems.

- Base proactive problem-avoidance around an early warning system that uses a feedback mechanism.

- Create a four-tier organizational support structure for problem management.

- Synthesize and correctly route information from feedback mechanisms to decision-makers in a timely fashion.

- Centralize operation services as an alternative way of lowering operations costs.

- Create a dedicated and centralized help desk that fronts all customer and user calls.

- Create a flight clock as the first step in automating a service-delivery environment. This outlines the manual operations required in a 24-hour period.

- Monitor each solution and business processes from an end-to-end view.

- Monitor the service-delivery environment outside of the firewall, into the Demilitarized Zone (DMZ), an area still within corporate control.

- Monitor strategic components critical to environment availability.

- Use Web management tools to accommodate the architectural differences to a traditional service-delivery environment.

- Configure the service-delivery environment for fast startups to reduce startup times

- Be cautious in claiming that a project is a success too soon after going live.

- Problems might not occur right after implementation, so monitoring broadly across the whole environment is critical after an implementation.

- Any environmental anomalies that occur should be investigated quickly using a cause-and-effect approach, since any delays might worsen the situation.

Refer to the case study in appendix A for more on a situation to avoid. Most of the points below are better visualized through the case study.

Questions You Can Ask Today

At this stage in the project, you should expect from IT an assessment of what is in place to protect the environment:

- A risk assessment of the overall problem-management methodology. (Refer to appendix C for more details.)

- An organizational risk assessment of the overall organization.

- A technical risk assessment of the operational tools.

- A risk assessment of the automated processes, the track record of the automated operator, and the expected results of switching the automated operator off.

- A summary of the results from implementation into the service-delivery environment.

- Recommendations from the operations services group about whether to remain live or not.

- A selection of feedback metrics as to how well the business service is responding. These need to be meaningful and representative to the business.

When the Unthinkable Happens

You have to plan for the unthinkable and create a business continuity plan for your online operation. With this you will be able to recover your online operation in times of disaster.

Dave Kulakowski,
Development and Technology Manager,
Honeywell Aircraft Landing Systems

Chapter Objectives

When you are done with this chapter, you will be able to create a business continuity plan for your on-line operation. With this, you will be able to recover your on-line operation in times of disaster.

In this chapter you will learn how organizations process their equipment and personnel through the disaster encounter and the subsequent recovery process. This chapter takes a "why-what-how" approach and examines why disaster recovery is critical, what disaster recovery entails, and how to determine whether you are in a disaster.

What Steps Do I Need to Follow?

There are four steps in the disaster recovery process:

1. Assess the damage.

2. Declare the disaster.

3. Enact the recovery.

4. Move beyond the recovery.

Why Is Disaster Recovery Critical?

The question, "Why disaster recovery?" might seem obvious. However, the majority of organizations who have discussed disaster recovery have not put disaster-recovery plans in place or prepared adequately.

What Is Disaster Recovery?

Disaster recovery is the concept of switching the on-line operation to an alternate service-delivery environment. However, it takes many shapes and forms, from the relatively simple recovery of data and files from a single application in a timeframe measured in days, to the relatively complex recovery of a complete business operation in a timeframe measured in minutes or hours.

How Do I Determine that I Am in a Disaster?

You are in a disaster when a problem does not respond to normal problem-recovery processes, as shown in Figure 7.1. A disaster can take three forms:

- Total (absolute and immediate)

- Rapid and imminent

- Slow and innocuous

When a disaster is recognized, contingency plans are invoked and a disaster is declared.

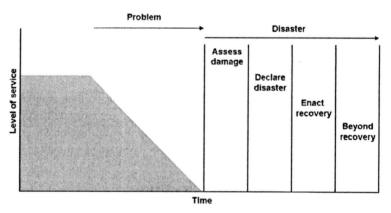

Figure 7.1: With time, a problem turns into a disaster, requiring the subsequent disaster-recovery steps.

Assess the Damage

Let's start by looking at *Titanic*'s situation at midnight on Monday, April 15.

Titanic's *Situation Worsens*

After the initial collision, the captain had ordered damage assessment reports, and two groups had gone out to investigate. The second group, led by the ship's architect and carpenter, returned with a much more detailed and accurate report than the first group. They reported major flooding in five compartments and recognized this was something that *Titanic* was not designed for. The grinding along the bottom had badly ruptured the outer skin, so flooding of the double hull had occurred. The different rates of flooding in six primary compartments indicated the top hull or tank top was also damaged. The damage was unexpected. It was beyond the expectations of the designer that something in nature could inflict so much damage.

A conference took place between the director, the captain, and the architect. The architect realized the extent of the damage right away and the seriousness of the director's and captain's actions in restarting the ship and sailing it forward. This action had forced the water up into the compartments, dramatically increasing the rate of flooding.

The architect realized the situation onboard *Titanic* had gone beyond recovery. He stated that the ship had 2.5 to 3 hours before completely sinking, and accurately determined that the problem could not be fixed. Too many compartments were ruptured and were rapidly flooding beyond the capacity of the pumps. The bulkhead walls, separating the compartments, had not been carried up to watertight horizontal traverses. Therefore, as the ship's nose went down, water spilled from one compartment to another rather like an ice cube tray filling with water.

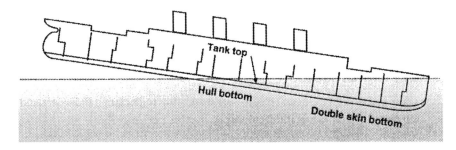

Figure 7.2: All the ship's safety functions failed, except the lifeboats, as water spilled over the bulkheads from compartment to compartment. This was a major compromise in the bulkheads as a safety feature.

Your On-line Operation

You need to recognize when a prolonged outage has gone beyond the four quadrants of the problem-recovery cycle discussed in chapter 6. Then, you need to assess the damage. This is not always obvious, as in *Titanic*'s situation, where both the director and captain ignored that they were verging on a disaster. The Outage Classification table, Table 7.1, lists the outage classes that are a potential for disaster. However, the probability varies by class. For example, an environmental outage involving the destruction of facilities is more likely to turn into a disaster. (Refer to appendix B for more details.)

Table 7.1: Outage Classes

Class	Classification of Outage
Physical	This includes physical faults or failures of the technology in the environment.
Design	These errors include system or application-software design failures and bugs.
Operations	These errors are caused by operations services staff because of accidents, inexperience, lack of due diligence, lack of training, not following procedures, or even malice.
Environmental	This covers a wide range of failures, from those in power supplies, cooling systems, and network connections, through natural disasters and terrorist activities.
Reconfiguration	Known as "planned downtime," this includes downtime required for scheduled maintenance, software upgrades, or migrations to new technologies, as well as configuration changes like adding or databases, or adding clients.

Your investments should be made in proportion to the likelihood of these disasters. Though needs to be given to the types of environmental outages and natural disasters that could possibly happen where your on-line operation center is located. The scale of disaster is important to consider as well. For example, if a relatively minor storm, fire, or flood knocks out your on-line operation, your customers are going to expect some contingency of service relatively quickly. In today's world, you need contingency for all of these, even the most catastrophic disasters.

Declare the Disaster

There is a need for extensive and clear leadership to declare the disaster and communicate the plan for recovery at different stages.

Communication on Titanic

With no resolution to the problem of major flooding, no problem recovery could take place. Only the captain and a few officers knew the extent of the damage and were resigned to the ship sinking. Their next step should have been to invoke a disaster-recovery plan and communicate it to all onboard. However, no formalized disaster-recovery plan was in place. No "abandon ship" command or formal declaration of a disaster was given. The captain just gave orders to the officers to uncover the lifeboats and get the passengers and crew ready on deck.

Titanic's captain knew the seriousness of the situation relatively quickly from the collision, but did not communicate this through the ranks of crew and passengers on board. This increased the confusion, particularly in the lower ranks of the crew. For example, the engine room sent some engineers to the boat deck, and the bridge sent them back down to the engine room.

There are number of possible explanations for the poor communication:

- The ship had very limited communication, with no alarm or public-address systems. Important information was communicated to passengers by word of mouth, the crew knocking on each cabin door and common room. Considering there were hundreds of cabins, it could take up to an hour for the crew to alert all passengers.

- A question remains as to what the crew was alerting passengers to, since the crew didn't have accurate information on the situation. It is likely that varying degrees of information were passed. The experienced captain believed in the safety systems of the ship and might have found the architect's verdict very hard to accept because everything appeared so normal in the first hour. The captain acted almost as if the situation was "business as usual."

- The captain realized that the carrying capacity of the lifeboats was inadequate, with only enough room for about half of the estimated 2,223 people on board. Perhaps better to keep things calm, and allow the lifeboats to be filled in an orderly manner when the timing was right. The ship's hierarchical structure and segregation of classes meant that first-class passengers had the best access to the boats.

- The captain feared widespread panic. He and the other officers were aware of the French liner *La Bourgogne*, which sank 14 years earlier. With room in the lifeboats for only half the people onboard that ship, widespread panic had broken out. The captain knew he could save the maximum number of lives by loading only those who were lucky enough to reach the boats. So, he avoided informing all the passengers, specifically in third class, of the situation.

Communication in Your Organization

Unlike *Titanic*, if you need to declare a disaster, invoke a well thought-out communication plan that clearly communicates with different audiences. This is probably as important as your recovery plan, for several reasons:

- Communicating internally with your employees can greatly help control the impact of the disaster. Also, the speed of communication is essential. For example, get information to customer-facing employees first, so that they can inform customers.

- Communicating externally with your customers is essential. The plan for customer communication needs to cater to customer segments using different channels, depending on the scope of the problem or disaster. A customer-retention strategy might need to be offered.

- You might also need to consider communicating with the press, depending on how serious the loss of service has been. For this, you need to identify key messages, how these are communicated, and through what channels. Many companies have been caught off guard when roving reporters trap unaware employees with questions.

Enact the Recovery

At this point, it is clear that *Titanic*'s captain and officers did not have a plan to follow. The best they could do was to bring some order to prevent widespread panic and chaos. The envisioned scenario for disaster recovery, at the time of the design, was to transfer passengers through lifeboats to another ship and then deliver them to port. The lifeboats would ferry passengers back and forth to the rescue ship, requiring a much smaller total lifeboat capacity. This scenario was based on the perception the ship could not possibly sink, but would float in an incapacitated state waiting for help.

Under maritime convention, there should have been a plan that brought everyone onboard to the lifeboat deck, loaded them into the lifeboats with places to spare, lowered the lifeboats safely, and put them adrift with experienced crews to handle them.

Without a Plan, What Do We Do?

Keeping in step with *Titanic*, the earlier chapters of the book have deliberately not included a plan for disaster recovery, to highlight the impact of not having a plan. If you had followed *Titanic*'s course of actions to this point, you would be in a sorry state indeed. You would have been giving lip service to availability and now would have a full-scale disaster on your hands. Your employees would be looking to you for the answers. As your team was running around trying to figure out what to do next, your help desk would be overwhelmed with customer calls.

Titanic's *Failure to Enact Recovery*

Let's go back to *Titanic* and see what happens when you don't have a plan.

Begin Recovery

Only 40 minutes into the disaster, six compartments were flooded, and only a handful of the crew knew the full extent of the situation. Information was still not well communicated to the majority of crew or passengers.

Onboard *Titanic*, the bridge was the command post. It had remained intact, sustaining no damage. As a result, all major decisions and actions, such as directing appeals for help through wireless distress call, slowing down the flooding by shutting watertight doors, and preparing the rockets for firing, continued to be directed from this location.

Lowering the Lifeboats

About 65 minutes into the disaster, the captain gave the order to start filling and lowering the lifeboats. There was a major delay in getting the lifeboats down, indicating a hesitation to launch the boats until as late as possible. It is likely the officers reacted slowly for several reasons: the ship was believed to be unsinkable, the gravity of the situation was not apparent, and everything appeared so normal at the time.

Very few signs of the disaster were visible to most of the passengers. The lifeboats were filled on a first-come, first-serve basis from the top decks, and these were mainly first- and second-class passengers. As a result, although each lifeboat had a capacity of 65 people, only 28 very reluctant people were lowered in the first one. At this point, the first of eight distress rockets was fired.

Lowering a lifeboat was hazardous, as it had to make a 60-foot drop. If the lifeboats were overloaded, they would buckle in the middle under the weight. As the ship listed to port, the distance from the edge of the ship to the lifeboat increased, making the jump into the boat very hazardous, as shown in Figure 7.3. On the starboard side, the lifeboat bounced along the side of the ship dangerously. The first three lifeboats left with 27, 41, and 28 passengers, and only the tenth lifeboat launched was full, 80 minutes after the collision.

Human Responses to Events

The extent of the damage was not visible at first. The sea was calm, and a slight list of five degrees was not unusual during the crossing. Onboard, the perception existed that the ship could withstand collisions with a dozen icebergs and still remain afloat. Many passengers arrived on deck, but wandered back to their warm cabins. It took a great deal of persuasion to get the women passengers into the cold lifeboats, leaving their husbands and the warmth of the ship.

Warning Signs Increase

One hour into the disaster, the warning signs were much more obvious.

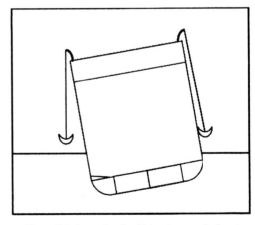

Figure 7.3: Lowering the lifeboats was challenging as the ship started to list to port, with the uneven flooding of the cells in the double hull.

Third-class passengers and stokers who had managed to get up from the decks below had seen the seawater rising up the floors first-hand. They were quite ready to fill the lifeboats. Panic did not break out on *Titanic*, however; passengers for the most part filed into lifeboats in an orderly fashion. A number of crew (325) and officers (50) remained at their posts, working in holds, boiler rooms, and throughout the ship, ensuring electricity was available for as long as possible. They consequently died.

Last Desperate Acts

The temperature of the air was freezing. The sea temperature was actually below the freezing point, and survival time in these temperatures was 20 to 30 minutes. Everything that could possibly float was thrown overboard, in the hope of use as a floating raft. The ship finally sank at 02:20. So much time was lost early on that the last two Englehardts (lifeboats much smaller than canvas lifeboats) were not launched properly and used as floating rafts. A few of the lifeboats, which rowed away from the sinking ship, returned to the site before *Carpathia* arrived at 03:30, from the position shown in Figure 7.4. The lifeboats searched for survivors in the icy water, and amazingly, some were found.

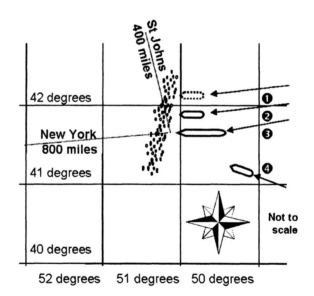

Figure 7.4: Titanic's disaster and rescue scene outlines the position of the disaster and the overall directions from which ships came to the rescue: ❶ California's position as given at the testimony; ❷ California's likely position; ❸ Titanic's foundering position; ❹ Carpathia's first position, 58 miles away.

How to Fail as Titanic *Did*

Let's see what happens when you don't have a plan for your on-line operation, and what you need to consider as a next step.

Begin Recovery

A major outage in a service-delivery environment can start so innocuously that, in the first hour, your organization might not even be aware of it or its implications. For example, only a less-critical part of the environment might be down, so it goes unnoticed. However, outages tend to have a "knock on" effect because of interdependencies between applications, and very quickly, other parts of the environment can become affected. This leads to a disaster in a very short time.

What Is the Cost of Disaster Recovery?

The associated costs of disaster recovery vary, based on the window of recovery (time), the elements of the disaster, and the degree of recovery required. As part of your plan, you need to carefully determine these.

What Is the Maximum Disaster-Recovery Window Acceptable?

The disaster-recovery time or *recovery window* drives the cost, as business revenue lost is usually directly proportional to the time. Your team should assess the downtime cost on an application-by-application basis, and determine the point where the business could slip into bankruptcy. The recovery window is the major variable in disaster planning, and should be based on the maximum window the business can possibly afford. As part of your plan, you need to carefully determine this window.

What Elements from the Environment Need to Be Recovered?

Distributed systems and client-server based environments have further complicated the disaster recovery picture, where organizations have to look beyond the mainframe operation to the broader desktop environment. For example, a relatively unimportant server in the marketing area might actually be very strategic to the business. As part of your plan, you need to carefully determine these strategic elements.

What Degree of Disaster Recovery Is Required?

Until the early 1990s, disaster recovery focused on an organization's data center, and recovering all of the center's applications or systems, regardless of their individual value to the organization. Today, most businesses have their operations on-line, and realize that it makes no sense just to recover these, without recovering the business processes that use them. For a business to continue, employees must have a place to work, with the necessary equipment. This *business continuity* is an essential part of your plan.

Beyond the Recovery

There is a final step that should be considered when everything else fails, and recovery is impossible. The bottom line is you might have lost the ship, but you can still save the shipping line.

How Titanic *Could Have Enacted a Recovery Plan*

Let's go back to *Titanic* and speculate what could have happened if a disaster-recovery plan was created that had carefully thought out the possible scenarios. What is important in this exercise is the shift in thinking and the overall process undertaken:

- The first assumption of the White Star planning process would have been the acceptance that safety systems could fail, and therefore the ship was fallible. This massive shift in thinking would build the plan around evacuating passengers and crew off the ship. This would require enough lifeboat seats for all.

- The second assumption would have centered on how quickly the ship could sink, and therefore the window of evacuation. This would hone the efficiency of the evacuation enacted by the crew within the window. It would require effective lifeboat-launching equipment and a crew trained in its use.

- The third assumption would have considered how quickly a rescue ship could pick up the evacuated passengers and crew from the lifeboats. This would require processes to ensure distress calls were put out quickly. Also, the lifeboats would have to be seaworthy enough to withstand the Atlantic and carry supplies to ensure survival.

How You Should Enact Your Recovery Plan

Clearly, today's businesses cannot afford environmental failures of the scale of *Titanic*. To ensure their continued survival, they must develop business-continuity or contingency plans that reduce the risk of environment downtime and the potentially catastrophic loss of services and data. Business-continuity planning determines how a company will keep functioning until its normal facilities are restored after a disaster.

Business continuity is a holistic approach to disaster recovery that goes beyond just the technology, to recover the whole business operation. For example, replicating the business operation includes the supporting infrastructure of organization, staff, all the processes and procedures, hardcopy records and documentation, and physical facilities. This encompasses how employees will be contacted, where they will go, and how they will keep doing their jobs.

An effective business-continuity plan outlines a disaster-recovery method, including the procedures a company should follow for restoring business services and critical business functions. This is difficult because of the nuances and anomalies found in business operations. The plan should define responsibilities and give guidance to those who will be executing it.

The Business-Continuity Planning Process

Usually, the business side leads the business-continuity planning process, in which disaster planners work with individual business functions, groups, and employees to identify critical business processes and supporting applications. These are developed into separate contingency plans for each business function. This increases ownership dramatically. The requirements for normal processing are usually simple to identify, but this is not the case with exception processing. Around 80 percent of the work is in ensuring standard business procedures are followed through the switchover. Many organizations might not have all their procedures documented in a run book, listing all daily activities, tasks, and information flow. This requires additional time.

A corporate team oversees that duplication of effort is minimized between business functions, and that resources are evenly allocated. The planning process starts with the following:

- Selecting the business function and services that are most critical to survival.

- Reviewing the potential types of disasters that are most likely to affect the environment.

- Determining recovery windows for each business function and service.

- Identifying the risks associated with the recovery of each business function and service.

- Analyzing the cost-benefit ratio of each recovery method supporting the window.

- Coordinating and testing the plan to uncover obstacles hampering the effort.

A business-continuity plan should answer questions like these, for an emergency:

- How would employees be located, communicated with, and then transferred to alternate worksites?

- How would employees' assignments change?

- Where would customers go for services?

- What power, heat, telecommunications, and transportation services would be needed?

- What about electronic and physical security?

- How would emergency purchasing be handled?

The benefits of business continuity include the following:

- Business-process criticality is ranked, so resources are used effectively.

- The recovery of noncritical applications and services does not interfere and consume valuable recovery time.

- Critical applications and services can be recovered in parallel.

- Applications and services that run on different systems can be recovered on the same system.

- Recovery methods are more focused, since end-users create their own plans and therefore have some responsibility and ownership.

The Business-Continuity Plan

In developing a business-continuity plan, each of the recovery steps breaks down into a fairly sizeable list of activities, tasks, and considerations. There are a variety of disaster-recovery methods from which to choose, including *cold sites*, *hot sites*, and *on-line ready sites*. A special section at the end of this chapter, "Disaster Recovery: It's How You Look at It," is devoted to these details. Typically, the window of recovery helps determine which method best meets business needs.

The process of business continuity is highly dependent on the flow of information, specifically communicating the plan to the organization. Then, each business function or group is responsible for communicating its part of the plan with team members. This did not happen on *Titanic*.

Finally, the plan should be updated as changes are made in the organization and the service-delivery environment. The change-management process should manage the plan.

Practice Going through the Plan

It is critical to put the plan into operation, and regularly practice switching operations to a disaster-recovery site. It's like practicing for fire alarms. Going through the steps shown in Figure 7.5 irons out any problems:

- The damage-assessment team determines the extent of the damage and the type of recovery required.

- A command post acts as a focal point. It locates employees and coordinates various groups.

- The recovery team and support staff (IT and business operations) are put into an alternate site.

- The recovery team leads the effort to rebuild the support infrastructure.

- The service-delivery environment is duplicated with replicate technology at the alternate site.

- The data is recovered to a point in time as close to the disaster as possible.

- The applications providing the business services are reinitiated.

- The alternate business services are delivered.

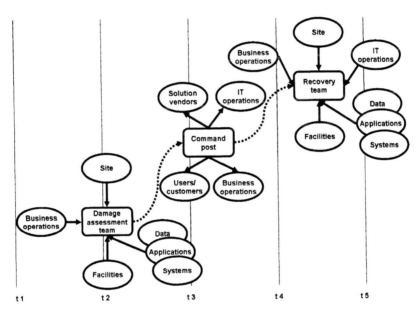

Figure 7.5: The disaster recovery starts with damage assessment, continues with setting up a command post, and completes with the recovery.

Disaster Recovery: It's How You Look at It

The following sections look at different aspects of disaster recovery in detail, so that you can competently navigate the planning process with your technical workers and vendors.

Do you think that disaster recovery is a simple term that is not open to interpretation? Think again. There are many approaches to disaster recovery, each of which is appropriate for certain business environments. Choosing the right one requires analyzing the cost of downtime to the business and weighing that against the cost and capabilities of each method.

Disaster recovery in today's service-delivery environments is usually a complex operation. However, with certain advances in concepts such as distributed computing and the replication of data, the operation has been much simplified since the days of the large mainframe.

For critical on-line applications, the window of recovery is likely to be measured in minutes and hours, rather than days and weeks. Studies for business-critical on-line applications have determined that the average recovery window is less than an hour. Of disaster-recovery methods given in Figure 7.6, only the on-line ready site is capable of supporting a recovery window of that size.

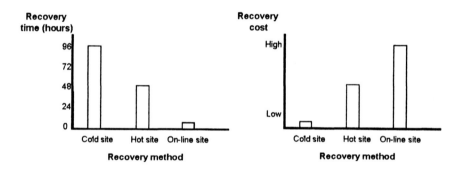

Figure 7.6: The cost of recovering a site is proportional to the disaster-recovery method and the recovery time.

Cold Sites

Typically, a cold site provides a computer-ready room reserved for a company's service-delivery environment, as well as space for business operations. It usually contains power distribution systems, telecommunications wiring, a raised floor, and a temperature control system. Equipment can be brought in by the organization, or more commonly, through a disaster-recovery service provider.

A mobile cold site consists of a computer-ready trailer that can be set up in a company's parking lot. This approach minimizes travel for operations employees, who might be personally affected by the disaster. It also allows a decentralized organization to engage one disaster-recovery vendor for all of its operations.

The cold site's design should minimize the effort required to deliver and assemble the environment at the site. Ideally, arrangements for quick delivery should be made with a service provider, so that operations can be restored before losses become unacceptable. Some service providers offer short delivery lead-times for an additional fee through environment-access guarantees. Creating an alternate business operation at a cold site can take anywhere from 2 to 10 days. This is by far the least expensive recovery method.

Hot Sites

Typically, a hot site is a preconfigured alternate data center that, unlike a cold site, is fully equipped, powered up, and maintained by an operational staff. Mobile hot sites, consisting of trailers with fully configured systems, are also available, offering the same advantages as mobile cold sites, along with the convenience of an already-installed system.

Switching business operations from a disaster site to a hot site involves retrieving database tapes from archival storage, transporting the tapes and the organization's own operations staff to the site, restoring the data to disk, and restarting the applications. Moving business operations to a hot site can take from one to two days. The hot site's recovery window is typically measured in days, rather than hours.

Inherent Risk of Hot and Cold Sites

Vendors of hot-site and cold-site services, to be viable financially, typically overbook their facilities, signing up more subscribers than they could support at one time. This approach is normally acceptable because only a few customers are likely to need support at any given time. However, in the case of a widespread disaster, such as a hurricane, earthquake, or flood, the vendor can support only a limited number of its subscribers, usually on a "first-come, first-served" basis.

All hot-site and cold-site vendors make this risk of contention clear to prospective subscribers. For organizations that consider the risk unacceptable, private hot-site data centers or on-line ready sites are more appropriate disaster-recovery solutions.

On-line Ready Sites

An on-line ready site is an environment in which a complete, continuously updated copy of the database from an organization's primary environment is maintained on duplicate disks located elsewhere. The duplicates can either be remote standalone disks that are connected to the primary environment, or they can be part of another complete environment. An on-line ready site can be located near the primary site, for convenience, or across the country, to minimize the effects of wide-area or regional disasters.

Because the backup database is always updated immediately, an on-line ready site limits data loss from an environmental disaster to as little as one second. This is different from the other methods, where recovery of data is usually time-consuming. Also, an on-line ready site maintains the confidentiality of the organization's information, as this information does not need to be entrusted to a third-party service provider. The three types of on-line ready sites are shown in Figure 7.7

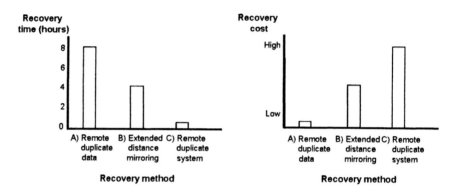

Figure 7.7: The disaster-recovery time is very different for the three on-line ready recovery methods.

On-line Ready Site with Remote Duplicate Data

In an on-line ready site with remote duplicate data, an organization maintains duplicate data disks at some distance from the primary service-delivery environment, but connected directly to it, to prevent data loss in the event of a site-based disaster. If necessary, the backup disks can quickly be connected to a different system to support continued business services with almost no loss of data.

On-line Ready Site with Extended-distance Mirroring

This is similar to the previous concept, except the extended-distance mirroring (*EDM*) feature allows the mirrored disks to be located several kilometers apart, connected by fiber-optic cable, as shown in Figure 7.8. Typically, EDM is not part of another system. EDM can be a valuable disaster-recovery tool when a primary system and disk are disabled by a disaster affecting a single building, such as a fire or burst water pipes, or a power failure affecting one or two city blocks.

If the remote mirrored disk is located near another complete system, such as the organization's development system, the disk can be connected to the nearby system immediately, and the application can resume processing. If no nearby system is available, a system-access guarantee can be agreed on with development, and access quickly provided.

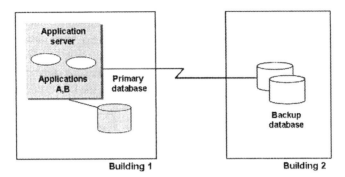

Figure 7.8: Extended-distance mirroring (EDM) maintains a current duplicate database on mirrored disks located several kilometers from the primary site.

On-line Ready Site with Remote Duplicate System

An on-line ready site with a remote duplicate system is a fully operational environment, complete with systems, applications, telecommunications facilities, and staff, and a continuously updated copy of the database on a remote network node. It can be located at any distance from the primary node, and can provide full environment-recovery within minutes.

The main advantage of a remote duplicate database facility (*RDF*) is the recovery-window capability that can be met because there is no bulk data movement, as found with a hot backup. It allows organizations to implement the extremely rapid disaster-recovery necessary for critical on-line applications. Another advantage of this type of on-line ready site is that an organization can use the duplicate environment for other normal operations, as a read-only resource. For example, it can be used to look up current data for inquiry purposes or decision support, to process heavy batch-reporting loads, or to consolidate data from multiple sites to a central site.

The backup site for the secondary environment can be located at any distance from the primary site. Automated telecommunications-link software ensures RDF remains active and automatically restarts sending data when a connection is reestablished. RDF can support on-line ready sites in three ways:

- A backup environment can support a primary environment, as described above.

- Two primary application databases using RDF can support each other in a reciprocal arrangement, as shown in Figure 7.9.

- A single secondary environment can back up multiple primary sites. This is an economical approach for large enterprises with distributed data processing centers.

In addition to supporting an on-line ready site for unplanned outages, RDF can support planned environment switchovers, to eliminate environment downtime during hardware and software updates. RDF software sends audit-trail information through transaction-monitoring software to a secondary environment, where the database is dynamically updated to reflect all changes made to the primary database. RDF offers the highest degree of disaster protection.

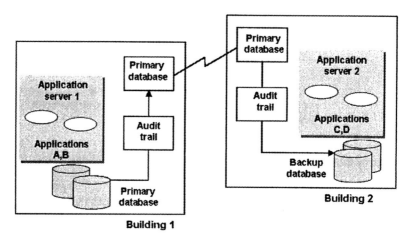

Figure 7.9: The remote duplicate database facility (RDF) maintains a current duplicate database in another environment. The facilities can act in a reciprocal arrangement.

Best Practices

The many organizations around the world that use remote duplication with two separate data centers (one primary, one backup) can switch applications over to the backup environment in less than 30 minutes, using internal staff.

Financial institutions that use remote duplication have been able to switch critical electronic-funds transfer (EFT) applications in a short time and finish all EFT processing in one day, without asking for any extensions and with no loss of interest to the bank.

In the automobile industry, which supports three shifts per day on factory production lines, the recovery window is excruciatingly expensive. For example, with tight schedules related to two-day turnaround on custom orders, manufacturers simply cannot afford any type of downtime. So, these manufacturers use RDF on backup environments, for planned reconfiguration maintenance, as well as for disaster recovery. Manufacturers can switch from production to backup environments in less than 10 minutes.

Conclusion

The following sections summarize the major points of this chapter and how they relate to your business today. For more information on these concepts, search the Internet for these keywords and phrases: *disaster recovery, cold and hot sites, RDF, business continuity*, and *contingency plans.*

Major Points, Considerations, and Titanic Lessons

- Much precious time was lost in the first hour after the collision. The disaster assessment took 20 minutes, and it took another 45 minutes before the captain gave the order to start filling lifeboats with "women and children first."

- Poor communication impeded passengers and crew from reacting, although this could have been deliberate to avoid widespread panic.

- The hierarchical organizational structure and the physical segregation of classes on the ship helped restrict the flow of information.

- Many passengers got up, and then went back to bed with the perception that they were safe. The first lifeboat left only half full because of passengers' reluctance to get in.

- The crew carried out orders, but for a long time was skeptical that anything serious was going to happen. In short, even if a disaster-recovery plan were available, it would have been very poorly executed.

- The launch of 16 lifeboats took over 90 minutes because the order was given late, and the crew was not very familiar with the drill. There was not enough time to launch the last two Englehardts, which were floated off upside-down. Even if more lifeboats had been in place, there would probably not have been enough time to launch them.

Best Practices for Your Organization

- Once you have declared a disaster, ensure that it is enacted upon according to the plan and followed by staff without hesitation. This requires a good communication plan.

- In most hierarchical organizations, the upper levels of the organization have greater visibility and timeliness to information. As a result, they should be able to make a better and more rapid assessment.

- Ensure that disaster-recovery plans are easily accessible throughout the organization.

- Nominate operations services as "guardian" of the disaster-recovery plan.

- Ensure that adequate training is available to staff to follow disaster-recovery plans.

- Practice and rehearse disaster-recovery plans regularly—at least annually.

- Establish off-site locations and command posts to run all your operations from. Most organizations use facilities in other cities as backup command posts, or go through a service provider.

- Establish clear channels through processes for communicating information during a disaster.

- Regularly review any business changes, and update the plan to include them.

- Avoid procrastination in an outage or disaster situation. Proceed with a shutdown, rebuild, and restore to achieve a stable state. Waiting is likely just to further increase your losses.

- Take responsibility and respond to the customer, the public, and the press, to manage your organization's image.

Questions You Can Ask Today

At this stage in the project, you should expect back the following answers from IT:

- A risk assessment of the current disaster-recovery or business-continuity plan and procedures in place. (Refer to appendix C for more details.)

- An alternative analysis of business-continuity plans, based on degrees of recovery and costs.

- For a new business service, a summary of how the incoming solution will be recovered in a disaster.

C H A P T E R 8

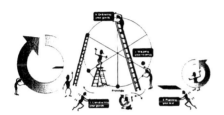

Conducting
a Post-Mortem

We can all learn from our activities and especially our mistakes. Conducting a structured post-delivery review provides a disciplined approach to ensure we have the facts to enable us to improve our performance in future, both during a project delivery and throughout the business lifecycle. This represents a small investment in the lifecycle costs, but provides the evidence for a massive reward.

Michael N. Crosby,
Founding Partner and Vice President of Delivery,
Sionet International Limited

Chapter Objectives

In this chapter, you learn how to go through a post-mortem of your on-line operation and service-delivery environment following a major unplanned outage. This will not only allow you to focus the learning energies of your organization on problem prevention, but to improve the required levels of service and availability.

A post-mortem is an investigation of the sequence of events leading up to a disaster, a major outage, or even a serious problem. As shown in Figure 8.1, it provides an insight into the factors contributing to the disaster and helps determine the root causes that otherwise would not surface.

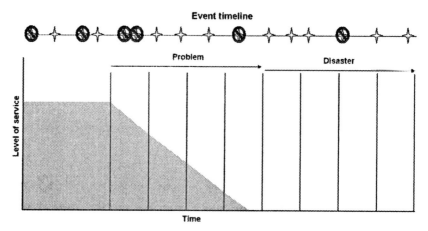

Figure 8.1: A post-mortem outlines the sequence of events as they occur on a timeline in an environment. Events are actions or observations, akin to the entries in a ship's log. The circled events are significant or problematic events that are at the core of the investigation.

What Steps Do I Need to Follow?

These are the three steps you need to take in a post-mortem for a major unplanned outage in your on-line operation:

1. *Discovery*—What went wrong? What should have/have not happened but did/did not? For this step, you need to do the following:

   • Collect the evidence (metrics).

   • Build the timeline of events.

   • Create the problem statement.

   • Determine contributing factors.

2. *Analysis*—Why did it go wrong? What were the contributing factors? What were the root causes of the contributing factors? For this step, you need to do the following:

   • Categorize the events.

   • Analyze the root causes of events.

3. *Corrective actions*—How can it be prevented from going wrong again? For this step, you need to do the following:

- Identify corrective actions to root causes.

- Evaluate your organization's support ability.

- Implement the changes.

To get started, let's look at these steps using *Titanic* as a backdrop. It is unlikely that you will experience a disaster on the scale of *Titanic*, but to consistently meet your SLAs, it is important to undergo post-mortems for all your outages, even small ones. As you go through this exercise, keep in mind some of the major outages listed in this book's introduction.

Discovery

This first investigation step collects the evidence, builds the event timeline, and articulates the scope of the problem. The purpose of this step is to determine what went wrong.

How to Collect the Evidence (Metrics)

Following *Titanic*'s disaster, both the U.S. and British authorities investigated, effectively conducting two post-mortems. A great detail of evidence was collected for these investigations. For example, the U.S. inquiry called 82 witnesses within one week of the disaster, including specialists and technical experts.

Likewise, you will need to call witnesses and collect as much evidence as you can through data and metrics. This needs to be done quickly, as it can get lost—or worse, disappear. Pulling this information together is necessary to create the event timeline.

Required Metrics

Two forms of metrics contribute to the event timeline: hard (or quantitative) and soft (or qualitative) metrics. These metrics can be internal or external to an organization.

Hard metrics are system-generated, can be part of the output of a service, and are collected through manual or automated processes. Examples include reports, error messages, transactions, and statistics. To help uncover this type of data, where not readily available, you might need to perform on-site "archaeology." These metrics tend to be explicit, timestamped, and accurate, but they usually require aggregation. Reports for these metrics include operational logs, service problem reports, service change requests, service level reports, environmental metric reports, and service outage reports.

Soft metrics include input from witnesses, customers, employees, or independent bodies. These are solicited through interviews, meetings, workshops, focus groups, and surveys. These tend to be subjective, difficult to collect, and prone to error, but they can be very insightful to root causes. They can be collected as witness testimonies, employee feedback, customer feedback, intermediary feedback, marketing feedback, "word on the street," and market perceptions of organization and services. The significance of all these metrics is that they can very accurately help piece together the event timeline.

Operational Logs

One of the objectives of the U.S. inquiry was to recreate the ship's log through the evidence gathered, and reconstruct the event timeline. Likewise, the operational logs in your service-delivery environment highlight the sequence of events. Therefore, they are probably the most important piece of documentation. Typically, these are handwritten, but assisted through automated tools.[1] Other useful documents include operational run books, end-of-shift reports, or standard operating procedures.

Service Problem Reports

Two types of groups handle problems and complaints: the help desk, which supports internal groups, and the call center, which supports customers. Both groups are responsible for problem management (opening, tracking, and closing problem tickets), compiling problem metrics in a database, and generating service problem reports. In collecting evidence, there are a number of things to look for in these reports:

- What major problems preceded the outage (looking back one to three weeks)?

- What problems led directly to the outage?

- What type of calls (as listed on the inventory model in Figure 2.7) preceded the outage?

- Which type of problems occurred most often: application, database, operating system, server, or network? What percentages of problems were unresolved?

- What was the average recovery time for problems and the time spent in each quadrant of the recovery clock (discussed in chapter 6)?

---

1. Sequences of operational commands as entered by operations at a console.

Service Change Requests

The business generates service change requests for the IT organization when it requires enhanced functionality or bug fixes (discussed in chapter 4). In collecting evidence, there are
a number of things to look for in these reports:

- What changes preceded the outage (during the last two months, based on the
  frequency of changes)?

- Is there any correlation between changes and unplanned outages?

- What percentage of changes are small, medium, large, and emergency?

- Which part of the operation is static/dynamic and has the least/most number of
  changes?

Service Level Reports

Service level reports are associated with service level objectives and agreements. They provide metrics on how the services are performing. In collecting evidence, you need to review
the following:

- What were the levels of service prior to the outage (looking back one to two
  weeks)?

- Were there any anomalies?

- Are the SLAs and SLOs currently met?

- Have any uncontrollable factors affected performance and meeting SLAs and
  SLOs?

Service Outage Report (Previous Outages)

The purpose of the service outage report is to provide a high-level summary of previous
outages. As shown in Table 8.1, the report quantifies the outage in terms of User Outage
Minutes (*UOMs*), penalties, and costs, and provides some insight to impact on the business,
and root causes. You should look back at least over a two-year period as part of the
post-mortem.

Table 8.1: Service Outage Report

Service	Time of Outage	Average Duration	Impact	Total UOMs	Root Cause	Class[a]	Outages	Penalty	Cost of Outage
1	Mon to Fri	8 hours	Minor	20,000	Poor messages	2	9	Lost clients	$20,000
2	After 06:00	2 hours	Minor	5,000	Faulty batch	2	3	User cash payments	$10,000
3.1	Mornings	2 hours	Severe	75,000	Process not followed	3	60	Lost contracts	$150,000
3.2	Anytime	16 hours	Severe	75,000	Cut line	3	2	No mgmt bonuses paid	$150,000
3.3	Anytime	1.5 hours	Very severe	90,000	Faulty install	3	20	Lost contracts	$200,000
3.4	Mon-Fri 09:00-15:00	24 hours	Very severe	85,000	Process not followed	3	10	Lost contracts	$200,000
4	After 18:00	12 hours	Severe	40,000	Sabotage	3	2	Penalties to government	$80,000
5	After 00:00	20 hours	Very severe	95,000	Operator error	5	2	Lost clients	$120,000

In collecting evidence from these reports, there are a number of things to look for:

- How do downtime figures (UOMs) relate between partial and full outages? For example, which has a greater user impact, many smaller or fewer larger outages? (For full outages, the cost of the impact is very often much greater than the actual outage-duration time because of user impact.)

- Do planned downtimes extend or overrun because of problems? (Unplanned downtime extensions indicate flaws in the change-management process.)

Environmental Metric Reports

A number of operational and business metrics can be automatically collected in the service-delivery environment:

- Operational metrics include error messages created by applications, devices, or components in a down or abnormal state. These indicate the health of the

2. Discussed in Appendix B.

environment and are similar to the ice warnings sent to *Titanic*. High peak error-message fluctuations indicate potential catastrophic environmental failures.

- Business metrics are transactional. They can be compared to the life-blood of an organization, where the flow increases and decreases depending on the varying service demands over time. Transaction metrics collected on a month-to-month and year-to-year basis are invaluable in building up very accurate trends.

These metrics provide an insight into the conditions and behavior of the environment. Combined, they give very detailed event-timeline information.

Witness Testimonies

The U.S. inquiry for *Titanic* had the authority to subpoena witnesses—including British nationals, such was its importance. The inquiry called up the director, officers, crew, and passengers from all three classes.

In your organization, testimonies from witnesses can help piece together a minute-by-minute chain of events leading up to the outage. Witnesses can generally be found in the support organization, employees, customers, and intermediaries.

Employee Feedback

Employees are usually customers of the organization too, and they can readily provide very realistic feedback related to their service experience and outage. Typically, the feedback is more honest, and there is no reluctance in providing it, as it benefits the employee in the long term. In gathering evidence, the following questions should be asked:

- What was your level of satisfaction prior to the outage (looking back one to two weeks)?

- What was the impact of the outage on you?

- How often do you use the service, and does it meet your expectations?

- How does it compare to competitive services?

Customer Feedback

Customers, like *Titanic*'s passengers, are an obvious source of feedback for service experience and outages. Their feedback can be collected through focus groups, third parties, phone interviews, e-surveys or questionnaires, etc.

It is important to target customers so that you know which segment they are a part of and the value of that segment to the organization. It is also important to recognize that individual aspirations make the feedback highly personalized.

Intermediary Feedback

Organizations providing services through an intermediary like a dealer or agent have a more simplified task of collecting feedback. Typically, it will be aggregated through the intermediary. The same questions as above could be asked, as well as questions related to any regional differences and whether these are significant. Useful feedback could also be solicited from distributors or suppliers who work closely with internal departments.

Marketing Feedback

Marketing departments are a further source of customer information. They are very interested in customer-satisfaction indexes and the impact on customer acquisition and retention. In gathering evidence from marketing, the following questions should be asked:

- What was the level of satisfaction prior to the outage (looking back one to two weeks)?

- Overall, how did the outage affect customer satisfaction?

- How did it affect the most valuable or top (most profitable) customers?

Word on the Street and Market Perceptions

Finally, external source information is useful. The following questions should be asked:

- Have any press, industry, or trade articles been written about the outage?

- How has the press depicted your organization and services? Have industry analysts compared your services to the competition?

How to Build the Event Timeline

With the evidence in hand, you can now compile the findings to create an event timeline, looking at the sequence of all events right up to the point of impact and beyond. *Titanic*'s event timeline is shown in Table 8.2.

Table 8.2: Event Timeline for the Titanic Disaster from Sunday, April 14 to Monday, April 15

Event ID	Time	Event	Description
E1.1	00:00-21:00	Seven ice warnings received during the day.	During the course of the day, many ships sent telegram warnings of ice.
E1.2	21:40	Last ice warning from *Mesba*, sailing in front of *Titanic*.	"...Heavy pack ice and a great number of large icebergs."
E1.3	23:25	Visible signs of ice.	Air temperature down.
E1.4	23:30	Officer Murdoch takes position on forward rail.	Regular change in officer shift.
E1.5	23:40	Lookouts see ice looming 40 to 50 feet above water.	Lookout phones the bridge with the warning "iceberg right ahead."
E1.6	23:40	Officer Murdoch orders engines to stop and "hard-a-starboard."	Officer Murdoch has around 37 seconds to react. Ship reacts very slowly.
E1.7	23:40	Officer Murdoch orders "hard-a-port."	The direction was switched to port around the iceberg (an S-turn).
E1.8	23:45	Captain arrives on deck, orders damage-assessment reports.	Two groups leave to investigate damage.
E1.9	23:46	Water damage in the fore peak and cargo holds in the bow.	Rushing water forces escaping air to throw open hatch covers.
E1.10	23:48	Director arrives on deck and asks what the damage is.	Thought ship had dropped a propeller.
E1.11	23:50	First group, led by Officer Boxhall, returns.	Inaccurate report of no major damage found.
E1.12	23:51	Director and captain order engines restarted.	Ship is floated off the ice shelf.
E2.1	00:00 (Monday)	Lawrence Beesley notices the deck starting to tilt.	Water has poured in and risen 14 feet in the front part of the ship.
E2.2	00:20	Second group led by architect returns with assessment report of unrecoverable situation.	Captain, director, and architect are aware that ship has only a few hours, but this is not widely communicated.
E2.3	00:20	Captain orders lifeboats uncovered, and passengers and crew readied.	No "abandon ship" order is given. There is only room in the lifeboats for about half of the 2,227 people onboard.
E2.4	00:20	First distress call sent.	*Titanic* radios a distress call.
E2.5	00:25	*Carpathia* picks up distress call 58 miles southeast; estimated arrival time three to four hours.	*Carpathia* changes course and heads full-speed to the rescue. No communication of this information is given to passengers and crew.

Table 8.2: Event Timeline for the Titanic Disaster from Sunday, April 14 to Monday, April 15 (continued)			
Event ID	Time	Event	Description
E2.6	00:45	First distress rocket sent.	Officer Boxhall sends the first distress rocket. Eight rockets are fired through night.
E2.7	00:45	First few lifeboats leave half-empty.	A lifeboat with capacity for 65 people pulls away carrying only 28.
E2.8	01:15	Ship is noticeably listing.	The tilt of the deck grows steeper. Lifeboats leave more fully loaded.
E2.9	01:40	Most forward lifeboats lowered.	Passengers move to the stern of the ship.
E2.10	02:05	Last lifeboat lowered	Over 1,500 people are left onboard.
E2.11	02:15	Two Englehardts are floated off.	The Englehardts float upside-down and are used as rafts.
E2.12	02:15	Wireless Operator Phillips sends last message.	"TITANIC TO ALL SHIPS. ENGINE ROOM FULL UP TO THE BOILERS."
E2.13	02:17	Power	All power is lost.
E2.14	02:18	Ship breaks in two.	The rear part of the ship starts to right itself from the angle of tilt.
E2.15	02:20	Ship disappears completely.	Survivors in icy water freeze to death.
E2.16	03:20	Lifeboats return.	Lifeboats return to the site to pick up survivors.
E2.17	03:30	The rescue ship *Carpathia* sighted.	*Carpathia's* rockets are sighted by survivors.
E2.18	04:10	*Carpathia* arrives.	*Carpathia* picks up the first lifeboat.

The details of your event timeline would obviously differ a lot from this example, but the format would be essentially the same.

How to Create the Problem Statement

Before you can start to hone in on the timeline and root causes, you need to select the events that had the most impact on the disaster. In other words, you need to determine those that were "problematic." To select them, however, you need to carefully define a problem statement, as there might be ambiguity to what the problem was or if several problems occurred simultaneously.

Your first question about the *Titanic* disaster might be "Why did *Titanic* not reach New York?" The answer simply is it ran onto an ice shelf and foundered after it sailed off. However, it is important to phrase the question in a meaningful context to the organization.

Let's take a look at how this is done, starting with *Titanic*'s survival figures, shown in Table 8.3.[3] They were shocking from the perspective that so many third-class passengers perished, especially women and children.

Table 8.3: Survival Figures by Class

Steerage of Passenger		Number Onboard	Number Saved	Percentage Saved
First class	Men	173	58	34
	Women	144	139	97
	Children	5	5	100
Second class	Men	160	13	8
	Women	93	78	84
	Children	24	24	100
Third class	Men	454	55	12
	Women	179	98	55
	Children	76	23	30
Total passengers		1308	493	38
Total crew		898	210	23
Total		**2206**	**703**	**32**

After the disaster, the public had relatively little sympathy for White Star and its economic loss. Therefore, the focus of the U.S. inquiry was "Why was *Titanic* such a tragic disaster, with so many lives lost?" The emphasis was on learning lessons and preventing future catastrophes.

Likewise, in your organization someone might ask "Why did we have a 12-hour outage?" when the question would be better phrased as "Why did we lose $2 million, over 200 premier customers, and get a scathing report in the national press because of the 12-hour outage?"

---

3. Presented in the British Inquiry report the 16 primary lifeboats had room for 65 passengers per boat giving a total capacity of 1120. The 4 Englehardts provided extra room for 30 per boat to a total capacity of 120. In all the total capacity was 1240, around 50 percent of numbers on board.

How to Determine the Contributing Factors

Once you have carefully articulated the problem and its scope, you can start looking at the contributing factors. These are still general statements, and refer to overall conditions.

There were several contributing factors to *Titanic*'s disaster:

- Officers failed to slow the ship down and prevent the collision with the ice shelf.

- The director and captain sailed the crippled ship off the ice shelf for Halifax.

- Recovery undertaken poorly by officers and crew.

Contributing Factor 1: Officers Failed to Slow Ship

There is little doubt that had *Titanic* sailed more slowly, a collision would have been unlikely. The possible causes for this contributing factor were as follows:

- It was believed that the built-in feedback mechanisms would provide early warning signs of ice.

- Numerous ships in the vicinity would provide ample radio warnings of ice.

- Visibility conditions were perceived excellent, so danger would be seen in advance.

Contributing Factor 2: Crippled Ship Was Sailed Off Ice Shelf

The director and captain ordered the engines restarted, and floated the ship off the ice shelf, with the hope of limping back to Halifax. There is little doubt that this one action was the most significant event of all.

The possible causes for this contributing factor were as follows:

- The collision seemed innocuous, with no signs of visible damage and no casualties.

- The director and captain believed that no serious damage had been sustained beyond what the safety features could cope with.

- The first damage-assessment report recounted no serious damage.

- The director and captain were hasty in not waiting for the second damage-assessment report from the architect that recounted catastrophic damage.

- The director saw an opportunity to extend the legend of *Olympic*-class ships further in that the ship could even save itself after a collision, by getting back to Halifax.

Contributing Factor 3: Recovery Undertaken Poorly by Officers and Crew

The statistics for the number of third-class passengers lost were horrendous when compared to the total numbers aboard the ship. There is little doubt that, had the officers and crew helped the third class and diligently filled the lifeboats full, an additional 750 people could have been saved. The possible causes for this contributing factor were as follows:

- No business continuity plan was in place, so full recovery was impossible.

- Information flow cascading to crew and passengers was very slow, or even purposely restricted.

- Officers and crew were slow to respond because of disbelief in the situation.

- Third-class passengers had great difficulty in getting to the boat decks.

Analysis

You are now ready to proceed with a detailed analysis, which will lead you to the root causes of the disaster. The purpose of this step is to determine why it went wrong. The first element of this step is to select the events that had the most impact on the disaster, or were most "problematic."

How to Categorize the Events

Use the contributing factors to review and categorize the events as follows:

- *Problematic*—Likely to have contributed to the disaster.

- *Unsure*—Could have had both a negative or positive impact.

- *Positive*—Likely to have prevented or limited the disaster.

The problematic events from Table 8.2 related to the contributing factors are as follows:

- The officers failed to slow the ship down and prevent a collision with the ice-shelf (events E1.1, E1.2, E1.3, and E1.5).

- The director and captain tried to sail the crippled ship off the ice shelf for Halifax (events E1.9, E1.10, E1.11 and E1.12).

- Recovery was undertaken poorly by officers and crew (events E2.2, E2.3, E2.4, E2.6, and E2.7).

How to Analyze the Root Causes of Events

You are now in a position to start to determine the root causes of the problematic events. A problematic event itself is not the problem, but rather the conditions that allowed it to happen are. Once the conditions are identified, then it is relatively straightforward to identify the root causes. Let's stay with the three contributing factors.

Contributing Factor 1: Officers Failed to Slow Ship

The events relating to the officers' failure to slow the ship are listed in Table 8.4.

Table 8.4: Problematic Events Related to Contributing Factor 1

Event ID	Problematic Event	Significance	Conditions	Root Causes
E1.1	Seven ice warnings received during the day.	No action taken.	Officers failed to piece these warnings together to determine the ice field's size. Messages are passed ad hoc.	Lack of clear procedures to collect messages and chart the ice field.
E1.2	Last ice warning from *Mesba*, sailing ahead.	No action taken.	No requirement for radio operator to pass message back immediately.	Lack of clear procedures between wireless room and bridge.
E1.3	Visible signs of ice.	No action taken.	Officers ignored danger. Ice-bucket test was positive.	Business pressure to better *Olympic's* crossing time, and feedback distrusted.
E1.5	Lookouts see ice looming 50 feet above water.	Warning sent too late for ship to stop.	No extra lookouts posted on the prow. Lookouts were missing binoculars.	Officers saw no reason to post more lookouts; visibility conditions perceived excellent.

Without a doubt, a lower speed would have prevented the disaster, an opinion derived by naval architects and engineers. The iceberg's impact would have been minimized, and with less damage to the hull plates, fewer compartments would have flooded. However, the officers were so confident in their ship's handling that, despite numerous warnings, they chose to press full-speed ahead. Let's take a look at why, by further expanding the possible causes:

- The officers gained experience through sailing *Olympic*. In operation for 11 months, they had encountered similar conditions and were very familiar with the danger.

- Built-in feedback mechanisms would provide early warning signs of ice. The officers were vigilant for ice, and used tests like the ice bucket.

- Numerous ships in the vicinity would provide ample radio message warnings of ice. After all, they were sailing along busy sea routes with other ships only miles away.

- The visibility conditions were perceived excellent. The sea was very still and the night sky very clear, so danger would be seen in advance.

Contributing Factor 2: Crippled Ship Was Sailed Off Ice Shelf

The events relating to the director's and captain's decision to sail the crippled ship off the ice shelf are listed in Table 8.5.

Table 8.5: Problematic Events Related to Contributing Factor 2

Event ID	Problematic Event	Significance	Conditions	Root causes
E1.9	Water damage in the fore peak and cargo hold.	No action taken.	Officers ignored warning signs.	Disbelief in seriousness of situation.
E1.10	Director arrives on deck to check damage.	Director saw opportunity to extend legend.	Director assumed operational authority over captain.	Business pressures to maintain perception of greatest liner ever.
E1.11	First group led by Officer Boxhall returns.	Inaccurate report of no major damage.	Seemingly innocuous collision with no visible damage.	Group likely not expecting any serious damage.
E1.12	Director and captain restart engines.	Most significant decision taken.	Acting on sparse or bad information, director and captain are reluctant to wait.	Ability to override procedures and rule of good seamanship.

The director and captain, convinced that no serious damage had been sustained, restarted the engines and floated the ship off the ice shelf, with the hope of limping back to Halifax. Let's take a look at why, by further expanding the possible causes:

- The collision seemed so innocuous, with no signs of visible damage and no casualties. For most individuals on *Titanic*, there was no warning that anything was wrong. The impact was no more than a vibration and grinding noise that grounded the ship.

- The resounding belief was that the safety features could cope with the damage. The water pumps and double hull were keeping up with the flooding. The bulkheads were sealed with electric doors.

- The first damage-assessment report was incorrect because Officer Boxhall's group did not descend enough decks to properly observe the damage.

- The director and captain were too impatient for the second damage-assessment report because of business pressure to arrive in Halifax within a specific timeframe to the estimated arrival time in New York.

- The director saw an opportunity to extend the legend of *Olympic*-class ships further, in having the ship save itself. He was under business pressure to maintain perception that *Titanic* was the greatest liner ever, and to avoid embarrassing publicity if distress calls were put that the ship was grounded on the ice shelf.

Contributing Factor 3: Recovery Undertaken Poorly by Officers and Crew

The events relating to the crew's poor recovery efforts are listed in Table 8.6.

Table 8.6: Problematic Events Related to Contributing Factor 3

Event ID	Problematic Event	Significance	Conditions	Root cause
E2.2	Executive aware that ship had few hours left.	Limited passenger awareness of disaster.	Information was not widely communicated.	Fear of panic. Communication systems were very poor.
E2.3	No "abandon ship" order given.	Limited passenger awareness of disaster.	Information flow was very slow or even restricted.	Fear of panic. Ability to override procedures.
E2.4	First distress call sent out.	Call sent 40 minutes into disaster.	Reluctance to face up to situation.	Business pressure. No continuity plan in place.
E2.6	First distress rocket sent.	Rocket sent 65 minutes into disaster.	Reluctance to face up to situation.	Business pressure. No continuity plan in place.
E2.7	First few lifeboats leave half-empty.	Lifeboats lowered 65 minutes into disaster.	Crew could not persuade passengers to board.	Disbelief in seriousness of situation.

The officers and crew were unable to enact a smooth recovery. The statistics for third-class passengers lost were horrendous compared to the total numbers aboard. Also, had the officers and crew filled the lifeboats full, an additional 750 people could have been saved. Let' take a look at why, by further expanding the possible causes:

- No business continuity plan was in place, so full recovery was impossible. A plan was thought unnecessary because of the confidence in the ship's safety features.

- The crew was preoccupied in helping first-class passengers to the boat deck and lifeboats.

- Cascading information flow was very slow, and the captain failed to give concrete orders like "abandon ship." The crew lied to the third-class passengers about the extent of the damage so that they would return to their quarters.

- Officers and crew responded slowly because of the disbelief that the ship was in danger, and only realized something was wrong as disaster signs appeared after the first hour. There was an overconfidence in the ship and its safety features.

- Third-class passengers had great difficulty in getting to the boat decks, because:

  - The class system on the ship exasperated the problem of movement. The lower the class, the further and deeper into the ship was the accommodation.

  - Third-class passengers were physically restricted by gates and barriers from wandering outside of their class because American immigration regulations specified that immigrants on ships be segregated from other classes, for health reasons.

  - Many of these gates were locked while the ship sank because the crewmembers in charge of the gates were unavailable.

  - Many third-class passengers themselves accepted their "lower position" in the socially created hierarchy, which further reinforced the segregation.

Corrective Actions

The purpose of this step is to prevent the disaster from happening again. Once root causes are evaluated, they can be tested and rationalized into true causes, and solutions determined.

How to Define Corrective Actions to Root Causes

Let's stay with the three contributing factors to *Titanic* in defining corrective actions.

Contributing Factor 1: Officers Failed to Slow Ship

The root causes of the officers' failure to slow the ship are as follows:

1. *Clear procedures were lacking.* This clearly hampered the ability to pass messages to the bridge and for the officers to chart the ice field's size. Had one of the officers been able to put together all the ice warnings, it is very likely the size of the ice field would have been better understood. These warnings were eventually communicated through the ship's hierarchy to the captain, but they were not adequately acted on.

2. *Business pressure to better* Olympic'*s crossing time influenced action.* The director was determined to prove *Titanic* was a better ship. However, the natural environment is anything but predictable and should not have been treated in such a cavalier manner, no matter how experienced the operation. Other ships in the region had pulled up for the night.

3. *Officers distrusted feedback data.* Data from feedback mechanisms was distrusted, discounted, or just ignored by the officers if it didn't fit in with their perceptions. This was especially the case with the captain, who was clearly a technophobe and tended to operate by instinct. However, some data, like the result of the ice-bucket test, was fabricated.

4. *Officers saw no reason to post more lookouts, visibility perceived excellent.* Visibility was, in fact, very poor because of the haze caused by the cold weather, and with the calm sea, there were no breakers to identify icebergs on the horizon. Overconfidence in the ship's operational capability resulted in lookouts posted without binoculars, while officers kept their own. No extra lookouts were posted to the ship's prow.

Root cause 2 is likely the true cause. A remedy could have been to play down the significance of the maiden voyage and have a "burn period" of shorter trips. Then, later in the summer, when icebergs were less likely, reschedule the voyage and take a more southerly route. However, there were great financial pressures to get *Titanic* operational quickly.

Contributing Factor 2: Crippled Ship Was Sailed Off Ice Shelf

The root causes of the decision to sail the ship off the ice shelf are as follows:

1. *Officers and crew disbelieved seriousness of situation.* After the first hour, there was still a disbelief in the situation by the officers and crew, a common disaster trait.

2. *Business pressures were to maintain perception of greatest liner ever.* The director callously exploited a very risky opportunity to save face by turning a problematic situation into a positive one, in his mind.

3. *First assessment group was not expecting any serious damage.* The investigation was hurried and not done thoroughly. The executives were looking for exactly this type of evidence to use to their advantage.

4. *Executives could override procedures and rules of good seamanship.* The director used his position to take control of the operation and all key operational decisions, without adequate relative experience, to the detriment of the organization. The captain was intimidated by the director, even with the overwhelming evidence of the dangers. The overriding authority of the director, captain, and the hierarchical culture made it impossible to challenge.

Root causes 2 and 4 are likely the true causes. A remedy could have been to establish SLA (to deliver passengers safely) and then establish responsibility firmly with one group alone (operations services) to meet these without any interference from executives whatsoever.

In a critical situation, it is easy to lose control and make rash decisions on too little information. Hence, the operations services group needs to follow processes like the problem-management process. It is likely they would have refused to take action before examining more evidence, and the ship could have stabilized on the ice shelf. This would have been long enough for rescue ships to complete a full recovery of the majority of the passengers.

Contributing Factor 3: Recovery Undertaken Poorly by Officers and Crew

The root causes of the poor recovery efforts are as follows:

1. *Panic was feared.* This was inevitable, as many of the third-class passengers on the lower decks, where the flooding was most apparent, were well aware of the disaster very early on. In many organizations, outages are first noticed by customers.

2. *Communication systems were very poor.* The crew had to alert passengers by knocking from door to door, which took up to an hour. On the upper decks, a level of calm was kept, as the crew was close by and helpful, unlike the lower decks, where the signs were more visible.

3. *No business-continuity plan was in place.* A disaster-recovery plan had not been carefully thought out for all scenarios.

Root cause 3 is likely the true cause. A remedy could have been to establish a disaster-recovery plan, carefully thought out for all possible scenarios. The plan would be well communicated and regularly practiced.

How to Evaluate Your Organization's Support Ability

If your outage or problem is particularly severe, affecting service levels, you should consider the question, "What is your organization's ability to run your on-line operation and support services"? As part of the post-mortem's corrective actions, you now have an opportunity to review the support organization's ability to support the on-line operation. This is not an extensive exercise, but it is rapid, as you will have to take short-term actions. The question relates equally to an internal or external service provider.

SEI Capability Maturity Model

There are a number of techniques available to help evaluate your organization's support ability. One of the most significant and widely accepted as a best practice is the Software Engineering Institute (*SEI*) Capability Maturity Model (*CMM*). The SEI at Carnegie Mellon University developed the model, based on industrial-engineering process concepts and research, to classify the maturity of an IT organization. It was based on the idea that an organization's maturity can be measured by the processes it has in place and how they are used. A process, in this sense, is a leverage point for an organization's sustained improvement. The CMM provides a structure that measures organizational maturity through its process capability, and its ability to support services.

Process Gap Analysis

You can assess an organization's processes in terms of what is in place (current state) and being used through Table 8.7. For a more detailed assessment, you might have to measure the processes, analyze the measurement results against the process performance objectives, and then review the processes for effectiveness and suitability.

In parallel, you also need to assess (future state) what might be required to support the future service-delivery environment, and your organization's process needs and objectives. For this, you need to do the following:

- Identify the policies, standards, and business objectives applicable to these processes.

- Determine the organization's process performance objectives and any associated metrics, such as problem recovery times and change success rates.

- Examine relevant process standards and models for best practices. (Refer to chapter 4, 5, and 6 for more details.)

Table 8.7: Process Gap Analysis

	None in Place	Individual, Home-grown	In Place, Followed	In Place, Measured	In Place, Improved
Chapter 4					
Planning	✓				
Assess Risk		✓			
Determine Alternatives		✓			
Define Test	✓				
Chapter 5					
First-stage Test					
Complete Tests	✓				
Review Results	✓				
Reassess Risk	✓				
Final-stage Test					
Load in Increments		✓			
Test Each Increment			✓		
Monitor All Increments		✓			
Chapter 6					
Problem Detection			✓		
Problem Determination			✓		
Problem Resolution			✓		
Problem Recovery		✓			

You should do this assessment in conjunction with your co-workers and vendors, as it can provide a sound measuring tool for ongoing improvement of processes and support capability. Completing the future state helps set targets and priorities for improvements.

Table 8.8 shows the complete SEI Process Maturity Model and its five levels. Each maturity level indicates an organization's process-acquisition capability. The term *quantitative management* implies a process that is statistically managed through measures and analytic techniques, so that the performance of the process is predicted. A baseline for a well-run on-line operation requires a maturity level of 4 or 5. Most organizations operate at level 1 or 2, so level 3 is an achievement.

Table 8.8: SEI Process Maturity Model for Supporting On-line Operations

Level	Characteristic	Key Recommendations	Result
Level 5: Optimizing	Continuous process improvement.	Maintain organization at optimizing level.	High productivity, low risk.
Level 4: Managed	Measured process (quantitative management).	Changing technology, problem analysis, problem prevention.	
Level 3: Defined	Process defined, institutionalized (qualitative).	Process management, process analysis, quantitative quality plan.	Medium productivity, risk.
Level 2: Repeatable	Process dependent on individuals (intuitive).	Training, practices, reviews, testing process, focus on standards, process groups.	
Level 1: Initial	No process (ad hoc/chaotic).	Project management, planning, configuration management.	Low productivity, high risk.

Other Indicators of IT Maturity

Once you establish a level, you should review how your support organization scores when it comes to projects. For this, you need to complete an organizational gap analysis. The way an organization handles projects, specifically multiple or enterprise projects, is very indicative of maturity. Signs you should look for include the following:

- A centralized governing body, such as a project management office, that runs multiple projects with a successful project track record of over three years of meeting business needs.

- A strong working relationship with the business community and users.

- The use of project best practices like PMBOK (*Project Management Book of Knowledge*) and PMI (membership in the Project Management Institute).

Organizational Gap Analysis

You can assess an organization's IT skills and experience against the skills required to support the service-delivery environment and the processes required using the criteria in Table 8.9. The criteria for assessment relate to service levels and whether your support organization has clear SLOs, and is tied to these through measurements and customer SLAs. For example, is team or individual performance directly linked to SLAs through organizational penalties or rewards?

Table 8.9: Organizational Gap Analysis

Support Organization	Track Record on Projects	Strength and Right Skills Mix	Experience	Individual Skills	Certification Paths	Use of External Help
Solution Services						
Development Group	Poor	Good	V. Good	V. Good	None	Some
Development Support	Adequate	Poor	Good	Good	In place	None
Technical Services						
Automation	Adequate	Adequate	Poor	Poor	In place	None
Specialist	Good	Adequate	Good	Adequate	None	Some
Operations Services						
Operators Team 1	Good	Poor	Good	Good	None	None
Operators Team 2	Good	Poor	Good	Good	None	None
Operators Team 3	Good	Adequate	Good	Good	None	None

External Service Provider and Hosting

Building up organizational skills and implementing processes can become a challenge for many organizations. Outsourcing Web mission-critical applications has become a popular option with many organizations. This is certainly a solution for organizations willing to allow a contracted host provider to take the responsibility of maintaining a site and its supporting applications, according to service uptime and performance levels. Careful consideration needs to be made as to how critical the site and applications are, agreed-to service levels, and how the host provider views availability (measured in terms of UOMs).

How to Implement the Changes

You have just completed an organizational and process gap analysis. You have evaluated your organization's ability to run your on-line operation and support services, and it falls short. You have process and organizational changes to implement. How do you do this?

Simple. You have just come full-circle, and you are now ready to go back to chapter 1. The process is continuous, just as the lifecycle figures have indicated throughout the book. You need to start at chapter 1 and work through each chapter again, verifying what is in place, using these chapters to provide the standards and model for best practices, and making the changes accordingly.

Conclusion

The following sections summarize the major points of this chapter and how they relate to your business today. For more information on these concepts, search the Internet for these keywords and phrases: *metrics analysis, root cause analysis, project post-mortems, service level agreements*, and *Software Engineering Institute*.

Major Points, Considerations, and Titanic Lessons

- The officers failed to map a clear chart of the ice field. The importance of collecting and integrating signals to complete a clear picture was missed.

- Right until the disaster signs appeared, after the first hour, there was a disbelief in the situation by the captain, officers, and crew. This is a trait common to disaster.

- Based on the finding of the post-mortem, there were three key contributing factors to the disaster:

   1. The officers failed to slow the ship down to prevent the collision.

   2. The director and captain sailed the crippled ship off the ice shelf.

   3. Recovery was undertaken poorly by officers and crew.

Best Practices for Your Organization

- Proceed with a post-mortem after any major outage, but also consider it as a standard operating procedure for all outages.

- Ensure critical metrics are automatically collected (like a black-box recorder).

- Collect metrics quickly. Don't let the evidence disappear.

- Always create an event timeline, as this is the starting point for the post-mortem.

- Closely examine downtime figures (UOMs) from reports, to differentiate between partial and full outages.

- Determine what type of outage has a greater user impact: many small or few large.

- Determine whether planned downtimes extend or overrun because of problems. If so, this indicates flaws in the change-management process.

Questions You Can Ask Today

At this stage in the project, you should expect back the following answers from IT:

- Procedures in place for post-mortems.

- The process for compiling availability metrics.

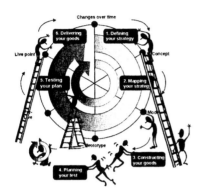

The Maiden Voyage Ends

Chapter Objectives

When you are done with this chapter, you will be able to assess your overall IT project and take away important lessons for your next IT project.

Congratulations. You have now completed the maiden voyage through your project's lifecycle. You have navigated the first six chapters, which required you to create and maintain your on-line operation. In chapter 7, you encountered a worst-case scenario of "when the unthinkable happens," something *Titanic*'s architects did not expect. Chapter 8 provided you with the tools for a post-mortem. This chapter reviews the book's key points.

The preface to this book advocated you, as a business manager, to be a full participant in the proposed IT project, since you might be responsible for it, its funding, and its deliverables. Your goal is to ensure that the IT project not only meets the short-term goals of the required functional objectives, but also the longer-term goals of the required financial and service-level objectives.

The book presented you with a project lifecycle model and an analogous case study, to use as tools. Conceptually, *Titanic*'s cradle-to-grave project lifecycle is not much different from those used in IT projects today. (Refer to appendix E for approaches to on-line operation projects.) Purists in the IT industry might beg to differ and steep modern projects in IT jargon and complexity, but fundamentally, they are the same.

Reviewing Titanic and Your On-line Operation

In reviewing *Titanic*'s case study, by the project-construction stage, decisions were made in the architecture and design that compromised and negated principal safety features, like the height of the bulkheads. The logical explanation is that assumptions were made by the White Star architects that the advanced technology incorporated would protect *Titanic* from whatever nature handed out. The arrogant view evolved that *Titanic* was a huge lifeboat. *Titanic*'s designers made the mistake of believing the initial design assumptions, and not testing these far enough. Such was the confidence in the safety of the ship that by the end of the project, disaster recovery and business continuity plans were considered superfluous.

In the early stages of your IT project's lifecycle (discussed in chapters 2 and 3), hundreds of granular decisions are made by your team. Some of these decisions might seem innocuous or insignificant. As the project takes shape, assumptions are formed. It is very easy to stray off the path in one stage and make dubious decisions, but still meet the goal of that stage. For example, underestimating the costs of nonfunctional requirements is a common problem that should have been factored into the business case (discussed in chapter 1). The impact of a poor decision might not be brought to light until later in the project, or even more likely months after the operation is on-line.

You need to ensure that a project stays true to its vision and direction through each stage of the lifecycle. It is unfeasible for you to micro-manage the project, so you have to ensure that everyone involved understands the project vision clearly, and is empowered to aggregate information, determine risks, and present critical issues at steering-committee meetings. Strategies like starting with a pilot or small project and then scaling each project lifecycle rapidly minimize the impact of poor decisions.

The belief in *Titanic*'s invincibility grew through the sea trials and into the maiden voyage, as the officers and crew went through the motions. By the end of the project, *Titanic* was the largest ship afloat and was billed as unsinkable. Everyone, from the captain, to the crew to the 53 millionaires onboard, believed this. Why else would the wealthy and powerful have filled the hold and safes with cars and riches, and come aboard on a potentially treacherous route? Fundamentally, they believed that man had conquered nature and there was little risk.

Likewise, your on-line project needs to include careful investment in planning, testing, and operating. It is easy to dismiss these stages in the project lifecycle and accept minimum testing, knowing that you will pay for it eventually when things do go wrong. On completing your on-line project successfully, it is easy to become very complacent and assume nothing will go wrong. After all, you have invested in the latest mission-critical technology, integrated reliable software, and marketed the solution extensively to your customer base.

The ship owners were very much driven by the pressing economic need to move *Titanic* into service. In reality, *Titanic*'s testing consisted of the maiden voyage across the Atlantic, fully loaded with passengers. This was a disaster waiting to happen. The poor operational readiness of the ship, coupled with the cavalier and arrogant attitude of its executives, violated all the basic rules of good seamanship.

Similarly, organizations today make a large number of assumptions that might prove incorrect when implementing operations on-line. Confidence that nothing can go wrong creates an atmosphere where little attention is paid to operational readiness.

Officer Murdoch came close to preventing *Titanic*'s initial collision through brilliant seamanship, when he almost pulled off an S-turn. However, he was under tremendous pressure not to slow down, and was forced to navigate a very risky run through a hazardous ice field. The operation of the ship was pushed beyond the limits that its safety features were designed for.

Similarly, it is very easy to attribute major outages or problems in your on-line operation to operator error or even a malfunction with the hardware or software. These explanations are simply not acceptable in today's world, where the stakes are so high. You need to ask why the operator made the error, what sort of pressure the operator was under, why the hardware or software went wrong, and why this was not caught in the testing stage of the project. The root causes to many problems are laid during the on-line operation project.

What You Can Learn from Root Causes

In reviewing *Titanic*'s post-mortem (discussed in chapter 8), 11 significant root causes were identified. Nine of these were related to organizational issues, two were related to the lack of procedures or plans, and none were related to technology. The following four root causes were most significant:

- The business pressures to better *Olympic*'s crossing time influenced actions, as the director was determined to prove *Titanic* was a more technically advanced ship.

- The director used his authority to take control of the operation and all major decisions, even though stringent guidelines and procedures were in place.

- No business continuity plan was in place, as it was thought unnecessary.

- The business pressure to maintain the perception of the greatest liner ever caused the director to callously exploit a very risky opportunity to save face.

It is clear that the true causes were related to business pressures overriding operational decisions, and very poor leadership. This is absolutely typical in today's on-line environments, where business pressures and overzealous leadership can override operational decisions. It is essential that you complete post-mortems for all major problems, closely look at the root causes in your on-line operation, and not accept superficial excuses.

In today's popular culture, we have come to accept that *Titanic* was just unlucky. The truth behind the root causes was falsified for political reasons. The failure of White Star's captain, officers, and crew to protect the ship should have resulted in a case of gross incompetence being brought against White Star. In effect, the British investigation knew that it would have to exonerate White Star to prevent rival German companies from dominating transatlantic shipping.

Why You Need to Take It Seriously

The British investigation shifted the blame onto the captain of the *California*, Captain Stanley Lord, who sat the night out. He was surrounded by ice, unaware of the disaster, and did not come to the rescue of *Titanic*. However, even if *California* had come to the call, it is highly likely that the rescue attempt would have been unsuccessful. The British government needed White Star. It saw a potential European war looming, and knew it would need large ships for transporting troops and materials. In today's world, *Titanic*'s disaster would undoubtedly have brought White Star down just through private lawsuits. In the business world, this has repeatedly happened. You need to consider these implications carefully, and their impact, when putting your operations on-line.

This can be summarized as the *Titanic* effect:

The severity with which an on-line operation fails is directly proportional to an organization's belief that it cannot. In other words, technology plus arrogance spells disaster.

Answers to Initial Questions

The preface indicated that this book would resolve six problems. Let's take a look at these problems and their solutions:

- *How can I improve the probability of success and mitigate the risk in my IT projects?* The book provides you a way to assess the real cost and risks of an IT project. For example, chapter 1 highlights the importance of determining the business rationale, hidden availability costs, and how to create a business case. Chapters 2 and 3 highlight how to identify and take appropriate actions to mitigate the risk and create an infrastructure to support this, in effect a balance between design and construction. Chapters 4 and 5 focus on planning and testing, and chapter 6 highlights the operational support investments. You can also look back o previous projects and assess their success by reviewing service-level objectives me annual User Outage Minutes achieved, the costs to accomplish these, and customer expectations. You now have a track record or baseline to offset requests for IT projects and solution investments.

- *How can I deliver my goods and services in an environment of uncertainty, in terms of the risk of doing business on-line, through intranets, extranets, the Internet, portals, or other electronic channels?* The risk of doing business on-line is expressed through the concept of availability, which is prevalent in all the chapters. Chapter 1 focuses on assessing the monetary exposure, and therefore quantifying the risk if your on-line operation is not available. Chapters 2 and 3 address the issues of dependencies and integration. Chapters 4 and 5 highlight how to set up a change-management process, services-level agreements, and service-level objectives. Chapter 6 outlines the operational requirements on a day-to-day basis, early warning systems, and how to meet the service levels.

- *How can I anticipate and mitigate service outages to save money, customer goodwill, and maybe my job?* One of the key objectives of this book has been to help you understand what is required to create an on-line operation so that it is run successfully and is resilient to service outages. The instant exposure of the Internet makes outages horrendously expensive and highly visible. Going on-line, therefore, is never easy. Likewise, business services become mission-critical through organizational or application interdependencies and the integration of legacy backend systems. e-Business integrates internal applications and then exposes them to the outside world. Meeting SLAs consistently requires an ongoing investment strategy that continually reevaluates and readjusts investment priorities, and this is central throughout the book.

- *How can I ensure my investments in individual IT projects related to business services are well-directed?* In putting operations on-line and establishing service levels, many organizations take the easier but ultimately more expensive option of focusing just on technology. They create redundancy through excess hardware in the environment. This book advocates an approach in which the focus is on identifying what is mission-critical and what is not, and where the weak points are that require protection (refer to chapters 1 and 2). You then take a holistic approach and ensure that the organization, processes, and technology carefully map to this. Availability is improved through all of these changes, including organizing more effectively, along an end-to-end view of the environment. The book provides you with a starting point to be able to rapidly complete a detailed breakdown of the costs.

- *How can I run with the IT-jargon "wolves" without being devoured?* Business has a clear role in the life of a new solution. For IT to be successful, business needs to take an active role. The section "Questions You Can Ask Today" at the end of each chapter highlights what you, as the business manager, require at each stage to make a go/no-go decision. On-line operations are the lifeblood of organizations, and this warrants the involvement of the business manager, at least on a steering committee. With a clear role for each group, business and IT can align. IT investments can be made in precise and incremental ways that the business side understands and fully supports.

- *How do I know what and how to measure?* When you are told your organization has achieved 99 percent availability, what does that mean? Does it refer to the availability of services, or the underlying hardware or network? Does it mean 99 percent of the time in a full calendar year, or in a prescribed 12-hour timeframe? In the Internet world, this simply does not work. A 24/7 operation means availability every day of the year for 24 hours a day, with no "ifs" or "buts." From chapter 1 onward, this book proposes a more meaningful metric, the User Outage Minute (UOM). This basic building block reflects a binary view of the service: either you have it or you don't. You can also better measure services and associate different values against them based on the user's wants and needs. You need to base your whole on-line operation on UOMs, and build everything throughout the operation to meet them.

In some industries, a few organizations have been able to provide close to continuous on-line operations. For example, financial institutions have been grappling with this problem for decades, specifically with electronic retail-banking services (cash, credit, and debit). They have become proficient in risk management and working towards measuring everything in terms of UOMs. This formula for success has followed the fundamental principles laid out in this book.

Summary

In summary, I leave you with a simple philosophy: project success is based on planning, making the right investment decisions, thinking through the consequences of going on-line and always having a contingency ready.

The photograph in Figure 9.1 shows *Olympic* and *Titanic* together for the last time. Both ships were identical, yet one ship had a 24-year career, while the other had one of only six days. Which reflects your project?

Figure 9.1: Olympic and Titanic, together for the last time.

Epilogue

A final word on the two enquiries, *Titanic*, White Star, and the survivors: Most authors and historians agree that the disaster had a significant effect on society. It did more than shake up maritime transportation. It jolted the public's level of confidence in technology and the industrial society.

U.S. Inquiry and Changes to Maritime Transportation

A disaster of *Titanic*'s proportion was probably the only single event that could shake up the shipping companies into making changes and introducing safety standards. The U.S. inquiry led to the following changes:

- The International Conference for the Safety of Life at Sea (SOLAS) approved the following resolution in November 1913: "When ice is reported on or near his course, the Master of every vessel is bound to proceed at night at a moderate speed or to alter his course, so as to go well clear of the danger zone."

- In 1913, the International Ice Patrol organization was created, financed by the nations that used the North Atlantic shipping lanes. The sea lanes were patrolled during the period of greatest iceberg danger, in the January-to-August timeframe.

- The number of lifeboats was increased on ships to "a place for every soul."

- After the sinking, Morse code was installed as the standard communication for ships at sea by most maritime nations. At an international conference, convened three months after the disaster, the SOS distress signal was adopted. The signal was adopted merely because it was an easily recognizable letter sequence of three dots, three dashes, and three dots. However, it became popularly known as "save our souls" or "save our ship."

- The wireless became accepted as an important safety device. Each ship required two radio operators to cover the 24-hour day. No longer was the wireless seen as a tool to entertain passengers.

- The southern Atlantic route was moved even farther south by 60 miles during the summer, to avoid any risk of iceberg collision.

- The German liner *Imperator*, built in 1912 after the disaster, was delayed by the addition of an inner skin, which extended above the water line in the forward compartments. The space between was 5 feet and was filled with water to test the tightness of the skins.

Titanic's *Impact on History*

Titanic was a product of the Industrial Revolution. Indeed, it was one the greatest technological superstructures of its time. The disaster not only sank this wonderful ship and caused a horrendous loss of life. It also had a huge impact on society and its attitudes, and brought the world population together for a short time. Later shipping disasters had a much greater loss of life. For example, the German ship *Wilhelm Gustloff* sunk in the Baltic in 1945, with at least 5,200 people. However, other disasters have not had the public attention that *Titanic* has.

The Fate of *Titanic's* Sister Ships

During *Titanic*'s very short career, she was said to have been the largest ship at that time. That honor reverted back to *Olympic* until the *Britannic* was launched on February 26, 1914. *Olympic* was nearly identical to *Titanic* and weighed slightly less, due to some improvements on *Titanic*. After the sinking, *Olympic* was refitted with a double hull above the watermark, making her the weight champion.

Britannic had all *Olympic*'s improvements, as well as other safety and convenience features, making her the largest. *Britannic* never entered passenger service. Right after she was completed, the British government invoked a clause on monies previously loaned White Star, and immediately had her gutted and refitted to be a hospital ship. She both entered and departed life as HMHS *Britannic*, and never filled the dream planned as RMS *Gigantic*. *Britannic* is still the largest wreck on the sea floor, sunk by a mine on November 21, 1916.

Olympic had an uneventful life, providing reliable service for White Star, with the following notable incidents:

- On the September 20, 1911, *Olympic* collided with the British Cruiser *Hawke* as the two proceeded down the Spithead Channel, 100 to 300 feet apart.

- *Olympic* was turned into a troop carrier during World War I and was attacked, but never damaged, by German torpedoes. She acquired the names "The Grand Old Lady of the North Atlantic" and "Old Reliable."

- *Olympic* was launched October 20, 1910, and arrived at Jarrow for scrapping October 13, 1935. *Olympic*'s interiors were sold off to various pubs around England.

- *Olympic* had been the largest ship in the world until *Queen Mary* was built in 1934.

Public Outrage

Both the captain and architect perished with *Titanic*. However, Director Bruce Ismay survived the disaster, to the shock of the public. He has been extensively criticized for this to this day. The general feeling was that he should have gone down with the ship. He was more responsible than anyone else onboard for the disaster. He left *Titanic* on collapsible boat C, and later defended his action to board the lifeboat by saying there were no other passengers waiting to get onboard. However, witnesses reported seeing Ismay push others out of the way to get on.

In 1912, Ismay resigned his position, but remained an executive with International Mercantile Marine until 1916. He lived a life out of the public view. He died at the age 74 from a stroke, in 1937. The British inquiry exonerated Ismay of improper conduct.

Appendix A:
Case Study for a New On-line Operation

This case study provides an insight into what could happen when an organization fails to take due diligence in creating a new on-line operation. It highlights how a chain of events and contributing factors can destabilize a mission-critical operation. The events described, which lead to a very severe outage, are based on actual events that occurred in a financial institution.

The organization had diligently invested over the years in a service-delivery environment to deliver a mission-critical operation. However, under tremendous competitive pressure to perform and deliver results quickly, the organization compromised—and paid the consequences.

The Organization

Titan is a (fictional) North American financial institution that provides retail financial services, including personal and commercial lending and deposits. The financial services are delivered through a network of 150 branches and an expanding geographic base supported by non-branch automated delivery from ATMs, telephone, self-service devices, and the Internet. Titan strives to be an alternative to the larger and "less caring" financial institutions.

Over five years, the growth of Titan's electronic business services has evolved the service-delivery environment to a mission-critical status based on fault-tolerant front-end processors (*FEPs*) and a high-availability host server. The growth of the Internet and emerging technologies has further extended the mission-critical aspects of the environment.

The Problem

In recent years, Titan has fallen under severe competitive pressure for its top retail customers. Through the use of emerging technologies, Titan's competitors are better able to target with superior products and service offerings Titan's most profitable customer segments.

Titan has had to react very quickly to retain its most valuable customer segments. It decided on a two-point approach: improve the range of products and services, and better target these at customers. Titan would extend its offerings through a partnership with an insurance provider. Each party would be able to target-market mutual customer segments. This required a "technology bridge" to provide collaborative information and leverage the common customer base.

The Solution

To enable this bridge strategy, a "partner portal" solution was drawn up, available to insurance brokers and financial advisors from the respective organizations. This would improve customer interactions and give both organizations a unified picture over the course of every contact its intermediaries had over the Internet, telephone, ATM, and in person. This access to contact history would help provide a consolidated view of customers across both organizations and various business units. This would help maintain and build a single business relationship for the entire customer base. The organization would benefit from increased customer loyalty, improved retention, productivity, and reduced costs, as shown in Figure A.1.

The project was driven by Titan's IT organization, namely solution services (as shown in Figure A.2), who were under some pressure to demonstrate success following a couple of errant projects. The solution would require the integration of pertinent customer information from both companies systems into one shared "data mart," readily accessible through the password-restricted partner portal. Both organizations could select information for sharing, and from its internal systems, extract, transform, and load the information into the data mart. Both organizations could use the portal as an interchange for collecting information on new customers through weekly updates. Brokers and advisors could relatively easily pass on new information on customers. This was one of the simpler approaches. The alternative would have required complex integration across the two organizations.

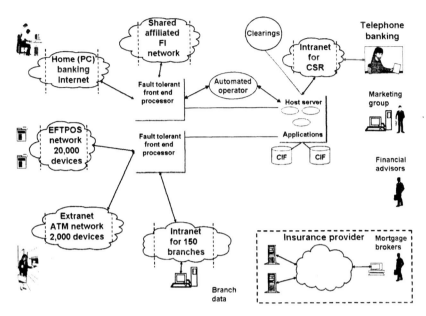

Figure A.1: In the existing service-delivery environment, the Customer Information File (CIF) holds the database of customer records. The insurance provider's systems (bottom right) are not integrated into the environment.

Solving the Problem

Solution services searched the marketplace for a ready-made solution to provide the required capability, or at least a solution that could be rapidly customized. They found a vendor that had created a similar solution for a financial institution in Europe to market profitable customers and increase the ratio of products. From the financial institution's viewpoint, the solution helped create a more accurate profile of the current state of a customer. It enhanced operations by improving cross-selling capabilities of multiple services to one customer through targeted marketing. The solution also provided the institution the ability to quickly cross-reference customers with all their financial products and services and build up a richer profile of customers and usage patterns. As a result, it enhanced the institution's ability to predict the products and services a customer was likely to buy. From the customer's viewpoint, the financial institution could offer a more personalized model to better serve the customer. The solution promised a lot for Titan.

Solution services reached an agreement with the vendor to complete a pilot. Titan would leverage the experience gained from the European project, pay royalties to the institution, and implement in a very short four-week timeframe. The vendor would install the technology for the pilot and, working with a third-party integrator, implement the application software taken from the European project. The integrator would then make some minor modifications and customize the application software to Titan's requirements—all fairly straightforward and requiring a relatively modest effort.

The project risk was assessed as low because the created services were not business-critical as there were no interdependencies with the mission-critical, transaction-based business services like ATM, POS, or home banking. As a result, the project timelines were condensed and the first stage of testing was omitted. Functional testing would be done on the pilot, which would then be implemented directly into the live environment.

Solution Creation

As the pilot got underway, the marketing department became interested. Marketing saw it as an opportunity to resolve some of its own business problems. The department was unhappy with response rates to most marketing campaigns, with a figure of under 5 percent because of lack of access to good, accurate on-line customer information.

Customer records were held in the Customer Information File (*CIF*) on the mainframe (host). However, the CIF lacked a lot of critical on-line information, such as an up-to-date snapshot of customer services and an indication of customer events required for marketing. Solution services, under pressure from the marketing department, agreed to meet this requirement and provide extended capabilities for direct-mail marketing and demographic branch telemarketing. Information would be extracted from the data mart, consolidated, formatted, and downloaded to the CIF. This extension was deemed low risk because, after all, the data from the data mart would be clean and have a high integrity.

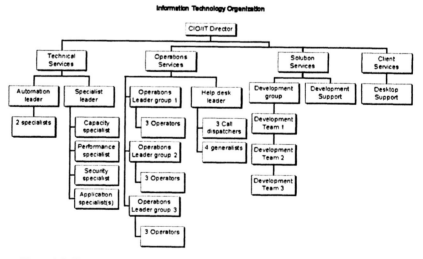

Figure A.2: Titan's Information Technology Organization.

Implementation

As the project neared completion, solution services requested operations services to implement the solution into the live environment in the next planned downtime window. This was a mere 48 hours away. Operations services was aware of the project, but expected the delivery time to take longer and undergo first-stage testing. Surprised, operations services insisted on postponing the implementation until the incoming change could be fully investigated and assessed for risk from an operational standpoint. However, the business pressures to go live were very high, and so this request was overridden with the help of the CIO. Solution services was adamant that the business risk was low.

At midnight on Sunday, operations services initiated the planned outage window and shut down the environment. The team went ahead and implemented the list of required changes. The planned outage went according to schedule and, surprisingly, everything came back up in a normal state. By early Monday morning, the new implementation, shown in Figure A.3, had been running smoothly without a glitch. After 12 hours of functional testing, the user acceptance team declared the implementation had passed acceptance. Solution services began to celebrate.

Meanwhile, in the operations center, the atmosphere was cautious. The team knew it was far too early in the implementation to objectively make a judgment. This was an implementation that had been rushed into service, bypassing the change-management process designed to protect the live environment. All the interdepartmental discussions and recommendations related to risky changes and following operating procedures had been ignored. The team carried out a thorough assessment of the live environment to accurately determine the impact of the new implementation. Operations remained extra vigilant for environmental anomalies or discrepancies.

Anomaly Noticed

On Tuesday afternoon, one of the junior operators noticed an anomaly on the host server. One of the processors was intermittently hitting a high utilization rate, even peaking at 100 percent. There was definitely a problem, and it would no doubt be affecting a number of applications, services, and, therefore, customers. The problem was immediately escalated to other team members. Neither the systems operators nor the network operators could identify its source. Everything was displayed as up and running, and appeared to be normal, except for a few application error messages that appeared from one of the application processes.

Based on previous experience, the operators knew they had to investigate the problem before it manifested into something serious. Like a ripple effect, these things have a habit of triggering problems in other parts of the service-delivery environment through bottlenecks and resource contention. Within the center, this was known as the "domino effect."

Some of the core application processes were stopped and restarted. After an hour or so, the messages reappeared, but the utilization on the processor had decreased to 80 percent. It was getting late in the evening, and the problem was now in a stable condition, as transaction rates decreased for that time of day. Further escalation was postponed until the morning.

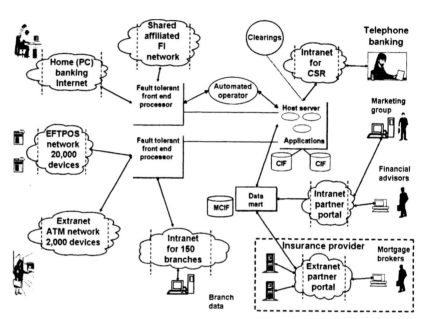

Figure A.3: In the new service-delivery environment, the insurance provider's environment is integrated with the data mart into Titan's environment (bottom right) through an extranet and a partner portal to provide access for insurance brokers. The financial advisors and marketing department access the data mart through the partner portal over the intranet. The host has a network link to the data mart to support the marketing department requirements and the interchange of data.

Everything Looks Normal, But with Some Dissatisfied Customers

On Tuesday evening, the operations center received calls from one of its competitors on the affiliated shared financial-institution network, which interchanges debit and credit transactions between competitive bank service-delivery environments. (For example, a customer might use a Titan debit card at a merchant supported by a competitor's network and POS devices.) One of the institutions customer's (a cardholder) had complained because she could not direct-debit her account through a retailer's Point of Sale (POS) device, the service provided by Titan. It led to an embarrassing situation in the store, where the retail clerk refused the customer.

The institution asked Titan to examine its debit services. The operators were still encountering application error messages, but there was no disruption within the live environment, everything was up and running, and so there was some concern and a degree of caution. The business-service failure for one retailer was related to resource contention and utilization problems.

Around 08:00 on Wednesday morning, the operators continued to escalate the problem. The help desk continued to receive calls from retailers complaining of loss of service and very dissatisfied customers. The symptoms of the problem were still randomly exhibited in the environment by high processor utilization on the host server and intermittent business-service failures in different locations.

Escalation, But Problem Disappears

The escalation process was moved up a level, so the operations-services managers got involved. This type of problem was not common, but had been encountered before. However, it was unusual for problems to be occurring so early in the week, when the transaction volumes were low. An investigation was set up, and more staff were allocated. The experienced management team decided on a top-down strategy that would start by looking at the whole environment. The team got to work, aided by technical services, who were dispatched to site.

By the end of the workday, there was no determination of the problem's root cause. However, the team determined that they could improve the situation by proactively managing the load balancing, and moving the resources around as required. On completion of these activities, all the dashboard indicators showed normal, and the problem just disappeared. The application error messages stopped, and there was a noticeable improvement in processor utilization. Relief swept over the operations center; maybe it was a minor glitch after all.

Further Problem Determination

Early on Thursday morning, the processor problem reoccurred. However, there were no application error messages. Throughout the day, the situation deteriorated, and the detailed investigation continued. By evening, the situation had become critical, and, to the surprise of operations, a work-around had not been found. The host server was all but at a standstill; of the four processors, three were at 100 percent, and one was at 80 percent utilization. The operators were confused because, apart from the very slow response rate, all the other indicators seemed normal.

Early on Thursday afternoon, one of the technical-services analysts investigated the automated operator. He noticed that it had been very busy. The level of interactions was way beyond what was expected in a normal period. Further investigation revealed a number of important things. First, the automated operator had attempted to resolve the worsening situation on the host server, but without much success. Unfortunately, its actions had obscured visibility from operations services. It had been acting on incoming messages without alerting operations, so everything seemed fine on the surface. However, because of the volume of incoming messages, the automated operator had reached a threshold and was in dire trouble itself. It had caught itself up in a continuous loop and was further affecting the host processor's utilization.

The team determined the best course of action was to reinitialize the automated operator and clear it from loop. However, a lot of risk was associated with this, as it had not been done in a long time. The automated operator was designed to support the environment and prevent problems from occurring. Turning it off could spark off a set of secondary problems in the environment. The overall situation was becoming desperate, so a decision had to be made quickly.

Automated Operator Turned Off

The automated operator was turned off, but this action just worsened the situation. Incoming credit and debit transactions were being rejected, and the help desk and operations center phones were ringing continuously. Worse still, this was the beginning of the peak period for transaction volumes. Thursday was busy, but Friday and Saturday were the busiest shopping days, especially since it was before Christmas. The team only then realized how dependent the environment had become on the automated operator. For years, automation had progressed at a breakneck speed, driven by a small team. The objective was to drive down costs and improve the environment operability. Only on one previous occasion had the automated operator been switched off, and the consequences had been manageable. However, this shutdown exemplified how much had changed in a short time and the dangers of indiscriminate automation.

By Friday morning the situation became intolerable, as client services were flooded by retailer calls. Years of painstaking relationship-building was being eroded, as retailers switched to other financial-service providers. Late in the morning, the First County Bank advised Titan that it was disconnecting Titan from its network due to poor service and failure to accept customer transactions. The bank also proceeded to inform other member financial institutions sharing the affiliated network of the situation. This was becoming very embarrassing for Titan's IT management.

The Scope of the Problem

The team had determined the scope of the problem. There was a huge transaction build-up (mainly POS transactions) on the link into the host server from the FEP servers and the network that connected all the POS devices out in the field. The POS transactions received by the FEP server were queuing on the server, waiting for authorization from the host server. The FEP server applications had a time limit; if a transaction was not returned in time, it was registered as a reversal and sent to the log file. The POS device was likely to decline the transaction with "no authorization" for the cardholder if the wait time was too long. (This depended on the intelligence of the POS terminal; some would wait indefinitely.) The retailer or consumer was likely to swipe the card a second or even a third time, adding to the number of transactions generated and further increasing the length of the queues, thus worsening the situation. The log files on the FEP servers were likely to get quickly filled in such a situation.

Once transactions were reversed in a debit situation, the capacity was doubled. The link bottlenecked with transactions and ran up the host server resources to a maximum. This alone seemed to be causing the processors to peak at 100 percent utilization. After a while, the only processing the environment completed was transaction reversal, and effectively the host server ground to a standstill. By any measurement, this was the equivalent of a full outage, as shown in Figure A.4.

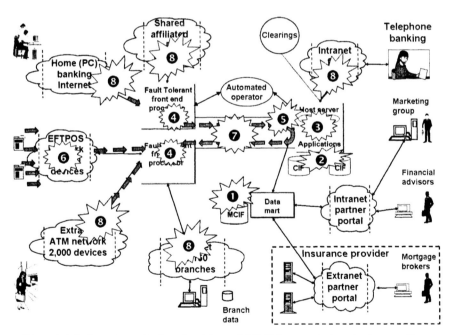

Figure A.4: In the outage situation, the data mart CIF (1) is corrupted, and subsequently corrupts the host CIF (2). As a result, applications behave abnormally (3) and cannot process incoming retail POS transactions routed via the FEP (4). The host fails to process the transaction volumes, and so rejects individual transactions back to the retailer with "no authorization"(5). The retailer re-swipes the card, thus increasing the volume build-up (6). Eventually, the transactions bottleneck in the FEP and the link to the host, driving the host processors to 100% utilization, effectively an outage (7). All the major banking service are affected (8).

At this point, the team had determined that the cause of the problem was the automated operator, and had found a solution. The problem related to inconsistencies in the rules base that created multiple, diametrically opposed actions. It was put back on-line, but it was still failing to cope with the huge overload of application errors and reacting to these without much effect, further masking the problem instead of resolving it. No one had envisaged such large volumes of incoming error messages.

Call in the Cavalry

Throughout the day, various financial-institution members had been advising Titan they were disconnecting Titan from their networks. Titan would be faced with stiff penalties, which drew the attention of senior executives and staff outside of IT. By the afternoon, the team was running out of options, and all the available staff were involved in the investigation. The only other option was to go to all the external service-delivery suppliers for help. The team was still decongesting the network's entry point into the host by increasing the number of processes handling the bottleneck and the priority of those processes.

The third-party integrator who had been hired to help implement the project arrived, and, following a quick debriefing, proceeded with a root-cause analysis. Its objective was to determine why the transactions were being reversed and why the host was timing-out transactions.

The team reviewed the files on the host from the point where the transactions were being rejected. Following a logical process map and using an inventory model, they noticed that the data mart also accessed the transaction authorization files. The data mart was being used to update the host CIF with information collected from the insurance brokers and financial advisors. This was too much of a coincidence. The data mart had to be contributing to the problem. It was the only recent major change in the environment. To confirm this, the team scrutinized a list of all the most recent changes to the service-delivery environment. Within a short timeframe, it was determined that the data mart had corrupted several critical files on the host CIF, and this was causing the host applications to behave abnormally by timing-out on incoming transactions. The team recommended to cut the data mart's link into the host. The impact was assessed, and this recommendation was enacted.

By evening, the situation had improved, with processor utilization at a more normal level. Transaction rejection had decreased, and the database specialist had started to evaluate the extent of the corruption. The team completed a risk assessment of the situation and determined the high financial losses to-date. To avoid further costs, the team would have to proceed with a full shutdown and reinitialization of the host at the earliest possible moment.

To Shut Down or Not

It was just past midnight on Saturday morning, and the operations services managers were still meeting. They recognized the need for a *cold load* of the environment, which involves shutting the environment completely down, powering off, and then restarting everything. Perhaps they would even need to restore the *system image* on the host, to replace the potentially corrupt image. This is typically a major activity, measured in hours.

The operations services managers hesitated to do this, for two reasons. First, Saturday was the busiest day of the week for most retailers. Second, not enough was known about the overall problem, and there were a lot of unknown variables. The risk was enormous. If anything should go wrong with the cold load and restoration, there would not be enough time to get through Saturday, the most critical day of the week for Titan's merchants and clients. Besides, the situation had improved when the data mart had been disconnected, and the evening had ended on a much calmer note.

The managers reviewed the risk and decided to proceed through Saturday without any further changes, and then go through a cold load on Sunday morning. Through further analysis, the team would get to the root of the problem. The operators were split on this difficult decision. Many of them were worried that so much corruption had occurred it was only prudent to move back to a clean environment. However, the situation had improved, there were a lot of unknowns, and Saturday was a critical day for Titan's clients.

Loss of Control

The operators were ready and vigilant at 09:00. The morning shift proceeded smoothly. Utilization rates appeared fairly normal, and there were no retailer calls. However, around lunchtime, the situation changed abruptly for the worse. Without much warning, the utilization rates on the host shot up. The operators determined that system resources had started to become very scarce. By mid-afternoon, the situation had become as precarious as the day before. The help desk was swamped with calls from very angry retailers and dissatisfied customers. Titan's management were also calling the operations center, which had the effect of inhibiting progress, rather than helping, as anxious managers distracted the team with questions.

The operators diagnosed that the CIF on the host was so badly corrupted that a number of the applications were behaving abnormally. The host was *thrashing* as it moved from task to task without completing any. As a result, the processor utilization rates reached 100 percent, and the environment appeared in a down state to the clients and the user community. It was 16:00, a peak period on a Saturday.

The options were very limited. The domino, or ripple, effect was occurring, with problems spreading to other applications and servers. The team started taking down the least critical applications in an effort to maintain some of the more critical business services. This was agreed to by the business side. There was no point in trying to maintain all business services, but to cut the losses and focus just on the most critical. The signs were encouraging, as the utilization rates dropped by 30 percent and the resource situation improved. At this point, the operations services managers decided that they would proceed with a cold load at midnight.

Shutdown, Restoration, and Back On-line

Just past midnight on Sunday morning, the team shut down the host server. For 72 hours, the live environment had been in a partial down state, although up to 80 percent of the users would have viewed it in a complete down state, as various business services were unavailable to them. This was the busiest period of the week for retailers. From a business perspective, the situation was unacceptable, and Titan was going to be liable for many stiff penalties and costs if not direct lawsuits. Technically, the host server had not been completely down, but it was hampered in handling business-critical transactions. The situation also had an adverse impact on the FEP servers, which also needed to be shut down and reinitialized.

The team agreed to get the environment up and running by 09:00. A nine-hour planned outage window would allow for a controlled shutdown of the host server and FEPs and a full restoration of the system image of the CIF from week-old tapes. However, the CIF would then require a roll forward, as daily information was updated. This would take most of Sunday, but at least the system would be up and running. There was no room for mistakes. The data mart had corrupted the CIF, but the extent of the corruption had not been determined.

Over six hours, the team restored the master CIF. The host was made available to a test team, to scan for operational functionality, inconsistencies, and any corruption. After three hours of thorough testing, they gave the go-ahead to go back on-line. At approximately 09:00, the environment was brought up. However, the data mart remained completely detached from the live environment. The team was not willing to take the risk and put it back on-line without thorough testing. The team would force this decision to the highest level in the corporation. For the next few days, the environment was closely monitored. A couple of "hiccups" occurred, but these anomalies were fixed by small initializations.

Recovery Meeting and Press Statement

By Sunday afternoon, the previous day's problems had reached the attention of the CEO. The first action of the CEO's office was to call each of the executives directly at home to meet at 06:00 the next morning. On no account was anyone to talk to the press. Some serious damage control was required to pacify some of Titan's top retail clients.

By Monday, the executive group was fully aware of the extent of problems and met to consider a mitigation strategy, with the financial losses so high. They prepared for likely liability actions and wrote a press statement to be issued by the public relations office. A few disgruntled users had called the press during the last 24 hours, and the CEO's office received the first of many calls from client executives. The executive group developed a clear story based on two themes. First, new, untested technology had been provided by an unscrupulous vendor. Second, poor decisions were made by operations services. Titan had to appease clients quickly and curb any further bad press. The executives believed that the vendor could easily ride out the storm and just drop the solution. Here is there statement:

> _Titan wishes to apologize to its customers for any inconvenience caused by the loss of ATM and Direct Debit services over the 25th and 26th of November. The loss of service was due to a computer malfunction caused by the implementation of new technology, and inadequate operational procedures. Measures have been taken to ensure this problem does not reoccur._

Reaction to the press release was very positive. At least the institution came clean and had taken action by dismissing operations services staff, even though they were fairly blameless compared to the CIO, marketing, and support services.

Lessons learned

There are a number of major lessons to consider:

- _Wrong business drivers for success_—The rationale for the project was misguided. The CIO and IT organization, criticized for poor customer service, were motivated to find a quick win. However, they did not look at the core problems carefully, articulate business requirements, or define the potential costs and possible risks. In addition, the marketing department's requirements took the project further off track. The solution was too loosely attached to the business problem, too many assumptions were made, and too few questions were asked. The project was not well qualified, with no risk assessment undertaken. The initiative should have been business driven. By the time of construction, it was apparent that solution services was motivated to drive the project quickly through to implementation, without completing all the project stages. They kept tight project control by not disclosing information.

- _No track record or North American references from vendor_—This should have set off alarm bells. Solution services were also depending on the vendor to provide resources, hence reducing internal resource requirements.

- _Product implementation versus construction_—Organizationally, there was confusion over the project's type. Solution services saw the project as a product implementation initiative rather than an integration, construction, and assembly initiative. As a result, project ownership and responsibility was not clearly laid out.

- *Eventual testing based on application or functional testing*—The testing should have included integration, simulation, operational, and other types of testing (as discussed in chapters 4 and 5). Solution services dismissed the testing phase as irrelevant, but they were too inexperienced in ascertaining its importance and should not have been put in a position to make this decision.

- *Operations services brought in too late and kept out of the project by solution services*—Experience indicates that operations services are the best-positioned group to own the change-management process, based on their day-to-day interactions with the environment. Solution services should have handed over a functionally tested change to operations for assessment, and then took a step back as a battery of tests was invoked. The change-management process should outline all the responsibilities.

- *No stopping the implementation*—Operations services completed a risk analysis of the implementation, but it was too late to have an impact. The project could not be halted, even with the serious misgivings of operations services. The change-management process lacked the political support in the organization at a senior level and the "teeth" to be effective. The process needed a strong champion.

- *"Don't count your chickens…"*—Problems might not occur right after an implementation. Solution services celebrated success too early, when they should have kept monitoring the whole environment for at least a week, especially if the implementation was deemed a high risk.

- *Investigation delayed*—Any environmental anomalies or problems should be investigated quickly and thoroughly, using the problem-management process to ensure there are no delays.

- *Problems with the automated operator*—The automated operator inhibited operations services from effective problem-determination, as it obscured the problem. As a result, operations were flying almost blind, with little visibility into the environment and what was really happening. Shutting it down worsened the situation because of the dependencies on it.

- *Uncontrolled changes*—The service-delivery environment was designed for high availability, but even with this high level of protection, it was susceptible and at risk uncontrolled incoming changes. This is very common where organizations invest in high-availability technology, but fail to match this in their processes and organization

- *Procrastination to shut down*—Only a complete shutdown, rebuild, and restoration from an archived image restored the environment to stability. Procrastination to proceed with the shutdown and restore further increased the outage losses. Operations services were just onlookers.

- *Management response needed*—Executive management had to respond to customers, the public, and the press to preserve the company's image. An outage as visible as this could not be swept under the carpet.

Conclusion

The Titan environment was designed as a mission-critical operation with high availability. Even with large investments in technology for protection, it was affected by a poorly managed on-line operation project that made major compromises. Executives could have prevented the disaster if the right questions were asked at the right time, and corrective actions taken.

Many organizations perceive the running and operation of a service-delivery environment as mainly a technical discipline, with little business and customer interaction. This has isolated and marginalized the role of operations services in the mainstream of many organizations, and the status of operations services has subsequently been downgraded compared to the more prestigious solution services. The Titan case study demonstrates how operations services are ignored and taken out of the decision process. In reality, the operations services function is very much focused on the business, its services, and its integrity. Operators are the last people to touch the business service before it reaches the customers, and so are best positioned to improve quality and prevent a service outage or disaster.

In many organizations, the operations services group fails to get well-organized. High business growth, pressures to keep operating costs down, and underfunding lead to operations services working in a pressured environment, acting reactively and chaotically. The group meets service levels, barely, but becomes adept in keeping operational problems "under the covers," so that they don't affect users and can possibly go for long periods without coming to the attention of management. Occasionally, however, a major problem leads to an expensive and prolonged outage, and leaks out. As a result, the overall costs far outweigh any savings. Underfunding is counterproductive, as the large effort required in keeping operations services going is detrimental to staff morale.

Also, many organizations have the perception that automation will eventually replace human operators through autonomous and self-healing environments. However, this is unlikely in today's perpetually changing environments, which require ongoing changes managed through a well-defined process.

Appendix B:
Outage Classes

The following table divides outages into five classes. Four are related to unplanned downtime caused by faulty systems, poor design, operator error, or disasters. The fifth relates to planned outages due to reconfiguration.

Table B.1: Outage Classes and Classifications Table

Class 1. Physical Outages

There is a complete loss of external power; internal batteries protect memory for a few hours.

There is a dual-system component failure, when two components fail simultaneously.

External data communications fail; equipment outside of the environment can fail.

A database fails to read or write, or a network router fails.

The emergency power-off switch is hit by mistake.

Class 2. Design Outages

Software is improperly coded.

A processor fails, caused by a memory-management error.

LAN software fails.

The database is corrupted by a program.

Table B.1: Outage Classes and Classifications Table (continued)

The system is poorly designed for operators.

Environmental startup files are problem-prone, so objects are brought up incorrectly.

A device like a tape floods the system with messages.

An application fails to receive an acknowledgment and hangs, due to poor integration.

A transaction in an incorrect state pulls down the Transaction Monitoring Facility.

Class 3. Operations Outages

Screens are accidentally deleted from production files.

An operating system is incorrectly installed so that users are unable to log on.

The wrong file is purged, crashing the environment.

An incorrect command is issued, causing the application to stop.

Alerts and problems go unnoticed.

Fixing something causes another problem, for example, lack of care using passwords.

An operator takes erroneous actions based on poor information.

Class 4. Environmental Outages

The infrastructure fails because of power lines, cooling systems, or network connections.

Natural disasters occur, such as hurricanes, earthquakes, floods, or fire.

An accidents occurs, such as damage caused by construction crews.

The system is the victim of intentional acts of violence, such as arson, terrorist bombings, and riots.

A fiber-optic cable is cut, bringing down the network.

The power goes out throughout the city.

A fire at a branch office destroys the automated teller machines.

Class 5. Reconfiguration Outages (Downtime Required for Maintenance)

Backup copies of data are made.

Technology migrations and reconfigurations are performed.

Communications are reconfigured.

Major new services, application releases, or software upgrades are installed.

The database is reorganized, restructured, or backed up.

A client is added or moved.

Appendix C:
Business Case for *Titanic*

The following diagram supports *Titanic's* business case in chapter 1. The focus was on increasing revenue through superior service, and decreasing costs. A staggering 75 percent of the total fare revenue was based on first class.

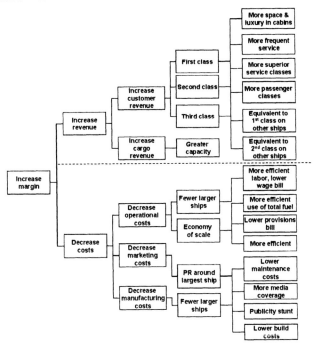

Figure C.1: White Star's business case for the 3 liners.

The following table outlines a profitability analysis White Star might have used in mitigating the construction of the three liners, based on the total projected cash flow on a pre-tax basis. A breakeven point is reached five years into the project, in 1912. The numbers are based on a maximum carrying capacity of 100 percent. An average 70-percent capacity would have been more realistic.

1909	1910	1911	1912	1913	1914	1915	1916
			Atlantic Crossings				
0	0	8	17	17	17	17	17
0	0	0	6	17	17	17	17
0	0	0	0	0	6	17	17
0	0	8	23	34	40	51	51
			Projected Revenue from Fares				
0	0	7,830,000	22,511,250	33,277,500	39,150,000	49,916,250	49,916,250
0	0	1,974,000	5,675,250	8,389,500	9,870,000	12,584,250	12,584,250
0	0	272,160	782,460	1,156,680	1,360,800	1,735,020	1,735,020
0	0	40,000	115,000	170,000	200,000	255,000	255,000
0	0	10,116,160	29,083,960	42,993,680	50,580,800	64,490,520	64,490,520
			Solution Investments and Operatinal Costs (fixed and variable)				
9,000,000	9,000,000						
		900,000	900,000	900,000	900,000	900,000	900,000
		360,000	1,035,000	4,000,000	4,600,000	6,000,000	6,000,000
		1,986,320	5,710,670				
		709,400	2,039,525	400,000	460,000	600,000	600,000
		80,000	230,000	400,000	460,000	600,000	600,000
9,000,000	9,000,000	4,035,720	9,915,195	5,700,000	6,420,000	8,100,000	8,100,000
			Profit				
-9,000,000	-9,000,000	6,080,440	19,168,765	37,293,680	44,160,800	56,390,520	56,390,520

Appendix D:
Risk in On-line Operation Projects

Risk is "the chance of injury or loss or bad consequence." It equates to the chance of financial losses. The unavailability of on-line operations is expressed in cost and customer dissatisfaction. It requires a set of procedures for reviewing, monitoring, auditing, and signing off risk. The processes are intended to achieve the following:

- As early as possible in the project, identify potential risks associated with unavailability and on-line operations that are sufficiently high to warrant actions.

- Ensure that the associated risks are fully identified, evaluated, eliminated, and contained to provide a sound basis for providing acceptable on-line operations.

- Prevent the implementation of change that could disrupt business services, and provide a baseline for continued risk avoidance and contingency measures.

Risk Management Processes

PMBOK (the *Project Management Book of Knowledge*) defines risk management as four processes:

- Risk identification

- Risk quantification

- Risk response development

- Risk response control

Risk Identification

Identify the risks that are likely to affect on-line operations. The following categories simplify identification and ramifications:

- *Business risk*—What are the risks to the business operations, services, or users?

- *Project risk*—What are the project risks that need attention? What are their impacts on the project? Who is the project prime? What is his or her experience, track record, and approach?

- *Technical risk*—Is the on-line operation built for availability? Will it integrate readily into the existing service-delivery environment? What is the impact?

- *Process risk*—What is the impact on the processes protecting the environment? Is the change-control process set up to handle incoming changes, like the on-line operation?

- *Organizational risk*—Is the organization set up to support the on-line operation's availability? What is the impact on the organization? Does it have the skill sets?

- *Automated risk*—What is the impact on automation supporting the environment? Will the automated operator recognize the new on-line operation and take actions?

- *Contractual risk*—For a new on-line operation, what are the additional contractual penalties and liabilities that need to be understood?

In addition, the risk of *financial cost* is applicable to all the above risks.

Risk Quantification

As shown in Table D.1, identified risk categories are evaluated for size and probability of materializing.

Table D.1: Identified Risk Categories

Risk Size	Definition	Consequences
Very high	The ability to maintain business services is in doubt.	Major organization exposure through financial loss, breach of contract, and loss of credibility.
High	Business services will probably be affected.	Significant exposure due to downtime, contractual liabilities, and loss of customer credibility.
Medium	There is a potential impact to business services.	Likely to damage organization's position and require additional funding/resources to meet customer expectations.
Low	There is a minor negative impact to business services.	Easily resolved, but must be addressed to avoid "knock on" effect.
Unknown	There is not enough information to make an assessment.	Always used with an estimate of criticality, such as "High/Unknown."

Percentage factors are used to express the probability of risk: unavoidable (100%), negotiable (80%), preventable (50%), and containable (20%).

Risk Response Development

The responses to qualified risks fall into these categories:

- *Avoidance*—Eliminate the risk or take action to remove the threat.

- *Mitigation*—Reduce the risk by taking action to limit the possibility of occurrence.

- *Acceptance*—Accept the consequences and develop a contingency plan.

After each risk is ranked, it has to be assessed on merit and addressed accordingly. The urgency of action depends on the risk quantification, which determines the resolution time required, as shown in Table D.2.

Table D.2: Identified Response Time for Risk Categories		
Size	Time to Implementation	Time Available for Resolution
Very high	Immediate	None
High	Within 10 days	5 days
Medium	Within 20 days	10 days
Low	Within 30 days	25 days
Unknown	Treat as very high	Get more information

The following tools are used to deal with risk:

- *Procurement*—Products and services to respond to the risk.

- *Contingency planning*—Steps to be taken if a risk should occur.

- *Alternative strategies*—Changes to a planned action.

- *Insurance*—Financial coverage.

Risk Response Control

Address the risk by executing the risk-management plan and organizing tools to monitor and evaluate the response. Tools to deal with risk include workarounds and additional risk-response development.

Questionnaire for Assessing Your On-line Operation

The questionnaire in Table D.3 is designed to help assess the availability of your on-line operation. It should be referenced throughout your project. The questions are broad, and they will require input from your IT staff. Each "no" answer scores a point, so the total score can be compared to a baseline to determine acceptability. The questions are organize according to the inventory model introduced in chapter 2.

Table D.3: Identified Risk Categories

A	Services	Y	N
A.1	Can the environment (server/network) handle the maximum number of users?	0	1
A.2a	In a failover[1] situation, can the backup environment handle the maximum number of users for all the services?	0	1
A.2b	If not, are some services unavailable for the duration of the problem?	0	1
A.3	Is response time acceptable to users? Could response time be improved?	0	1

A score of more than 1 indicates high availability risk and the need for further evaluation.

B	Applications	Y	N
B.1	Are the applications sensitive to detect and react to a failover situation?	0	1
B.2	Are the applications capable of automatic startup of a failed process?	0	1
B.3a	Are the applications well-behaved and isolated from each other?	0	1
B.3b	Can the failure of one application adversely affect another application? (For example, a non-critical application, like a shareware package, might affect business applications.)	0	1
B.3c	How intelligent are the applications in handling errors? What happens if an application runs out of resources, such as disk space?	0	1

A score of more than 2 indicates high availability risk and the need for further evaluation.

C	Database	Y	N
C.1	Is on-line maintenance (such as creating indexes, adding columns, or moving partitions to different disks) possible without stopping services?	0	1
C.2a	Can business services remain on-line while the database is backed-up?	0	1
C.2b	If not, does stopping the application slow down response?	0	1
C.3a	Is the granularity of recovery at volume level, so only that database portion is unavailable?	0	1
C.3b	If not, at what level is it? The higher the level, the less available the application. Knowing what part of the database is out of service is important for help desks.	0	1
C.4	Does database recovery from a full outage take longer than 60 minutes?	0	1
C.5a	Can the application continue to operate in the presence of a database failure?	0	1
C.5b	If a disk volume is down, can the application run (informing user of missing data)?	0	1
C.6a	Can the database/application environment be maintained on-line (for things like the regeneration of a new image) without requiring a shutdown?	0	1

---

1. Failover is the ability of a function to switch over to an alternative location and continue to operate.

Table D.3: Identified Risk Categories (continued)

		0	1
C.6b	Can a device be integrated without affecting the applications that are currently executing?	0	1
C.6c	Can the environmental limits be raised on-line without an application shutdown?	0	1
C.6d	Can the application manage and allocate resources without shutdown?	0	1

A score of more than 6 indicates high availability risk and the need for further evaluation.

D	**Middleware**	**Y**	**N**
D.1a	Does the middleware support resource load-balancing around users/servers?	0	1
D.1b	Does the load-balancing prevent overloading a critical service?	0	1
D.2	Can the server dynamically handle increased loads and start up more servers?	0	1
D.3	Does the middleware support failover to a backup service?	0	1
D.4	Does the application use transactional integrity (where the whole transaction occurs or nothing occurs), to avoid data corruption and hence a possible outage?	0	1
D.5a	Does the application make use of two-phase commit[2] or replicated data?	0	1
D.5b	If not, could improperly synchronized data cause an application outage?	0	1
D.6	Does the organization make use of integration servers and enterprise application integration for integrating disparate applications?	0	1

A score of more than 3 indicates high availability risk and the need for further evaluation.

E	**Operating system**	**Y**	**N**
E.1a	Are the system files held on a separate file system? (Not applicable for all systems.)	0	1
E.1b	If not, could a runaway process cause an outage? If the file system runs out of space and creates temporary files or spool print jobs, will the system crash?	0	1
E.2	Can disk space be added on-line without affecting the database or application?	0	1

A score of more than 1 indicates high availability risk and the need for further evaluation.

F	**Network**	**Y**	**N**
F.1	Different types of redundancy increase availability by providing alternative paths, e.g., a complete duplication of network hardware requires an evaluation of the cost against the benefit. Alternate redundancy is to have a smaller, but less costly connection method, like a dial-up backup or an older front-end processor.		
F.2	Is there physical redundancy in the network? This is a critical networking issue.	0	1

2. Two-phase-commit ensures that all the "transaction writes" to a database either occur or not, so that the database is consistent.

Table D.3: Identified Risk Categories (continued)

	Do the following components have physical redundancy:		
F.2a	Host nodes?	0	1
F.2b	Host adapters?	0	1
F.2c	Wiring hubs?	0	1
F.2d	Bridges/routers?	0	1
F.2e	Communications lines?	0	1
F.2f	Front-end processors or switches?	0	1
F.3	Select the most applicable recovery from hardware failure, from the following options:		
F.3a	User intervention requires an operator or user to interact with the environment, for example, to place a call, turn a switch, or plug a cable into a different connector.	2	
F.3b	Programmatic recovery involves an automated programmer recognizing that a failure has happened, and then taking actions to recover from the failure.	1	
F.3c	Automatic recovery through the network is done without intervention by people or programs. It is desirable and similar to F.3b, but not custom, so it is lower-cost.	0	
F.4	Do the network protocols support error detection and recovery at different levels? For example, the TCP protocol of TCP/IP will detect missing packets and request a retransmission of them, whereas the UDP protocol does not, but if the application using the protocol handles error detection and recovery itself, then UDP is sufficient. The layer below TCP also needs to be considered. For example, if TCP/IP is running over a LAN, then packets could be lost. If, however, it is running over the X.25 protocol, then there is a smaller chance of loss because of the built-in X.25 functionality. Another issue is whether the protocol can recover automatically from failures/errors, or report the error to the application and let the application recover. This is similar to F.3c.	0	1
F.5	Are there enough paths with sufficient capacity in the backup network/paths?	0	1

A score of more than 4 (adding the two columns) indicates high availability risk and the need for further evaluation.

G	Network Configuration Issues	Y	N
G.1	Is there automatic detection and reconfiguration when failures are fixed?	0	1
G.2	Do backup facilities have to be preconfigured, or are they automated?	0	1
G.3a	Does reconfiguration happen automatically? Manual reconfiguration requires manual reconnection, while "automatic" reconfiguration causes network interruptions.	0	1
G.3b	Is there an issue with resource consumption for the standby configurations (such as preconfigured alternate paths versus automatically detected ones)?	0	1

A score of more than 2 indicates high availability risk and the need for further evaluation.

Table D.3: Identified Risk Categories (continued)		
H	**Operations**	**Y** **N**
H.1	Are tape backups cycled regularly (such as daily or weekly)?	0 1
H.2	Are backup/recovery tests run on a regular basis?	0 1
H.3	Are tapes carefully labeled physically, with written labels?	0 1
H.4	Is automatic tape-labeling supported? Can mislabeled tapes be identified?	0 1
H.5	If software compression is used, is it available for replacement environments?	0 1
H.6	Is backup media sent to the recovery center (to facilitate off-site recovery)?	0 1
H.7	If a temporary system is used for backing up, are absolute filenames used? Relative pathnames could have bad results if restored to the wrong file system.	0 1
H.8a	Are custom-developed scripts or batch files used to administer the system?	0 1
H.8b	How robust are they?	0 1
H.8c	Are they prepared for every contingency? If a recovery script fails to back up data, would it delete it? Operations scripts need to be simple and easy to maintain.	0 1
H.9a	Do on-line maintenance and administrative functions affect response times?	0 1
H.9b	If so, will applications be affected?	0 1
H.10a	Are the recovery procedures automated?.	0 1
H.10b	Are they fully automated? For example, is manual intervention required?	0 1
H.11a	Are system errors (event messages) identified for most situations?	0 1
H.11b	Are they logged or displayed on an operations dashboard?	0 1
H.11c	Is that station continually manned?	0 1
H.12	Are all the important and necessary errors logged?	0 1
H.13a	If network management is used, do the server, database, network and application all send traps (exceptions) to the operations dashboard?	0 1
H.13b	Are these traps cryptic? Can operators identify and correct them?	0 1
A score of more than 4 indicates high availability risk and the need for further evaluation.		
I	**Security**	**Y** **N**
I.1a	Is the security level adequate for the applications?	0 1
I.1b	Is the security level adequate for the users?	0 1
I.1c	Is the security level adequate for the environment?	0 1
I.2	Could disgruntled or careless employees bring down the entire environment?	0 1
I.3	Are there known security risks in the environment operating system? FAQs are available on the Internet for most commercial operating systems.	0 1

Table D.3: Identified Risk Categories (continued)

		Y	N
I.4	Is the environment secure from all access points (LAN, WAN, dial-up)?	0	1
I.5	Is the superuser password secure? Is it restricted and not used day-to-day?	0	1
I.6a	Do users need shell access?	0	1
I.6b	If not, are they limited to required programs or shell access by "interrupting" a program?	0	1

A score of more than 3 indicates high availability risk and the need for further evaluation.

J	**Hardware**	Y	N
J.1a	Does the organization practice "a pair and a spare" for crucial hardware components?	0	1
J.1b	Can the organization expect to procure one of these parts in less than eight hours?	0	1
J.2	Is recovery time for downed equipment less than one hour?	0	1
J.3	Are there any black-box components (working components that are unknown)?	0	1
J.4a	Is the environment free of any unsupported components?	0	1
J.4b	Is there a contingency plan for their failure?	0	1
J.5a	Do multiple servers provide the same service?	0	1
J.5b	Are there failover capabilities?	0	1
J.5c	Is there simple redundancy? Does intervention require a user or operator?	0	1
J.6a	Does the hardware have multiple processors?	0	1
J.6b	Can one processor failure cause the system to fail?	0	1
J.6c	Can the services restart in a degraded mode?	0	1
J.7	Are there redundant network connections?	0	1
J.8	Are disks mirrored across different controllers?	0	1

A score of more than 3 indicates high availability risk and the need for further evaluation.

K	**Development and Physical Environment**	Y	N
K.1a	Is the development environment segregated from the live environment?	0	1
K.1b	Could the development environment/network cause an outage?	0	1

A score of more than 1 indicates high availability risk and further evaluation.

L	**Power**	Y	N
L.1a	Are there power surge-suppressers?	0	1
L.1b	Is all equipment grounded? Do asynchronous lines use a frame/signal ground?	0	1
L.1c	Are communication lines the correct lengths and properly shielded?	0	1

Table D.3: Identified Risk Categories (continued)

L.2	Are any uninterruptible power supplies in place?	0	1
L.3	Are they configured to send a "powerfail" signal to the server?	0	1
L.4	Will applications gracefully shut down when aware of impending power failures?	0	1

A score of more than 2 indicates high availability risk and the need for further evaluation.

M	Vendors	Y	N
M.1	With incumbent vendors, is it apparent who to call when something goes wrong?	0	1
M.2	Does the support agreement cover all components and times? Is 24-7 needed?	0	1
1M.3	Will the vendor(s) respond within four hours when something critical happens?	0	1
M.4a	Can the vendor provide assistance in an emergency?	0	1
M.4b	Even if the emergency is acknowledged as the customer's fault?	0	1

A score of more than 2 indicates high availability risk and the need for further evaluation.

Appendix E
What to Expect from Your Project

Your project is likely to differ somewhat from traditional IT development projects, since it relates to an on-line operation that is mission-critical. On-line operation projects are unique because they:

Deal with an ill-defined subject that lacks consistent organization and definition, and covers a broad range of topics, from technology, process, and organization.

- Are difficult to justify, as the benefits tend to be bottom-line, in improved operating costs, rather than top-line in improved revenue or profits.

- Need to deal with an organization's tendency to focus on technology and hardware.

- Affect most departments in an organization, and should involve all stakeholders. Strong executive buy-in is needed from the outset. (After a major outage, of course, this is relatively simple to achieve.)

- Require incremental proof points to demonstrate value and maintain buy-in.

- Need to transition into the mainstream of operations.

In addition, your organization is likely to have existing project methods that you need to follow or consider.

Checklist of Basic Questions about Your Project

Before the project is approved, your team needs to answer the following basic questions:

- What business-critical problems need to be addressed? Why is availability important?

- What are the project's objectives and its scope?

- What are the principal activities? How much effort is required, in terms of resources?

- What are the deadlines for project completion? How long is the envisioned effort?

- What are the investment requirements? What is the business case to support this?

- What indicates that the project is complete? What are the critical success factors?

- What are the metrics to measure the impact of the solution?

- What SLAs will the solution have to meet?

Approaches to On-line Operation Projects

An on-line operation project goes through a lifecycle, but the approach varies. The four approaches are shown in Table E.1 and Figure E.1.

Table E.1: Approaches to On-line Operation Projects

Approach	Description	Positive Aspects	Negative Aspects
Waterfall	All the major activities are in a one-step approach that completes like a production line.	A very traditional and well-understood approach to projects.	There are at least 12 months before benefits are realized. The project might also get off track.
Incremental	Evolved as cost of large software-development projects escalated. The most costly stages of constructing and testing are delivered in increments.	Addresses the shortcomings of the waterfall approach by delivering benefits in structured increments.	Not flexible to changes in architecture and design.
Spiral	Evolved through systems-integration projects that were required in fast-changing environments, where the approach is iterative with different organizational groups.	Addresses the shortcomings of the incremental approach by focusing on rapidly changing requirements in stages 1, 2, and 3 of Figure E.1.	Not flexible to changes in construction and testing.
Evolutionary	Combines the incremental and spiral approaches, where the solution is evolved in small evolutions. This provides a tailored fit to business needs.	Addresses the shortcoming of all the previous approaches.	More chaotic than traditional projects. Requires experience at each evolution completes.

The evolutionary approach is the most effective for on-line operation projects for the following reasons:

- It catches major flaws a lot earlier, and so is more cost-effective than other approaches.

- It creates something quickly, so adjustments to scope can be readily made.

- It gets executive buy-in and organizational support by showing early success.

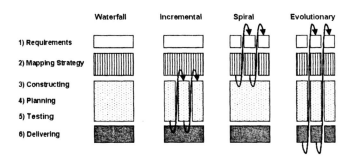

Figure E.1: Titanic's project approach was the waterfall. Yours should be evolutionary.

How to Decrease Project Risk

On-line operation projects have more risk associated with environmental failure. Many on-line operation projects fail because they do not follow a methodology that identifies and manages this risk. The evolutionary approach solicits and evolves business user requirements, and then constructs a prototype very quickly.

Making big announcements about a forthcoming project usually sets expectations very high, and the organization has to live up to these expectations. With *Titanic*, for example, the expectation was that it was the safest ship ever. Expectations need to be set for the project completion and shutdown.

The evolutionary approach is akin to a cycle repeatedly spinning around. At the start of a project, a *work breakdown structure* defines the activities, and groups them into cycles. Another view is a micro and macro approach, i.e., start small but scale fast. In each evolution, the model increases in functionality and availability. This approach allows the immediate testing of the working model early on. A feedback loop improves each evolution, by allowing lots of minor adjustments to be made quickly, which helps measure the overall progress and gauge the likelihood of success.

A Typical Project Team

Evolution 1 starts with a small team made up of a business consultant and solution architect. Evolution 2 adds a full-time project manager and specialists with different consulting skills. Evolution 3 includes integration specialists and development teams. The roles of the team members are as follows:

- *Project manager*—Responsible for the implementation and coordination of all the activities, and to complete the project on-time, on-budget, and to the client's satisfaction. Aware of UOMs and the impact of the project on the service-delivery environment. Directs all program-related activities and coordinates issues. Also responsible to the steering committee for the status of tasks and deliverables, and coordinates all related off-site activities necessary to complete the project.

- *Business consultant*—Responsible for the business requirements and justification of the project, establishing the value of business services, defining what is or is not an on-line operation, and the requirements for business availability. Takes the lead on stage 1 and acts as a guide to the solution architect in stage 2.

- *Solution architect*—Responsible for mapping the appropriate levels of availability to protect the business service, technical solution integrity, design of functions, and systems architecture. Also responsible for providing a consistent design philosophy for the development phases. Supports stage 1, takes the lead in stage 2, and acts as guide for stage 3.

- *Integration/development coordinator*—Responsible for all project construction and development; oversees integration teams, programming, documentation, and module testing. Works closely with the solution architect to ensure the development meets the architectural vision, functional requirements, conceptual design goals, and detailed design. Also works closely with the operations analyst to ensure that the implementation is free of technical complications. Leads stage 3.

- *Operations analyst*—A representative of operations services responsible for ensuring operations requirements are met and for coordinating subprojects oriented towards supporting the implementation and acceptance of the project. In this role, directs the teams for implementation preparation, documentation, implementation, production testing, and acceptance testing. Leads stage 4, 5, and 6.

- *Technical analysts*—Responsible for supporting requirements definition, design, test plans, programming, testing, and documentation. Supports stages 3, 4, 5, and 6.

- *Business user/service representative*—Works with the business consultant in stage and the operations analysts through stages 4, 5, and 6 for solutions acceptance.

- *Automation consultant*—Responsible for reviewing the solution's automation requirements and determining the relationship and impact on the automated operator.

- *Organizational and process consultants*—Required if the project needs organizational and process changes and alignments.

Project Effort for One Evolution

For each evolution, the project effort is increased. However, as shown in Figure E.2, the ratio of effort within the stages is consistent. In stage 1, the effort is concentrated up-front, but is ongoing through the evolution. Stages 4 and 5 (planning and testing) should be nearly as long as stage 3 (construction).

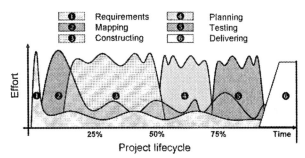

Figure E.2: The overall effort required in an on-line operation project cycles over time.

Project Shutdown

A traditional project depends on the completion of all objectives, measured through *Critical Success Factors* (CSFs). In on-line operation projects, this is not necessarily the case. The measure of success is through UOMs, which might take six months to collect.

Project Transition to Operations

The time gap to project benefits is important. The project should not just gently wind down and allow a post-project state to resume. The project needs to transition to operations and a continuous improvement program.

Education and Training Requirements

As part of the transition, operations need to be in a "ready" state. This goes beyond the experience gained in the previous evolutions. It is centered around education and training requirements.

Deliverables for Your Project

Table E.2 describes the deliverables by stage for your project, where the lead for a deliverable is indicated by the ● symbol, and those involved are indicated by ◗.

Table E.2: Project Deliverables

Project Task	Service Reps	Business End Users	Business Sponsor	IT Sponsor	Project Manager	Business Consultant	Solution Architect	Integration Coordinator	Operations Analyst	Technical Analysts	organization Consultants	Process Consultants	Workflow Consultants
Business	●	●											
Project Management													
Project Definition													
1 Organizational Readiness Assessment	◗	◗	◗	◗	●	◗					◗		
2 Preliminary Project Scope	◗		◗	◗	●			◗					
3 Preliminary Business Case/Justification			◗	◗	◗	●							
4 Risk Assessment Document	◗		◗	◗	●				◗				
Project Planning and Management													
1 Project Identity	◗	◗	◗	◗	●								
2 Project Resource Plan			◗	◗	●								
3 Draft Project Plan					●								
4 Project Change Management			◗	◗	●								
5 Project Communication Plan			◗	◗	●								
6 Program to Measure Success			◗	◗	●								
7 Process to Manage Scope					●								
8 Project Definition Report					●								
Stage 1: Requirements													
Requirements Definition			◗			●	◗						
1 Business Problem Definition			◗			●	◗						
2 Business Solution Definition			◗			●	◗						

Table E.2: Project Deliverables (continued)

Project Task	Business		Executive		Project team					Special Teams			
	Service Reps	Business End Users	Business Sponsor	IT Sponsor	Project Manager	Business Consultant	Solution Architect	Integration Coordinator	Operations Analyst	Technical Analysts	Organization Consultants	Process Consultants	Workflow Consultants
Stage 1: Requirements (continued)													
3 Business Case, Cost/Benefits Analysis						●							
4 Service Availability Needs						●			▶				
5 Likely Service Level Targets						●			▶				
6 Business Process/Evaluation Data		▶				●	▶						
7 Business Requirements Deliverables		▶				●	▶						
8 Completion Criteria		▶				●	▶						
9 Project Scope						●	▶						
10 User Acceptance/Project Review Documents					▶	●							
Stage 2: Mapping Strategy													
Architecting for Availability													
1 Functional Requirements Deliverables		▶				▶	●						
2 Non-Functional Requirements Deliverables		▶				▶	●						
3 Logical Architecture Model							●				▶		
4 Physical Architecture Model							●				▶		
5 Inventory Model							●				▶		
6 Interdependency Model							●				▶		
7 Test Physical Models						▶	●	▶			▶		
8 User Acceptance/Project Review Docs.		▶				▶	●				▶		

Table E.2: Project Deliverables (continued)

Project Task	Business		Executive		Project team					Special Teams			
	Service Reps	Business End Users	Business Sponsor	IT Sponsor	Project Manager	Business Consultant	Solution Architect	Integration Coordinator	Operations Analyst	Technical Analysts	Organization Consultants	Process Consultants	Workflow Consultants
Stage 3: Constructing													
Evaluating Availability Options													
1 As-Is State Model							●	▸	▸	▸			
2 To-Be State Model						▸	●	▸	▸	▸			
3 Gap Analysis of Availability Alternative							●	▸	▸	▸			
4 Selection of Potential Protection Document							●	▸	▸	▸			
5 User Acceptance/Project Review Docs.					▸		●	▸		▸			
Designing													
1 Design Specifications							●			▸			
2 Prioritized Project Scope							●			▸			
3 User Acceptance/Project Review Docs.	▸				▸		●			▸			
Developing Custom Application and Custom-Packaged Solution													
1 Programs source Code									●	▸			
2 Documentation for User and Application manuals									●	▸			
3 Unit Test Plans and Results									●	▸			
4 User Acceptance/Project Review Docs.					▸				●	▸			
Selecting Configurable Solution and Off-the-Shelf Applications													
(Repeat for each selection area.)									●	▸			
1 Development of Evaluation Matrix									●	▸			

Table E.2: Project Deliverables (continued)

Project Task	Service Reps	Business End Users	Business Sponsor	IT Sponsor	Project Manager	Business Consultant	Solution Architect	Integration Coordinator	Operations Analyst	Technical Analysts	Organization Consultants	Process Consultants	Workflow Consultants
	Business		**Executive**		**Project team**					**Special Teams**			
2 Candidate Products Research								●		▷			
3 Development of Application Short List								●		▷			
4 Application Option Evaluation								●		▷			
5 Creation of Prototype for Evaluation								●		▷			
6 Application Recommendation						▷	▷	●		▷			
7 Presentation of Findings to Management					▷	▷	▷	●		▷			
8 Contract Negotiation					●				▷	▷			
9 User Acceptance/Project Review Docs.		▷			▷			●		▷			
Stage 4: Planning													
Planning													
Assess Risk					▷	▷	▷	●	▷	▷			▷
1 Specification Table					▷	▷	▷	●	▷	▷			
2 Risk Assessment Table					▷	▷	▷	●	▷	▷			
3 Categorization Table					▷	▷	▷	●	▷	▷			
4 Test-Depth Table					▷	▷	▷	●	▷	▷			
Determine Alternatives								●		▷			▷
1 Alternatives Table								●		▷			
Define Test								●		▷			▷
1 Test-Plan Table								●		▷			
2 Test-Scripts Table								●		▷			
3 Test-Environment Build Table								●		▷			
4 User Acceptance/Project Review Docs.		▷			▷			●		▷			

Table E.2: Project Deliverables (continued)

Project Task	Service Reps	Business End Users	Business Sponsor	IT Sponsor	Project Manager	Business Consultant	Solution Architect	Integration Coordinator	Operations Analyst	Technical Analysts	Organization Consultants	Process Consultants	Workflow Consultants
Stage 5: Testing													
First-Stage Test Phase													
Complete Test									●	▶			▶
1 Issues Table									●	▶			
Review Results									●	▶			▶
Reassess Risk									●	▶			▶
2 User Acceptance/Project Review Docs.		▶			▶	▶			●	▶			
Final-Stage Test Phase													
Load in Increments									●	▶			▶
Test Each Increment									●	▶			▶
Monitor Each Increment									●	▶			▶
1 User Acceptance/Project Review Docs.		▶			▶	▶			●	▶			
Contractual Obligations													
1 Service Level Objectives					●				▶				
2 Important End-User Measures					●				▶				
3 Service Level Agreements					●				▶				
4 Policies					●				▶				
5 User Acceptance/Project Review Docs.					●				▶				
Stage 6: Delivering													
Operations Management													
1 Organizational Support Structure									●	▶	▶		
2 Centralized Operations									●	▶		▶	▶

Table E.2: Project Deliverables (continued)

Project Task	Business		Executive		Project team					Special Teams			
	Service Reps	Business End Users	Business Sponsor	IT Sponsor	Project Manager	Business Consultant	Solution Architect	Integration Coordinator	Operations Analyst	Technical Analysts	Organization Consultants	Process Consultants	Workflow Consultants
3 Automation (Problem Resolution and Recovery)									●	▸		▸	▸
4 Fundamentals of Problem Detection and Determination									●	▸			
5 Fundamentals of Problem Resolution and Recovery									●	▸			
6 Preventative Action									●	▸		▸	
7 User Acceptance/Project Review Docs.		▸			▸	▸			●	▸			
Stage 7: Recovering													
Disaster Recovery													
1 Disaster Recovery Plan		▸						▸	●	▸			
2 Business Continuity Planning		▸					▸	▸	●	▸	▸	▸	▸
3 User Acceptance/Project Review Docs.		▸			▸				●	▸			
Stage 8: Post-Mortem													
Analyze Availability Data													
1 Discovery Step Summary							●	▸					
2 Analysis Step Summary							●	▸					
3 Corrective Actions Step Summary							●	▸					
4 User Acceptance/Project Review Docs.					▸		●						

Appendix F:
Glossary and Terms

Frequently Used Acronyms in the Book

ABM   Automated Banking Machine

AO   Automated Operations

AOM   Annual Outage Minute

API   Application Programmatic Interface

ATM   Automated Teller Machine

B2B   Business to Business

B2C   Business to Consumer

BAP   Business Availability Project

CIF   Customer Information File

CIP   Continuous Improvement Process

DMZ   Demilitarized Zone

EAI   Enterprise Application Integration

ECC   Error Correction and Checking

EFT/POS	Electronic Funds Transfer/Point of Service
EIS	Executive Information System
EMS	Event Management System
EWS	Early Warning System
GAP	General Arrangement Plan
IS	Information Systems
ISP	Internet Service Provider
IT	Information Technology
LAN	Local Area Network
MCIF	Marketing Customer Information File
MTBF	Mean Time between Failure
MTTR	Mean Time to Recovery
OSM	Object State Modeling
PCRA	Problem/Cause and Recommended Action
PMBOK	Project Management Book of Knowledge
PMO	Program Management Office
RAID	Redundant Array of Inexpensive Disks
RDF	Remote Duplicate Database Facility
ROI	Return on Investment
SEI	Software Engineering Institute (Carnegie Melon University)
SLA	Service Level Agreement
SLO	Service Level Objective
SPI	Subsystem Programmatic Interface
UOM	User Outage Minute
WAN	Wide Area Network

IT and Business Terms Used in the Book

3 by 3	A rule for automating three actions taken by three different people.
Annual Outage Minutes	The total number of system or environment outage minutes in a year that a business service is unavailable to all the users.
Application	A computer program that performs functions for users. It differs from program development suites, operating system programs, and system management tools.
Application integration	The use of a wide variety of tools and methodologies that allow multiple applications to work together.
Application server	The term has come to be implicitly associated with the support of component-based technologies like COM+ or EJB/CORBA.
Architecture	An abstract view of a system that divides it into components and describes the components themselves and the connections among them.
As-is state	The current state of the business or service-delivery environment.
Automation	A machine or system (automated operator) that follows a set of activities in a process, without human intervention.
Availability	A measure of "the service" being there, where high availability implies a higher degree of confidence that the service will be there. This book advocates a binary view of availability, i.e., the service is either available or not.
Benefits	Changes aligned with business needs that, when expressed in quantifiable terms, are an advantage for the organization.
Best practices	Processes or procedures regarded as effective and efficient, defined through experience or formal benchmarking.
Black-box testing	An outside view that looks at what is done rather than how it is done. It includes looking at the outputs and impact on the environment.

Business availability	A high degree of confidence that the business service will be there; that it is always available.
Business case	A logical, written expression of the business value of a project, intended to secure resource allocation, ensure results, and justify the decision to spend funds.
Business-critical environment	A part or whole of a service-delivery environment that is important to a specific part of the business, differentiated from mission-critical.
Business function	A series of work activities done by a person. For example, functions within the sales process include prospecting, qualifying, and proposal writing.
Business process	A series of business functions within defined boundaries, such as a sales process, invoicing process, or marketing process.
Business operations	The operations or functions followed by the business.
Business requirements	The specifications for business services, and the preferences and "information styles" defined by a business user or service recipient.
Business services	Electronic business services that are delivered to clients through channels like ATMs, kiosks, the Internet, and the phone.
Business-to-business	An e-business interaction (Internet-enabled transaction) between two commercial organizations.
Business-to-consumer	An e-business interaction (Internet-enabled transaction) between a commercial organization and a consumer, for example, Web-enabled banking services.
Business user	An individual or group within the organization, but outside of IT, that is the recipient of business services to help carry out daily tasks. Also called the *end user*.
Change management	The process of introducing changes into the service-delivery environment while maintaining environment integrity and the business-service continuum.
Client	The client server technology.

Cockpit	An operations control facility or a dashboard for running and monitoring services.
Component	A part of an environment, such as a piece of hardware or software. Components are identified and stored in an inventory model.
Concept	A perception or impression of what needs to be done in business terms.
Continuous improvement	A process aimed at optimizing and improving a technology, process, and organization to meet business objectives, using a feedback system.
Critical Success Factors (CSF)	The key business goals that must be performed well to achieve business success.
Customer	Any person or business entity that makes a payment to a merchant.
Customer Information File	The master database of records, typically on the host. It contains the primary customer information from which other databases copy.
Cut-over	The process of moving a service from one environment to another.
Deliverable	A tangible project output, like a report or document for the client.
Demilitarized Zone	The area outside of the firewall, but still under the control of an organization.
Disaster recovery	The recovery of services to an alternate service-delivery environment off site.
Distance mirroring	A technique of maintaining a current duplicate database on mirrored disks, located several kilometers from the primary site.
Domino effect	A problem that triggers a ripple effect in the service-delivery environment.
Dynamic testing	Testing that is carried out by executing the code of an element or solution.

e-Business	The Forrester group defines this as online/traditional business activities that use Internet technologies to support communication, collaboration, service, and trade.
e-Business services	An electronic business service available to thousands of customers which, when enabled for e-business, is available to anyone with Internet access. It also becomes much more tightly integrated with the other applications and technologies that the organization offers.
e-Commerce	The Forrester group defines this as using the Internet to: 1) identify suppliers; 2) select products or services; 3) make purchase commitments; 4) complete financial transactions; and 5) obtain service. Delivery may occur over or outside of the Internet. This encompasses both business-to-business and business-to-consumer activities.
Element	An aggregate of components introduced into the environment like a solution (hardware, operating systems, databases, middleware, and applications).
e-Markets	Online exchanges that bring together buyers and sellers of business product or services through Internet-based systems.
Entity	A technology, such as clients, networks, and servers; part of the inventory model.
Error messages	Electronic warning messages put out by systems.
Excel	A spreadsheet software for plotting graphs.
Extranet	An Internet-based network that serves an organization and selected suppliers, partners, or customers.
Failover	Different levels of transfer of functions, applications, services, and users from a failed to a running node in the environment. This can be manual or automated.
Function	An activity or a set of activities
Functional requirement	The specifications and preferences for functions, typically by a business user or service recipient.
High availability	A state where all unplanned outages are minimized or masked. Users have access to services and applications during normal operations.

Hosting	The outsourcing of applications or Web sites to a third party.
Hot-plug components	Components that can be removed or added to a system while the system is operational. Also referred to as *hot swap*.
Instrumentation	The conversion of error text messages to machine-readable messages.
Integration	A variety of techniques that allow multiple applications to work together.
Integrity	The accuracy, quality, validity, and authorized use of data.
Interface	A process or system (automated or manual) that facilitates data exchange.
Internet	A communication mechanism for exchanging information between individuals or organizations.
Interoperability	The ability of different elements to work together.
Intranet	An Internet internal to an organization.
Load balancer	Software and/or hardware used with multiple single servers to improve availability. Hardware-based load balancers use the "least used connection" method, whereas software-based ones use "application logic."
Manual	Implies a human following a set of activities in a process.
Marketing CIF	A Customer Information File or database of records used for marketing purposes.
Mean Time to Recovery	A clock that measures overall time taken from the failure occurring to recovering the service-delivery environment to its normal condition.
Merchant	An individual or business entity, like a retailer in the Titan case study, who has signed up for business services.
Methodology	A structured set of guidelines, activities, rules, or steps to assist people in undertaking the development of a solution.
Metrics	Countable entities or distinct observable events that occur in environments.

Metrics measurement	A logical group of metrics that have at least one dimension that can be normalized.
Middleware	According to the Gartner definition, runtime systems software that directly enables application-level interactions among programs in a distributed computing environment. All applications requests require a timeout facility and exception handling.
Mission-critical environment	A part or whole of a service-delivery environment that is absolutely critical to support the life of a business or the livelihood of an organization.
Model	An intellectual construct descriptive of an entity. It represents the logical relationship between objects graphically or schematically.
Nonfunctional requirements	Relate to the nonfunctions (opposed to functional requirements) that an IT system must satisfy from a qualitative perspective.
Non-stop	Something that never stops; refers to availability.
Object-state monitoring	The monitoring of critical objects or components, where each can be up, down, or pending, represented through a state diagram or a hierarchy.
Operations management	A group within IT responsible for a service-delivery environment meeting a pre-agreed service level.
Outage	Refers to any time a service recipient does not receive service within the conditions set by a Service Level Agreement or preset expectations.
Outage minutes	A recommended metric for measuring availability. It provides a far more accurate and granular view than percentage uptime.
Parameter	A component has parameters that can be configured.
Planned downtime	A period of time allocated to shutting down business services to allow for changes to the service-delivery environment, like configurations or upgrades.
Policies	Management directives defined as a set of guidelines.
Potential problem analysis	A technique for analyzing a situation and identifying potential problems that might arise.

Pre-production	A non-live environment used for change management.
Problem management	The process of prediction, detection, determination, resolution, and recovery of problems within the service-delivery environment, while maintaining the environment integrity and the continuum of the business service.
Problem ticket	A record used for tracking a problem through the problem-management cycle.
Process	A structured flow of activities that integrate people and technology.
Production	Another term for the service-delivery environment or the live environment.
Prototyping	A method that helps define requirements, user interface changes, or technical concepts.
Quick-hit opportunities	Short-term improvement opportunities that require minimal effort (not requiring full implementation) and show a financial return and measurable results.
Remote duplicate database facility	A current duplicate database maintained in another environment located remotely, which is dynamically updated to reflect all changes made to the primary database.
Risk	The exposure to loss, or the chance of injury or bad consequence.
Self-adjusting	Software or hardware that adjusts itself to a normal situation.
Self-balancing	Software or hardware that balances itself and its resources to a normal state.
Self-healing	Software or hardware that identifies a fault, analyzes it, and recovers from it.
Service deliverer	The person responsible for providing services.
Service-delivery environment	The overall combination of elements that delivers electronic business service(s). It implies the whole end-to-end environment (enterprise).

Service Level Agreement	A formal, written contract that is signed by all parties involved.
Service Level Objective	A criterion by which a service is measured, including service times, response times, and exclusions and penalties to be paid when the objective is not met.
Sideways scalability	The ability to scale the environment sideways rather than upwards.
Signal-to-noise ratio	The concept of seeing meaningful information through a sea of "noise" or redundant information.
Solution	Hardware, software, services, and processes that solve a business problem.
Static testing	The process of evaluating a program by a walkthrough of the code documentation, without executing the element or solution.
Tiering an environment	A three-tier architecture of Web/application/data services that enhances the environment availability by enabling sideways scalability of selected components. It allows for single failure-point removal through replication or redundancy, and failover links.
To-be state	The next state of the business or service-delivery environment in place.
Transaction	In the Titan case study, a payment initiated through a merchant's account, by either the merchant or the merchant's customer.
Two-phase commit	Ensures that all the transaction writes to a database either occur or not, so the database is in a consistent state.
Upgrade	The process of installing a more recent version of software or operating system, or of increasing resources like processors, memory, disks, or cards.
User acceptance	The acceptance of a solution by users, effectively leading to acceptance by the business owner funding the project.
User Outage Minutes	The total number of minutes a business services is unavailable to an individual user.
Value chain	A series of linked business processes that create value in both products and services.

Web-based	An application created to use Web and Internet technologies.
Web-enabled	An application that has a Web interface so that users can access it via a browser.
White-box testing	Testing that takes an inside view and looks at how something is done rather than what is done. It includes testing paths, conditions, exceptions, and error-handling.

Nautical Terms Used in the Book

Bow	The front of the ship.
Port	The left side of the ship.
Starboard	The right side of the ship.
Stern	The rear of the ship.

Appendix G
Credits and Sources

Photo Credits

Figure 2.6, the illustration of *Titanic*'s general arrangement plan, was used courtesy of the Encyclopedia Titanica (*www.encyclopedia-titanica.org*).

The following illustrations were used courtesy of the Ulster Folk & Transport Museum:

- Figure 2.9, shipbuilder's model of *Olympic/Titanic*.

- Figure 3.6, electric door of *Olympic*.

- Figure 3.8, keel of *Titanic*.

- Figure 3.9, fitting the propeller shaft.

- Figure 4.4, *Olympic*'s damage from HMS *Hawke* collision.

- Figure 5.5, starboard stern view of completed ship in Belfast Lough with tugs.

- Figure 9.1, *Olympic* and *Titanic* in slipways.

Bibliography

1998 MERIT Project. *Best Practices in Enterprise Management.*

Adams, Jonathan; Galambos, George; Koushik, Srinivas; Vasudeva, Guru. *Patterns for e-business: A Strategy for Reuse.* IBM Press

Bonsall, Thomas E. *Great Shipwrecks of the 20th Century*. New York: Gallery Books.

Bristow, Diana. *Titanic: Sinking the Myths*. KatCo Literary Group of Central California / June 1995.

Brown, David. *The Last Log of the Titanic*. McGraw-Hill.

Davie, Michael. *The Titanic: The Full Story of a Tragedy*. The Bodleyhead Ltd.

Eaton, John P.; Haas, Charles A.. *Titanic: Triumph and Tragedy*. Norton, W. W. & Company, Inc., March 1995.

Hyslop, Donald, Alastair Forsyth, and Sheila Jemima. *Titanic Voices*. New York: St. Martin's Press, 1998.

Lord, Walter. *A Night to Remember*. New York: Holt, Rinehart, & Winston, 1955.

Lord, Walter. *The Night Lives On*. New York: Holt, Rinehart, & Winston, 1985.

Maxtone-Graham, John. *The Only Way to Cross*. Barnes & Noble Books, 1998.

Spignesi, Stephen. *The Complete Titanic*. Birch Lane Press Group, 1998.

Thompson, Harvey. *Customer Value Management*. McGraw-Hill, 2000.

Wade, Wyn Craig. *The Titanic: End of a Dream*. New York: Rawson, Wade, 1979.

Wels, Susan. *Titanic: Legacy of the World's Greatest Ocean Liner*. Alexandria, VA: Time-Life Books, 2000.

Autonomic Computing, A Systemic View of Computing Modeled on Self-regulating Biological Systems.

Web Sites for Background Information

www.availability.com/, *http://www.tivoli.com/*—Availability

www.bredemeyer.com/index.html, *www-106.ibm.com/developerworks/patterns/*—Software architecture

www.ibm.com/services/e-business/ert-index.html, www.ibm.com/services/e-business/roi.html—Return on Web investment

www.incidents.org/—Tracks spread of viruses

www.infrastructure.com/—Infrastructure projects

www.managementscience.org/research/ab0107.asp—Use of project post mortems

www.optimizemagazine.com/—ROI

www.pm2go.com/—The Standish Group ("Chaos, a recipe for projects success")

www.pmi.org/—The Project Management Institute

www.qaforums.com/, www.benchmarkqa.com/—Planning and testing

www.cert.org/advisors/CA-2000-01.html#solutions—Testing for denial-of-service

www.research.ibm.com/autonomic/index_nf.html—Autonomic computing

www.sdmagazine.com/—Software development

www.techagreements.com/, www.metricnet.com/—Service levels

www.thebci.org/, www.contingencyplanning.com/—Business continuity

Index

Note: Boldface numbers indicate illustrations and tables.

Note: Boldface numbers indicate illustrations and tables.

critical component identification in, 43
extenuating circumstances testing and, 41-44
flow analysis in, 38-41, **40**
functional requirements in, 26
general arrangement plan (GAP) and, 32-36, **33**
granular components of physical model in, 32-36
guarantee delivery of required physical layout in, 44-45
individual component availability and risk in, 43, **44**
interdependency model in, 35-36, **35**
inventory model in, 34-35, **34**
logical storage and, 27-30
models for testing and, 37
movement of key elements and, 27-30
nonfunctional requirements in, 26-27
physical architecture in, 30-31, **32**
physical model testing and, typical operating
  environment, 37
single points of failure in, 40-41
steps in, 25-26
tiered or segmented service structures in, 29-30, **30**
user groups/business services model in, 36, **36**
user interface (UI) elements in, 26
"what if" analysis in, 41-44
worst-case analysis in, 41-44
maritime transportation, post-*Titanic*, 199-200
marketing CIF, 251
marketing feedback, 174
mean time between failure (MTBF), 39
mean time to recovery (MTTR), 39, 251
merchant, 251
methodology, 251
metrics, 169-174, 198, 251
  critical success factors (CSF) to measure progress in, 237
  customer feedback in, 173-174
  employee feedback in, 173
  environmental metric reports in, 172-173
  intermediary feedback in, 174
  marketing feedback in, 174
  operational logs as, 170
  required, 169-170
  service change requests in, 171
  service-level reports, 171
  service outage reports, 171-172, **172**
  service problem reports in, 170
  witness testimonies in, 173
  "word on the street" and market perceptions as, 174
metrics measurement, 252
micro design, 67
middleware, 34, 252
mirror sites, extended distance mirroring (EDM), 162, **163**
mission critical environment, 252
mitigation of risk in, 225
model of *Titanic*, **37**
models, 37, 65, 75, 252
modular design, 67-68

monitoring increments of online operations, 112-114
monitoring operations in, 134-136
movement of key elements and, 27-30

N
nautical terms, 255
navigation testing (Web site), 90-91
near collision of New York and *Titanic*, **113**
"noise" and signal-to-noise ratio in communications, 133,
  135-136
nonfunctional requirements in, 26-27, 252
nonstop, 252
North Atlantic and *Titanic* sinking, **108**

O
object oriented programming, 63
object state monitoring, 135, 252
Olympic and *Titanic*,199-200, **199**
Olympic collision with *Halleneck/Hawke*, 78-80, **79**, **80**
online ready sites in, 158, 161-164, **162**
  extended distance mirroring (EDM), 162, **163**
  remote duplicate data, 162
  remote duplicate database facility (RDF), 163-164, **164**
operating system, 34
operational logs, 170
operational testing, 93, **93**
operations analyst, 236
operations management, 252
operations run book for, 128-131
operations services involvement, 216
organizational and process consultants, 237
organizational gap analysis in, 188, **189**
organizational pitfalls in support systems, 125
organizational risk, 224
outage classification, 150, **150**, **219-220**, 252
outage minutes, 252
overconfidence vs. availability/success, 59-60

P
parallel and switchover testing, 96, **96**
parameter, 252
passenger/crew capacity of *Titanic*, **111**
percentage of availability vs. true availability, 16-22, **17**
performance management and, 124
performance reports, 116
performance testing, 90-91
physical architecture in, 30-31, **32**
physical architecture of *Titanic*, **31**
physical model testing and, typical operating environment,
  37, 41-44
physical outages, 219
pilots, 66

Note: Boldface numbers indicate illustrations and tables.

Note: Boldface numbers indicate illustrations and tables.

About the Author

Mark Kozak-Holland is a Senior Business Architect/Consultant. Mark has many years of international experience working with organizations in formulating projects and initiatives for developing and integrating solutions that leverage emerging technologies. He has been working with mission-critical solutions since 1985.

Mark is very passionate about history and sees its potential use as an education tool in business today. As a result, he has started to develop a "Lessons-from-History" series, which is for organizations applying today's Information Technology (IT) to common business problems. It is written for primarily business and IT professionals looking for inspiration for their projects. It uses relevant historical case studies to examine how historical projects and emerging technologies of the past solved complex problems.

Email: mark.kozak-holl@sympatico.ca
Web Sites: http://www.mmpubs.com/kozak-holland/
                http://www.lessons-from-history.com/

LESSONS FROM

HISTORY

About the "Lessons from History" Series

For thousands of years people have been running projects that leveraged emerging technologies of the time, to create unique and wonderful structures like the pyramids, buildings, or bridges. Similarly, people have gone on great expeditions and journeys, and raced their rivals in striving to be first; for example, circumnavigating the world or conquering the poles. These were all forms of projects that required initiating, planning, executing, controlling and closing.

The *Lessons from History* series looks at historical projects and then draws comparisons to challenges encountered in today's projects. It outlines the stages involved in delivering a complex project providing a step-by-step guide to the project deliverables. It vividly describes the crucial lessons from historical projects and complements these with some of today's best practices. It makes the whole learning experience more memorable. The series should inspire the reader as these historical projects were achieved with less sophisticated emerging technologies.

This series is for primarily business and IT professionals looking for inspiration for their projects. Specifically, business managers responsible for solving business problems, or Project Managers (PMs) responsible for delivering business solutions through IT projects.

Website: **http://www.lessons-from-history.com/**

Titanic Lessons for IT Projects

Titanic Lessons for IT Projects analyzes the project that designed, built, and launched the ship, showing how compromises made during early project stages led to serious flaws in this supposedly "perfect ship." In addition, the book explains how major mistakes during the early days of the ship's operations led to the disaster. All of these disasterous compromises and mistakes were fully avoidable.

Entertaining and full of intriguing historical details, this companion book to *Avoiding Project Disaster: Titanic Lessons for IT Executives* helps project managers and IT executives see the impact of decisions similar to the ones that they make every day. An easy read full of illustrations and photos to help explain the story and to help drive home some simple lessons.

ISBN: 1-895186-26-9   (paperback)
ISBN: 1-895186-23-4   (PDF ebook)

http://www.mmpubs.com/titanic

Churchill's Adaptive Enterprise

Lessons for Business Today

This book analyzes a period of time from World War II when Winston Churchill, one of history's most famous leaders, faced near defeat for the British in the face of sustained German attacks. The book describes the strategies he used to overcome incredible odds and turn the tide on the impending invasion. The historical analysis is done through a modern business and information technology lens, describing Churchill's actions and strategy using modern business tools and techniques. Aimed at business executives, IT managers, and project managers, the book extracts learnings from Churchill's experiences that can be applied to business problems today. Particular themes in the book are knowledge management, information portals, adaptive enterprises, and organizational agility.

ISBN: 1-895186-19-6   (paperback)
ISBN: 1-895186-20-X   (PDF ebook)

http://www.mmpubs.com/churchill

Winston Churchill, the Agile Project Manager

In May 1940, the United Kingdom (UK) was facing a dire situation, an imminent invasion. As the evacuation of Dunkirk unfolded, the scale of the disaster became apparent. The army abandoned 90% of its equipment, the RAF fighter losses were deplorable, and over 200 ships were lost.

Winston Churchill, one of the greatest leaders of the 20th century, was swept into power. With depleted forces and no organized defense, the situation required a near miracle. Churchill had to mobilize quickly and act with agility to assemble a defense. He had to make the right investment choices, pour resources in, and deliver a complete project in time to save his country. This audio looks at Churchill as an agile Project Manger, turning a disastrous situation into an unexpected victory.

ISBN: 1-895186-50-1   (audio CD)

http://www.PM-Audiobooks.com

 **The Project Management Audio Library**

In a recent CEO survey, the leaders of today's largest corporations identified project management as the top skillset for tomorrow's leaders. In fact, many organizations place their top performers in project management roles to groom them for senior management positions. Project managers represent some of the busiest people around. They are the ones responsible for planning, executing, and controlling most major new business activities.

Expanding upon the successful *Project Management Essentials Library* series of print and electronic books, Multi-Media Publications has launched a new imprint called the *Project Management Audio Library*. Under this new imprint, MMP is publishing audiobooks and recorded seminars focused on professionals who manage individual projects, portfolios of projects, and strategic programmes. The series covers topics including agile project management, risk management, project closeout, interpersonal skills, and other related project management knowledge areas.

This is not just the "same old stuff" on the critical path method, earned value, and resource levelling; rather, the series has the latest tips and techniques from those who are at the cutting edge of project management research and real-world application.

www.PM-Audiobooks.com

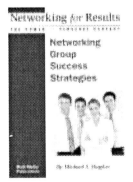

Printed in the United States
54013LVS00002B/11-20

9 781895 186734